COMMUNICATING NATIONAL INTEGRATION

To David Amienyi Edosomwan,
My dearest deceased father
Who taught me to always:
Listen to the voice of experience

Communicating National Integration
Empowering Development in African Countries

OSABUOHIEN P. AMIENYI
Arkansas State University, USA

ASHGATE

Published by
Ashgate Publishing Limited
Gower House
Croft Road
Aldershot
Hants GU11 3HR
England

Ashgate Publishing Company
Suite 420
101 Cherry Street
Burlington, VT 05401-4405
USA

Ashgate website: http://www.ashgate.com

British Library Cataloguing in Publication Data
Amienyi, Osabuohien P.
   Communicating national integration : empowering development
   in African countries
   1.Communication - Political aspects - Africa, Sub-Saharan
   2. Social integration - Africa, Sub-Saharan 3.Communication
   in politics - Africa, Sub-Saharan 4.Africa, Sub-Saharan -
   Politics and government - 1960-
   I.Title
   302.2'0967

Library of Congress Cataloging-in-Publication Data
Amienyi, Osabuohien P.
   Communicating national integration : empowering development in African countries /
by Osabuohien P. Amienyi.--1st ed.
      p. cm
   Includes bibliographical references and index.
   ISBN 0-7546-4425-1
   1. Africa--Social conditions--1960- 2. Social integration--Africa. 3. National
characteristics, African. 4. Communication--Africa. I. Title.

   HN773.5.A45 2005
   306'.096--dc22

                                                              2004026958

ISBN 0 7546 4425 1

Printed and bound in Great Britain by
Athenaeum Press Ltd., Gateshead, Tyne & Wear

Contents

List of Figures

List of Tables

Preface

Prior to the independence decade of the 1960s, social science literature was replete with conceptualizations and propositions about the construct of national integration.[1] A constant among these conceptualizations was the suggestion that modernization and industrialization were the keys to the achievement of national integration. Coleman,[2] Robinson[3] and others argued that modernization and industrialization stimulate activities that mobilize a society towards integrative behavior. They included actions such as the establishment of mass communications, the promotion and use of a common language (at least for commerce), and the sharing of common cultural experiences (including norms, attitudes and values). These actions had been partly responsible for national integration in several Western European countries in the 1950s.[4] At that time, they seemed a logical, general paradigm for achieving the integrative objectives of Third World countries in succeeding decades.

However, in the period immediately following the independence decade, attempts to replicate the Western-based theoretical formulations for integration in the emergent states of Africa, Asia and Latin America failed to yield the expected results. Research findings from data gathered in the developing countries generally supported the view, held at the time by a minority of scholars, that the emphasis on modernization, industrialization and the mass media would not be a sufficient cause, in and of themselves, for reducing tribal, racial and class cleavages.[5] In fact, empirical studies revealed that modernization tended to aggravate ethnic conflict in nation-building, and that the mass media generally reinforced existing attitudes rather than inculcating new ones.[6] Through this knowledge, and the rapid political changes that occurred throughout Africa in the post- independence period, it became apparent the problems and processes of national integration must be reexamined. Although a few case studies were published in the late 1960s and early 1970s, they did not fully account for the overwhelming variety of integrative patterns that were emerging in Africa; nor did they fully explicate the existence of specific dimensions of national integration.[7]

In the late 1970s, scholars at Northwestern University conducted a number of empirical studies on national integration in Africa. These studies were carried out across the main dimensions of the construct: values and identity, and linkages and structures. The topics examined ranged from assessments of the relationship between education and integration to extrapolations of the situations under which national integration can occur. However, as with their predecessors, their general findings, though quite instructive, did not fully establish the nature of the relationships that exist between communication and national integration.

Ogunade's[8] study on Nigerian media was perhaps the first attempt to state a direct relationship between communication and national integration, but his conclusions drawn strictly from philosophical data appeared to have limited external validity. Since 1987, more insight has been gained on the topic as numerous empirical studies[9] have supported Kuo's[10] earlier theories. Kuo stated that communication is important to the formation of a people, a community and a nationality, and that the communicative ability of a country is a determinant of the rate of national assimilation or differentiation. These latter studies have enhanced the definition of the national integration construct, as well as the measurement of the actual degree of the association between mass media and national integration. They have provided the knowledge that so far the integrative contents of African media have not contained the 'development' themes required to stimulate the feeling of belonging to a terminal community among the disparate groups,[11] nor have they been driven by any ideological direction.[12]

Although the reviewed studies have made immense contributions to the media and national integration literature, the central question of why some countries can avert or minimize internal communal conflicts to the point where they no longer pose a threat to their national integrity or survival, while other countries cannot, still remains unanswered. Furthermore, there is as yet no clear insight into why communication mitigates the negative consequences of internal communal conflicts reasonably well in some countries, but fails miserably in others. Perhaps, this anomaly can be explained by the absence of integrative communication models that countries, that have problems with irredentism, can easily access. The absence of such vital reference material is a significant handicap. It deprives national leaders and other concerned parties of an important educational resource for learning from the integrative communication successes and/or failures of other countries.

This book attempts to fill this gap by summarizing the existing knowledge on the use of communication in national integration and supplementing it with original ideas and strategies where necessary. The book is guided by following questions:

- What social, cultural, political and economic factors enhance or minimize the success of integrative communications?
- What adverse effect does the problem of national integration have on the developmental aspirations of countries?
- What specific roles should communication play in integrative endeavors?
- What conceptual or semantic difficulties are implicit in designed integrative communications and how are they overcome?, and
- What pragmatic research initiatives should national governments and international development agencies implement for integrative communication?

Communicating national integration must be viewed as an all-encompassing task that transcends official speeches in attempts to persuade a disparate population to cultivate national consciousness. It must encompass efforts to persuade leaders to eliminate policies that seek to promote spatial dislocation and cross-cultural interaction, and to arouse the audience to pay closer attention to integrative messages disseminated through the mass media. It must span the totality of all individual and collective actions and activities capable of resulting in the perception of non-integrative behavior. For example, some leaders in Africa consistently promote national integration in public speeches and writings, while their personal acts, actions, activities and adopted policies are decidedly sectional. Such leaders unwittingly communicate duplicitous integrative messages that are often not lost on the receiving audience who, more often than not, are apt to pay closer attention to the polarizing politics than to the integrative speech. However, if communicating national integration is to be effective, message sources must consistently 'say what they mean and mean what they say' in their words and in their deeds.

Notes

1 John Paden, *Values, Identities and National Integration*, Evanston, Illinois: Northwestern University Press, 1980.
2 John Coleman, 'Political Integration in Emergent Africa,' *Western Political Quarterly* 8 (March 1955): 44-57.
3 Robinson, 1974.
4 Karl Deutsch, *Nationalism and its Alternatives*, New York: Alfred A. Knopf, Inc., 1969.
5 John Coleman, 'Political Integration in Emergent Africa, 44-57.
6 Robinson, 1974.
7 John Paden, *Values, Identities and National Integration*.
8 Adelumola Ogunade, 'Mass Media and National Integration in Nigeria,' in *International Perspectives on News*, ed. Leon Atwood and S. J. Bullion, Carbondale: Southern Illinois University Press: 22-32.
9 See for example Osabuohien P. Amienyi, 'Obstacles to Broadcasting For National Integration in Nigeria,' *Gazette* 43 (1989): 1-15; Osabuohien P. Amienyi, 'Adult Perception of the Integrative Contribution of Mass Media in Nigeria,' *Southwestern Mass Communication Journal* 6 (1990)53-63; Osabuohien P. Amienyi, 'The Association Between Mass Media Exposure and National Identification in Nigeria,' *International Third World Studies Journal & Review* 2 (1991):337-346; Moses Osaghae, 'Political Integration in Nigeria,' Unpublished Ph.D. Dissertation, Texas Tech University, Lubbock, Texas, 1989; and Christina Drake, National Integration in Indonesia.
10 Eddie Kuo, 'Language, Nationhood, and Communication Planning: The case of a multilingual society,' in *Perspectives in Communication Policy and Planning*, ed. S. A. Rahim and J. Middleton, Honolulu: East-West Communication Institute, 319-335.
11 Alan DeGoshe, 1985.
12 Ogunade, 'Mass Media and National Integration in Nigeria,' p. 23.

Acknowledgements

No one can complete an undertaking as extensive as this without the encouragement and support of others. I owe a debt of gratitude to my dear friend and mentor, Harold Fisher, who stood by me through the four years that it took to complete the book. Hal generously donated his time to painstakingly verify the accuracy of information contained in it, making sure that the writing was fluid, sensible and free of ambiguities. His intimate knowledge of Africa ensured that the recommendations offered in the last chapter have meaning and functionality.

A special thank you is also extended to my friend and esteemed colleague, Marlin Shipman, who spent several hours, despite his busy schedule, to critique and copy-edit the book. His comments, questions and observations were thought-provoking and incisive. They challenged me to rethink many of my initial conceptualizations. The result is a vastly enriched book. Laura Cremeens, Secretary to the Dean of my college, made an invaluable contribution by formatting all tables in the book. Getting the tables to fit page specifications was a seemingly intractable challenge until Laura came to my rescue. I owe her a lot for her time, patience and meticulous attention to detail. I thank also all the research assistants I have worked with through the years. Most notable among these are Chen Jun, Takesha Holt-McMiller and Deajin Jeon. The numerous hours these industrious souls spent poring over library and online sources ensured that I always had the information I needed.

I am exceedingly grateful to my brother, Collins Airhihenbuwa, for his wise counsel in selecting a publisher and for sharing through his love the exhortation of our ancestors that 'blood is thicker than water'. His unwavering support for all of my endeavors provided the mental stability to finish the project. I owe a special debt of gratitude to my children in the United States: Brandon Osasere, Shaina Osaretin and Shela Osaro, for being the delight of eyes and for inspiring me to aim for the highest pinnacle of success. Shaina devoted many hours she could have spent frolicking in the summer sun proofreading the camera ready copies.

I am deeply indebted to one, whose kindness always keeps her close to my heart, Dorothy Madahana, and my dear friend, Michael Arunga, for providing the concrete examples used throughout the book. These examples have increased the intensity and efficacy of the arguments made. To my dearest friend of many years, Peggy Wilson, who has been the rock that gave me strength when my back was against the wall; I say thank you from the bottom of my heart.

This project was begun during my sabbatical in 2000, but it could not have been completed without the release time granted me by the dean of my college Russ Shain, the head my department Richard Carvell and the Associate Vice Chancellor for Academic Affairs office, V. Rick McDaniel. I am most grateful for this support.

I am deeply indebted to the love of my life, my wife, Sanoya Ann Lomax-Amienyi, whose unwavering devotion provided the psychological serenity that allowed me to think through every word I wrote. Without her persistent encouragement, this would have been a most tedious undertaking, indeed. She was the wind beneath my wings and the gentle tide that calmed any rough seas I encountered during the preparation of the manuscript. She, too, spent endless hours proofreading the final manuscript.

Finally, to everyone at Ashgate Publishing who made it possible for this discourse to reach the public in a timely manner, I say thank you. In particular, Brendan George, the social science editor, whose diligence, professionalism and warm personality endeared me to the company. The editorial staff, in particular Donna Hamer, Carolyn Court and Rosalind Ebdon, my copy editor, who painstakingly copy-edited the book and gave professional advice on formatting and layout. The meticulous attention to detail that these professionals gave the manuscript made it possible for the final product to be as clean as possible. I thank you all for your devotion.

Chapter 1

Understanding National Integration for Development

...To build a nation, it takes centuries; to destroy it, it takes only a day or two...

Nik Abdul Rashid bin Nik Abdul Majid
Executive Director of Melaka Musuems Corporation

The problem of social disintegration is so recurrent in Africa that the existence of many of its countries as viable national entities is subject to doubt. The threats to national cohesion assume many forms, including ethnic, regional, religious and class cleavages, to name a few. Africa does not have a monopoly of this problem, but it is fair to say that it has exhibited the most acute cases in contemporary history.[1] The persistent social discord and instability renders meaningless the numerous attempts to find lasting solutions to the problems that pervade African societies: poverty, pestilence, illiteracy, inadequate social infrastructure, poor health, unemployment and political disenfranchisement. All this and more make difficult the building of structures for solving these problems on solid ground.[2]

Yet, the problem of national integration has not received much attention in development projects executed by both national governments and international agencies working in countries of 'The South', especially those countries in Africa. Nor have the communication approaches and strategies presented by the development communication scholars offered any solutions. This author has noted[3] previously that the actual number of international and domestic development projects devoted to the core integration issues, such as the promotion of a common language, the development of political awareness, and the encouragement of integrative behavior, is less than five percent. Concomitantly, during the 1990s, less than seven percent of the World Bank's research efforts on The South's development focused on issues related to national integration (communication and information, education and transportation). Furthermore, of the five communication approaches and six strategies for development formulated by the development communication theorists (see Tables 1.1 and 1.2), only one—the ideological and mobilization approach—relates directly to national integration. It aims at developing political awareness; one of the core dimensions of national integration. Two other strategies—instructional broadcasting and entertainment education—address the national integration issue peripherally; they both aim at promoting 'social change', which their authors define to include the overshadowing or elimination of primordial sentiments in favor of embracing national sentiments or loyalty.[4]

Table 1.1 Development Communication Approaches

Development Strategies

Approach	Media Used	Goal	Assumptions
Extension and community development method	Interpersonal (handbills, letters, telephones)	To communicate useful and practical information on such issues as agriculture home economics, health, law and order, civic responsibility, sanitation and so on.	Social systems are interested in new ideas; there are sufficient resources to support development; there is a crop of education, intelligent and public supported leaders to motivate the masses to action.
Controlled mass media method	Mass media (centrally controlled)	To use mass media to promote development priorities set by government or party.	Mass media should support national development objectives.
Localized (decentralized) mass media method	Local mass media (community radio, etc.; interpersonal)	To create opportunities for access and participation for rural people.	A 2-way flow of messages is the best communications method for development.
Integrated approach	Interpersonal/ mass media	To generate ideas and discussions that would lead to understanding development objectives and each person's role in it.	Mass media can disseminate information but they cannot change attitudes or behavior. Mere dissemination of information is not a sufficient cause for positive personal action.

Source: Compiled from Moemeka, A. (1994). *Communication for Development: A New Pan-African Perspective*. Albany, New York: State University of New York Press

These findings are curious because numerous authors have suggested strongly that national integration is the crucial development issue for Africa. Accordingly, national integration is stated as a high priority on the development agenda of many African countries. In fact, many African officials readily admit that national integration is the most important consideration in the development in their countries. Why then is national integration so frequently neglected in developmental project planning and implementation, or addressed so indirectly or peripherally when it is included?

Table 1.2 Development Communication Strategies

Development Strategies

Strategy	Media Used	Goal	Assumptions
Open broadcasting	Radio/television (RTV)	To broadcast messages to an unorganized audience.	A good and relevant message is capable of being accepted by an individual on his or her own.
Instructional broadcasting	RTV	To organize use of RTV for social change and development.	A good and relevant message must operate on the principle of cooperation and guided listening.
Rural broadcasting forum	RTV	To use of RTV broadcasting with discussion groups.	Audience input is essential for effective development.
Radio schools	Radio	To offer fundamental, integral information that goes beyond reading and cognitive skills and try to change passive and dependent attitudes of people.	People must be aroused to action.
Radio animation	Radio	To promote a trained cadre of people in local communities.	Local communication must be used to find and define solutions for people's problems.
Entertainment education	Television	To use an entertainment communication program to transmit educational, instructional-development messages, to foster social change.	Change occurs when people see benefits from another's behavior.

Source: Compiled from Moemeka, A. (1994). *Communication for Development: A New Pan-African Perspective*. Albany, New York: State University of New York Press

Why is National Integration Ignored in Development Planning?

There are no obvious answers to this question, but three substantive factors seem intuitively plausible. The first is that African leaders, and their Southern counterparts, have yet to take direct control over the direction and shape of their country's national development. As it is widely known, international development agencies like the *World Bank*, *The United Nations Development Programme (UNDP)*, *The Food and Agriculture Organization (FAO)* and the *US Agency for International Development (USAID)*, wield enormous influence in shaping the nature, direction and focus of national development in Third World countries.[5]

They 'attempt to promote long-run growth of the least developed countries (LDCs) by building large projects, giving budgetary and balance of payments help, and funding a variety of research and planning efforts'.[6] Through the enormous economic, technological and humanitarian assistance they provide, they accentuate the interlocking elements that Third World countries should consider vital areas of focus in their development plans, and they establish the scale on which these elements should be addressed.

The second factor is that national integration construct is inherently complex. Like the construct—national development—of which it is part, the construct of national integration encompasses a broad array of interrelated cognitive, attitudinal and behavioral activities. These activities are usually classified with the same labels associated with the different levels of development. Hence, national integration also contains socio-cultural, economic and political dimensions. Perhaps when development agents address the socio-cultural, economic and political dimensions of development, they also reason erroneously that they are addressing the dimensions of national integration.

Such confusion is understandable because there is a lack of consistent scholarly research about national integration. During the independence decade of the 1960s, many books and articles were published about national integration.[7] Soon afterwards, scholarly interest on the topic waned presumably because, as Jacob and Teune[8] wrote, social scientists began to take the construct for granted; they thought they knew what an integrated society was when they saw it. Interest in this topic has been revived in recent years, as scholars whose native countries face serious integration problems have been motivated to revisit this critical issue.[9]

The recent studies show that though national integration and national development are symbiotically related, the objective of one should not be mistaken as the objective of the other. The goal of national development is to achieve an increase in a social system's capacity 'to fulfill its own perceived needs at progressively higher levels of material and cultural well-being'.[10] Meanwhile, the goal of national integration is to provide cohesiveness to permit constructive and development-oriented societal change to take place. Consequently, national integration is a substantive part of national development; its existence in a social system must depend upon the balanced synergism of historical-political, socio-cultural, transactional and economic forces. According to Drake, 'If one component [of national integration] is neglected or becomes out of balance, disintegrative forces may emerge that can threaten a state's stability or even its continued existence.'[11] And if a state is no longer in existence or if its existence is marked by persistent turmoil, the issue of national development becomes moot.

The third factor is that national integration operates at an emotive state of human behavior which makes it difficult to evolve strategies or projects. The decision to maintain affinity with one's social system and others in it is an emotional decision made at the individual level. As a result, its success or failure cannot be measured by post-project evaluations. However, the international agencies are more concerned with specific projects for which evaluations of success can be made. The World Bank, for example, is concerned with 'return-on-investment' and will seldom engage in projects that are risky. This may explain why many of the projects are agricultural or technical arenas because they can easily be evaluated for success or failure.

Also, national governments and international agencies' often believe that infrastructure is the critical factor in economic growth, scientific and technological advancement, and political stability. They reason that for development to occur in Third World countries, infrastructure (e.g. roads, ports, airports, power, water, etc.) must keep pace with the general economic development of the country. They believe that if infrastructure is allowed to lag, economic and social progress will be difficult to achieve. For these reasons, the majority of the projects sponsored or supported by the national government and international agencies are infrastructure oriented.

Importance of National Integration in Development

The substantial attention both national and international development theorists and planners devote to such pragmatic issues in national development as economy, health, industry, science and technology, trade, audience participation and agriculture gives the impression that such issues are the most critical considerations in the development of Third World countries. But that impression is naïve. Without question, the pragmatic issues are vital to 'the process of increasing the capacity of a social system to fulfill its own perceived needs at progressively higher levels of material and cultural well-being'.[12] However, it is quite obvious that whether the development of a holistic social system can derive from independent growths in the described sectors may depend on the absence of irredentism in the social system. In a social system where people in different geographical areas and of different ethnic, socio-cultural, religious and economic backgrounds do not generally feel themselves to be united or to function as one nation, development cannot be fully achieved. It is often either sluggish, haphazard, totally non-existent or simply tantamount to the satisfaction of the will and aspiration of a small minority of individuals or groups who tend to seek for themselves a greater share of the economic and political fortunes that otherwise should be used to improve the social system as a whole.[13]

Thus, the relationship that exists between the absence of irredentism in pluralistic social systems and the success of national development planning and social change in the systems is symbiotic. The nature of this relationship is explained by Christina Drake,[14] who writes:

> Cohesive forces are vital both to ensure the continued existence of the [social system] as one political entity and give political stability... For without some measure of integration, both human and material resources that are needed to raise living standards must be diverted instead toward coping with the centrifugal forces of regional disaffection and rebellion.

She adds that:

> The success of a country's economic development also depends to a considerable
> extent   on the strength of its integrative, cohesive bonds, so that the almost inevitably
> uneven spatial impact of development does not unduly exacerbate regional differences
> and tensions and lead to disintegration.

Agreeing with Drake, the Inter-Africa Group[15] pointed out that national integration
is the fundamental overriding issue in national development for any social system.
In its absence, the existence of the social system is called into question, and every
other development consideration or problem recedes into irrelevant. It would be
futile indeed to talk about issues such as education, literacy, economic growth,
political stability, agricultural productivity, or technological progress in the
absence of a society.

Other writers have also stated this relationship. For example, Mabogunje[16]
observes that the failure to achieve development in Third World countries may be
directly attributable to the inability to 'integrate a sufficient mass of population to
achieve the type of change-generating interaction needed to move the social
system to new and desirable heights'. Abernethy[17] notes that disparate peoples
and groups, who lack a strong sense of belonging to their country, are more likely
to permit conflicts among themselves to reach the point threatening the continued
existence of their country. Cowan[18] advises that Southern countries, especially the
pluralistic societies in Africa, must first address the problem of nation-building
before embarking on the goal of human development.

These writers reflect the apparent reality that systemic dislocations such as
revolutions or continual dislocation of civil authority, political instability, and civil
wars are an obstacle to achieving sustained national development. This was the
reality that prompted the first Prime Minister of the Federal Republic of Nigeria,
the late Alhaji Abubakar Tafawa Balewa, to acknowledge that 'national integration
is naturally uppermost in our minds as it is self-evident that planning and
prosperity can thrive only in conditions of peace and orderliness'.[19] The same
reality prompted the Indonesian government to promote the use of a national
language and other integrative policies.

It was this reality that prompted the visionary former leader of Tanzania,
Julius Nyerere, to exhort international development donors and agencies to deal
with the problem of hunger in Africa. He said it was better to teach Africans how
to fish rather than to give them fish for a day. The same reality underscores the
loss of lives and destruction of property in the war in Bosnia-Herzegovina, the
1995 genocide in Rwanda, and the ongoing political crises in Burundi, Liberia,
Nigeria and a host of sub-Saharan African countries. This reality makes it clear
that national integration must be addressed as the central crucial element for
obtaining healthy returns-on-investments made in all other sectors of national
development.

The irredentist-driven wars in Bosnia-Herzegovina, Rwanda, Burundi and
Liberia illustrate how the absence of national integration can impede economic and

political progress. No country in Africa better illustrates this than the Federal Republic of Nigeria. Since the British created Nigeria in 1914, the nature of its development has been defined by the centrifugal forces of ethnic and religious rivalry. The tribal and regional tension that drove the political upheavals in the early 1960s and culminated in the civil war of the late 1960s continues to provide today the institutional basis of political instability in the country. Ethnic distrust killed the only political initiative capable of planting the seed of Nigerian nationhood on sustaining grounds—the 1996 decree of a unitary state ordered by the then Head of State, General Aguiyi-Ironsi. The decrease continues to serve as the basis for placing the fulfillment of ethnic aspirations at the top of the list of policy considerations in socio-political and economic planning.

The philosophy of 'statism', one of the negative consequences of the creation of states, has continued to accentuate fundamental differences between Islamists and Christians. It has also become the basis for using civil unrest to draw attention to economic exploitation or neglect, and consequent environmental degradation. Because of irredentism, Nigerian development continues to stagnate. The average Nigerian's physical quality of life continues to decrease. For example, Nigeria's annual per capita income has fallen dramatically from 1000 dollars in the 1970s to 300 dollars today, even though its present population is much smaller than 1970s estimates.

Some argue that the problem the absence of national integration poses to the success of national development efforts is shared by developed and developing nations; however, Jahan notes an important distinction between the two. In developed countries, he writes, 'a well formed national ideology, a national elite, national institutions and national pride is already preexistent'[20] that prevents disaffection among groups. Latent parochial loyalties prevent such dissatisfaction from gaining sufficient momentum to undermine the integrity, stability or development of the social system.   For example, no matter the level of dissatisfaction ethnic groups might experience in the United States or Britain, the maintenance of the goals of the national system is still held in high esteem by most. On the other hand, in developing countries, no such 'sense of territorial nationality which overshadows—or subordinates—parochial loyalties'[21] exists to prevent individuals or regions undermining the development efforts of the system. Instead, at this considerations determine development priorities, resources, opportunities and rewards. This creates systemic imbalances, which hinder national development.

Meaning and Dimensions of National Integration

There is a certain degree of consistency in the various attempts to conceptualize the notion of national integration. For example, David Smock and Kwamina Bentsi-Enchill describe national integration as the development of identification with the national community that supersedes in certain situations more parochial loyalties. John Coleman and Carl Rosberg say integration is the progressive lessening of ethnic, cultural and regional tensions and discontinuities in the process of creating a homogenous political community. Henry Binder writes that the achievement of integration involved the evolution of a 'cultural-ideological consensus of a very high degree of comprehensiveness'. Amitai Etzioni (1965) believes that a community is integrated when it has:

- an effective control over the means of violence;
- a center of decision-making that significantly affected the allocation of resources and rewards; and
- a dominant focus of political identification for a large majority of national citizens who are politically aware.

Weiner sees national integration as specifically referring to 'the problem of creating a sense of territorial nationality which overshadows—or eliminates—subordinate parochial loyalties'. Together, these definitions suggest that for national integration to occur in a nation, a significant number of citizens must develop identification with the nation that supersede identification with ethnic, cultural or religious group, acquire political awareness, share common norms and values and develop attitudes favorable to the display of integrative behavior among peoples of different groups.

Within this context, analyses of the construct usually begin with the question: Do the people of a social system possess common ideals and believe these ideals are important? This question is foremost because, as Abernethy[22] has noted, when people believe they belong to a terminal community, whose values and institutions they consider worth preserving, they become less likely to permit conflicts that could threaten the existence of the community. Many attempts have been made through the years to answer this question in Africa, Asia and Latin America. The results of these inquiries suggest that national integration is a dynamic process[23] rooted in the constant interaction of people and is essential to continued interactions.[24]

The renowned African political scientist Ali Mazrui[25] identifies five interrelated aspects of national integration:

- the fusion of norms and cultures (including the sharing of values, mode of expression. Lifestyles and a common language);
- the promotion of economic interdependence;
- the narrowing of the gap between the elites and the masses, the urban and rural areas, rich and poor, etc (social integration);
- the resolution of emergent conflicts; and
- the sharing of mutual experiences so that people can discover that they have undergone some important experiences together.

Paden[26] coalesces these five aspects into four main dimensions of national integration: values, identities, linkages and structures. He defines values as the positive or negative perceptual and attitudinal realities or belief system that yields behavior of one kind or another. He notes that the critical value element in national integration is 'integrative tendency' (also termed integrative behavior). Deutsch[27] defines integrative tendency as the process whereby individuals or groups interlock their communication habits, share meaning, learn to predict each other's behavior and coordinate each other's action. When integrative tendency has been developed in a society, individuals or groups acquire the readiness to work in an organized way for common purposes, and to behave so as to achieve these purposes.[28] Integrative tendency, then, appears to be of primary importance in the generation and sustenance of patriotism and collective allegiance to a country.

Paden defines identities as the 'in-groups and out-groups ascription of labels or names to aggregations of people which may have social, political or economic relevance'.[29] This means that identities are the national or sub-national socio-cultural entities that people regard as their horizon. For example, an illiterate villager may regard his village as his horizon, not his nation. National identification requires the willingness to perceive oneself as a member of a national community, or to feel a sense of belonging to a country. This occurs at three levels; the verbal, the symbolic (as with the flag, national leaders, national icons, etc.) and the affective (or emotional attachment to the country and its leaders).

Linkages refer to the main facilities used to bridge any spatial divide between disparate communities. By their nature, linkage facilities encourage interaction between groups, and facilitate national identification and integrative tendencies. Important among them are links that facilitate all kinds of movement and communication across provinces, including land, sea, and air transportation networks, satellites, radio, television, telephone, and other kinds of electronic communications, migration and trade.[30] Data related to availability of these facilities are presented in Chapter 6. These facilities bring peoples from different geographic areas together thereby preventing ethnic isolation, which is antithetical to integration. They help Africans transcend spatial constraints that might have otherwise hindered interaction among cultural groups.

Drake[31] described structures as the historical, political, social and economic contexts that enable the planning and implementation of all other phases of integration. The commonality of structural experiences constitutes an important component for promoting a sense of unity and identity among people in different areas of a country and of different ethnic, socio-cultural, and economic backgrounds. In India, for example, a degree of national integration exists because common political and economic structures were established during the reign of Indira Ghandi and have been maintained.

Consequently, national integration is a multi-dimensional concept, with many inter-locking elements that operate independently to some degree but yet are also interactive, cumulative and generally complementary. It is also holistic in the sense that an integrated community is often more viable than each of its constituent parts. It is a highly complex phenomenon in the sense that what is integrative on the one hand may be disintegrative on another; and it is a dynamic construct in the sense that 'once integrated does not mean always integrated'.[32]

National integration seeks to produce intra-national unification and system stability. Intra-national unification is defined as 'the process or condition whereby functional unity is created among people who recognize some kind of common unity, such as the integration of their elites'.[33] Etzioni says that intra-national unification begins with the elites in the society putting aside their ethnic, racial, religious, regional or class differences to create an atmosphere where heterogenous units can feel some sense of interdependence and integration.[34] In countries where intra-national unification has been achieved, disparate groups are 'held together by mutual ties of one kind or another which gives the groups a feeling of identity and self-awareness'.[35]

Concomitantly, political scientists define system stability (otherwise seen as the absence of conflict) as the situation whereby a social system eliminates or minimizes potential sources of conflict. Abernethy[36] notes that when a society has transcended any and all forms of domestic conflict, it becomes unified. The conflicts that can threaten peaceful coexistence among discrete groups include ethnic tensions, civil unrest and military coups. Such occurrences may bring systemic breakdown, civil war, revolution and/or the dislocation of civil authority.

Every country strives to develop a stable and cohesive system in order to provide a society conducive for social, economic, technological and political development. To do so, they spend vast amounts of fiscal and political investments to avert conflicts. Yet, national integration does not mean the absence of tensions or conflicts in a society, in whatever form they may appear. In fact, sociologists have well established that tensions and conflicts are the elements that lend dynamism to a society. They have long held that conflict is the catalyst for social change. Since a society is dynamic, it cannot be devoid of tensions or conflict. The essence of national integration, therefore, is the establishment of 'institutions and modalities for the peaceful and satisfactory resolution of societal conflicts, whatever form they may take: class, ethnic, religious, regional, etc'.[37]

Strategies Previously Applied to National Integration

National leaders in pluralistic countries have applied two basic strategies to achieve a solution to the problem of national integration: 'cultural assimilation' (also called cultural syncretization) and 'multiple identities' (also referred to as unity-in-diversity).[38] But neither strategy has produced the necessary integration. Those countries that have chosen the cultural assimilation strategy have sought the coalescence of the cultures of sub-national groups into a centralized national culture or central political ideology. They have attempted to do this by assimilating the sub-national cultures either to 'a particular core cultural identity, or to the presumed characteristics and political affiliation of the culture of a dominant ethnic group'.[39] In some cases, this has meant superimposing the dominant ethnic group's culture upon members of smaller groups. In others cases, it has meant creating a new supra-ethnic identity that treats all ethnic groups as equal.[40]

A good example of the cultural syncretization strategy is the '*Pancasila*' in Indonesia. Described as the foundation upon which the Republic of Indonesia is built, *Pancasila* consists of two concepts: *Panca* and *Sila*. *Panca* means 'five' and *Sila* means 'principle'. Compounded into one concept, *Pancasila* has had far-reaching connotation by encompassing the various shades of identity, outlook and philosophy in Indonesia. It is the Indonesian national identity, the life outlook of the people and the philosophical foundation of the state. Its five principles are the belief in the one supreme God, a just and civilized society, the unity of Indonesia, people's sovereignty guided by the wisdom and ability of Representatives and advocates, and social justice for all Indonesians. Since 1978, *Pancasila* has been taught effectively in schools, and to all civil servants entering the civil service.

In 1999, violence in East Timor led to its successful secession of the province from Indonesia. Then, another province began clamoring for independence. This may suggest a failure of the *Pancasila* strategy. However, as a young Indonesian student[41] at an American university explained, it was not the strategy that failed. A failure of leadership caused the civil disobedience in Indonesia, the replacement of the country's leadership, and subsequent independence for East Timor. According to the student, Indonesians were incensed that their leaders failed to live up to the precepts of the *Pancasila*, which they expected the rest of the population to abide by. The leaders preached one sermon and lived another, and the Indonesian people corrected the situation by popular revolt. Thus, as this book argues, leadership by example is a way of communicating national integration.

The second strategy that national leaders in pluralistic countries have applied to achieve national integration is the philosophy of 'multiple identities'. This strategy was inherited as a colonial legacy in the many African countries where it has been implemented. These countries have attempted to cultivate the sense of political unity among diverse ethnic groups, while at the same time upholding and maintaining the social structures and cultural norms that make the groups disparate. Proponents assume that the acceptance of common political institutions is sufficient to make cohesive the disparate groups. The emergent political harmony, they assume, would produce the framework for economic unity and development.[42] Countries that have implemented the multiple identities strategy include India, Nigeria, Ghana, Kenya and among many others. While India has had some success with this approach, African efforts have been largely unsuccessful.

Take for example the implementation of the principle of ethnic balancing (i.e. the policy of reflecting the federal character), which requires that personnel from every state or province should be represented in national positions and offices, 'even in situations where it may be difficult to find suitably competent persons from every state'.[43] Although this policy was well intentioned in its goal of fostering ethnic harmony, it has nonetheless entrenched a culture of mediocrity across all levels of human endeavor throughout Africa. Because qualification and professionalism are sacrificed for political expediency in political and civil service appointments, civil servants feel no obligation to peg the career advancement against quality performance. The resulting apathy leads to gross negligence and dereliction of duty, and to competitive wrangling among various ethnic communities.

In Nigeria, for instance, the policy of ethnic balancing has further polarized the north and south. Northern Nigerians argue that the federal government has been tardy 'in using the quota principle to correct the imbalance in the federal bureaucracy that has resulted from the south's headstart in modern education'.[44] On the other hand, southern Nigerians counter that:

> use of the quota system in recruitment to the federal civil service, the police, the armed forces and other purely bureaucratic or technocratic federal institutions, has already made it possible for many persons from the North to occupy important positions without being required to possess the qualifications demanded from persons in the South seeking the same positions, and often at the expense of better qualified Southerners.[45]

To the southerners, the quota principle has been a major retarding factor in national growth and development, as it has entrenched a nonchalant attitude in the work ethic of Nigerian civil service employees. Employees have devised ways to avoid performing their duties altogether, or to get away with far less than excellent performance. Fela Ransom Kuti, a notable Nigerian musician and social critic, described this attitude among civil employees in his song, 'Rat Show'. He described how customers would go to the post office only to be ignored, their time wasted, before being told that there is no change for the smallest currency unit— fifty kobo. When the customer complains, supervisors defend the employee's reprehensible conduct by claiming that the employees are overworked. However, to the customer, it is usually apparent that the frivolous behavior of employees is because of the absence of honest competition in job hiring.

In a general sense, the national integration strategy that a country chooses can be used to classify the country as 'statehood' or 'nationhood'. Countries that apply the cultural assimilation strategy seek the status of nationhood; those that use the multiple identities approach seek statehood. Statehood centralizes power to maintain political stability, while nationhood aims to develop a national culture. The paramount goal of development in statehood is political and economic unity, whereas the developmental goals of nationhood include not only the presence of political and economic unity, but also the achievement of social, cultural and linguistic cohesion.

Theoretical Approaches to the Study of National Integration

Social scientists have studied the process of national integration from three universal theoretical perspectives. General systems theory analyzes whether there is a regular and continuing inter-connectedness in the subsets or elements of a system. Inter-connectedness is the main ingredient in the formation of value congruence in a system. Fischer notes that the formation of value congruence is why 'all ongoing social systems actually show a tendency toward a general system of common cultural orientation'.[46]

The transactional or communication salience theory of Deutsch, Toscano and others has also been used to explain both the degree to which people are connected and the way changes in the direction of communication affect the direction of integration. Deutsch notes that transactions are the first step to salience, which Fischer defines as 'the magnitude of flow of communication or goods which exceeds the null-model'. Deutsch[47] explains what happens when a community experiences many transactions:

> The people who have experienced these transactions will like them. When the transactions are highly visible, easy to identify and differentiate, people may form images of the community or of the group involved in the transaction. If these transactions were rewarded, the image of community may be strongly positive.

He says the perception of a sense of community allowed diverse groups to exchange norms, values and expressive symbols unconsciously. Fischer writes that such exchanges produce stability and integration in the social system.

Social scientists have used geographical relocation to study the problem of national integration. This 'Spatial' perspective sees integration as a function of the geographic distribution of people. According to Mabogunje, the movement of mass populations into different regions of a country is a significant way of achieving integration between a people and its territory, and also between different groups within the population.[48]

Based on the foregoing, any proposed communication strategy for national integration must necessarily derive from a combination of the knowledge gained from existing theories and approaches, the shortcomings of previous strategies and approaches, and the practical lessons learned from several decades of the experiences of developing societies. The theories and approaches help to identify the main areas for the proposed strategy; however, they do not offer much knowledge about the specific integration needs of each pluralistic society. These specific needs can be gleaned from the practical lessons learned from more than three decades in developing societies.

Since independence, the disparate peoples inhabiting many of the developing countries have maintained their primordial attachments of ethnicity, kinship and religion. In Rwanda, The Congo, Burundi, Nigeria, and even in the former Yugoslavia, people have not replaced their preference for ethnic protection with an acquired recognition of and appreciation for the supremacy of nationhood and its reliance on the goodwill of citizens. Yet, it seems that if tribal words and adjectives continue to be used in pluralistic countries, and the sense of nationhood continues to evaporate, the stability of these countries will remain threatened.

Communicating National Integration

African leaders rely heavily on mass media and speeches as weapons against division. Head projected this when he noted that practically all Third World leaders see the establishment of a national media service 'as a rite of passage into true nationhood, much like starting the national airline'.[49] Bourgault notes that the integrative function 'takes up the greater part of the media's energy and efforts'.[50]

Since mass media began in their countries, national leaders have implemented policies and issued statements that show they believe the mass media can facilitate national integration. In a 1987 address to the National Communication Policy Seminar held in Lagos, Nigeria's former Federal Minister of Information and Culture, Prince Tony Momoh, expressed the faith that African leaders have in the power of mass media to foster national unity. He told seminar participants that the media of radio, television and newspapers should not be seen as instruments for dividing the people of a country, but as tools 'for the promotion of national unity and integration'.[51] In many African countries, the integrative function is a required policy objective in the articles of association of national media organizations.[52] It is regularly articulated in the public speeches of media managers and national leaders.[53]

The belief held by African, Asian and Latin American leaders that the mass media are effective agents of national integration emanates partly from the works of scholars such as Deutsch, Bass,[54] Momoh[55] and Domatob.[56] Deutsch argues that the mass media are instruments for social mobilization, which is the key to the development of various kinds of integration. Bass suggests that people can develop common references by sharing mass media content. Momoh notes that because national interest supersedes any other interest, the mass media have 'a duty to win, maintain and perpetuate support for the nation'. Domatob believes that the mass media, which are generally perceived as instruments for education, information, entertainment and political socialization, should also be used to develop and preserve African cultures.

However, the attempts to use mass media to forge a sense of nationhood in African, Asian and Latin American countries have been largely frustrating. The mass media have continued to play the role of the devil's advocate throughout Africa. Since independence till now, the [mass media] have continued to contribute significantly to the disintegration of African societies. Media managers use the media to promote African societies weaker linkages: tribe, ethnicity, religion and political cleavage. They tend to emphasize alienation and polarization rather than unity through the broadcast of tribal and religious programs.[57] Thus, while media campaigns have achieved minor successes in such areas as the promotion of economic interdependence, adult literacy, urbanization and general social well being, after more than 40 years of self-determination, the majority of African countries have not evolved from tribal communities into nationhood. The ethnic structure that characterized their pre-colonial existence remains, and continues to be protected and nurtured.

For this reason, it is necessary to broaden the definition of communicating national integration to include all individual and collective acts, actions and activities that are capable of producing the perception of integrative or non-integrative behavior. This requires evaluation of all formal and informal channels of communication for their effectiveness, including interpersonal, small group, public speaking, the electronic media, and new media. Attention must be paid to non-verbal communication cues as well, particularly dress and behavior that sources intentionally or unintentionally use to contradict their integrative messages, thereby clouding meaning.

Scope and Organization of the Book

This then is a book primarily about the communications aspect of integration. Its analysis focuses exclusively on how well communication aids integration in Africa, and what could be done to make it more effective. Communication is one of many strategies to achieve national integration. However, perhaps it is the most important because it aids the effectiveness of all other strategies. But education, economic prosperity and political participation are other highly important integration strategies that should not be ignored.

This book's content is derived from the numerous works in political science and sociology. Where possible, the borrowed concepts are elucidated with examples from my personal experience in Nigeria and from interviews with colleagues from the Democratic Republic of Congo, Ghana, Kenya, South Africa and a host of other African countries. Because the integrative experiences of African countries are diverse, the examples presented here are not presumed to be all-inclusive. It is hoped, however, that this book will help readers to better understand the communicative practices that can better serve integration in Africa.

Appropriately, the book is structured along the dimensions of national integration. Part I contains three chapters that explore the effectiveness of communication used to promote each of the three dimensions of national identification: verbal identification; identification with salient national symbols, and affective identification.

Part II examines the communications practices used in the socio-cultural dimension of national integration. Within this context, Chapter 5 explores how effectively communication is used to create bonds through shared common historical experiences. Chapter 6 critiques the role communication plays to promote social interaction by examining the use of a common language, the pervasiveness of value and normative congruence, and elite integration. Chapter 7 explores the effectiveness of communications in economic development. Specifically, this chapter examines how communication can be used to integrate people at the grassroots into the national economy and to assess their understanding of their roles within the economy. Chapter 8 examines the various roles communication plays in political development.

Part III addresses the main theoretical considerations relating to communication for national integration: Chapter 9 discusses the need for research.

Chapter 10 examines the planning considerations related to integrative communication. Chapter 11 presents a model for integrative communications. Chapter 12 summarizes the content of the book.

Notes

1 Of the 52 or so countries on the continent, 32 or more have experienced some form of systemic instability, including civil wars. The 1995 'genocide' in Rwanda reportedly claimed more than one million lives. When the destruction of personal property and societal infrastructure are added to the loss of lives, Africa stands above others as a model of social disintegration.

2 The Inter-Africa Group, 'Social Development in the Horn of Africa: Challenges and Prospects, March 1995', paper prepared for the World Summit on Social Development, Copenhagen, Denmark, 1995, p. 6.

3 Osabuohien P. Amienyi, 'Communication and development quintessentials: The focus of development agencies and theorists', *The Journal of Development Communication* 9 (June, 1998): 1-16.

4 Ibid, p.12.

5 William J. Starosta, 'Communication and family planning campaign: An Indian experience'. in *Communicating for development: A new pan-disciplinary perspective*, ed. Andrew Moemeka, Albany, New York: State University of New York Press, 1994: 244-260.

6 J. Majewski, 'Third World development: Foreign aid or free trade?', *The Freeman* (1996): 1-6.

7 See for example the following works: John Paden, *Values, identities and national integration*, Evanston, Illinois: Northwestern University Press, 1980; R. Jahan, *Pakistan; Failure in national integration*, New York: Columbia University Press, 1972; Alan Liu, *Communication and national integration in Communist China*, Berkeley: University of California Press, 1972; Abraham Bass, 'Promoting nationhood in Africa', *Journal of Broadcasting* 13 (1969) 2: 165-169; Karl Deutsch, *Nationalism and its alternatives*, New York: Alfred A. Knopf, Inc., 1969; and Myron Weiner, 'Political integration and political development', *Annals of the American Academy of Political and Social Science* 358, March, 1965: 52-64.

8 Philip Jacob and Henry Teune, 'The Integrative Process: Guidelines For Analysis of the Bases of Political Community', in *The Integration of Political Communities*, ed. Philip Jacob and James Toscano, Philadelphia: J. B. Lippincourt Company, 1964.

9 Osabuohien P. Amienyi, *The relationship between mass media and national integration in Nigeria*, Unpublished Ph.D. dissertation, Bowling Green State University, Bowling Green, Ohio, 1989; Paul A. V. Ansah, 'Problems of localizing radio in Ghana', *Gazette* 25 (1985)1: 1-16; Christina Drake, *National integration in Indonesia*, Honolulu: University of Hawaii Press, 1989; Adelumola Ogunade, Mass media and national integration in Nigeria. in *International perspective in news*, ed. Leon Atwood and S. J. Bullion, Carbondale, Southern Illinois University Press, 1982: 22-32; and Moses Osaghae, *Mass media and political integration in Nigeria*, Unpublished Ph.D. dissertation, Texas Tech University, Lubbock, Texas, 1989.

10 Majid Tehranian, 'Communication and development,' in *Communication Theory Today*, ed. David Crowley & David Mitchell, (Stanford, California: Stanford University Press, 1994: 274-309.

11 Drake, *National integration in Indonesia.*
12 Tehranian, 'Communication and Development.'
13 Amienyi, Communication and Development quientessesntial,' p. 2.
14 Drake, *National integration in Indonesia.*
15 Inter-Africa Group.
16 Akin Mabogunje, *The Development Process: A Spatial Perspective*, New York: Holmes & Meier Publishers, inc., 1981: 250.
17 David Abernethy, *The Political Dilemma of Popular Education: An African Case*, Stanford, California: Stanford University Press, 1969.
18 Gray Cowan, *The dilemmas of African independence*, New York: Walker and Company, 1965.
19 Abubakar Tafawa-Balewa, 'Nigerialooks ahead', *Foreign Affairs* (1962, October): 131-140.
20 Jahan, *Pakistan; Failure in national integration*, p. 2.
21 Weiner, 'Political integration and political development'.
22 Abernethy, *The Political Dilemma of Popular Education.*
23 Minion Morrison, 'Ethnicity and Integration: Dynamics of Change and Resilience in contemporary Ghana', Comparative Political Studies 15 (1983) 4: 445-468.
24 Edward Spicer, 'Developmental Change and Cultural Integration', in *Perspectives in Developmental Change*, ed. Art Gallaher, Lexington: University of Kentucky Press, 1968.
25 Ali Mazrui, *Cultural Engineering and Nation-building in East Africa*, Evanston: Northwestern University Press, 1972.
26 Paden, *Values, identities and National Integration.*
27 Deutsch, *Nationalism and its alternatives.*
28 Abernethy, *The Political Dilemma of Popular Education.*
29 Paden, *Values, identities and National Integration.*
30 Ibid.
31 Drake, *National Integration in Indonesia*
32 Amitai Etzioni, *Political Unification: A Comparative Study of Leaders and Forces*, New York: Holt, Rhinehart and Winston, Inc., 1965.
33 Jacob and Teune, *The Integrative Process.*
34 Etzioni, *Political Unification.*
35 Jacob and Teune, *The Integrative Process.*
36 Abernethy, *The Political Dilemma of Popular Education*
37 The InterAfrica Group, 'Social Development in the horn of Africa'.
38 Henry Bienen, *The State and Ethnicity: Integrative Formulas in Africa*, in *State versus Ethnic Claims: African Policy Dilemmas*, ed. Donald Rothschild and Victor Olorunsola (Boulder, Colorado: Westview Press, 1983): 100-126.
39 Ibid.
40 Eddie Kuo, 'Language, Nationhood, and Communication Planning: The Case of a Multilingual Society', in *Perspectives in Communication Policy and Planning*, ed. S. A. Rahim and John Middleton, Honolulu, Hawaii: East-West Communication Institute, 1980: 122-126.
41 This text emerged from an informal conversation with an Indonesian student studying at Arkansas State University in the Fall of 1999.
42 D. K. Chisiza, 'The Outlook for Contemporary Africa', *The Journal of Modern African Studies* 1 (1963): 25-38.

43   Rotimi T. Suberu, 'Federalism and Nigerian's political future: a comment', *African affairs* 88 (1988, July): 431-438.

44   Ibid.

45   Ibid.

46   Fischer, 'The Impact of Political Socialization'.

47   Deutsch, *Nationalism and its Alternatives.*

48   Mabogunje, *The Development Process.*

49   Sydney Head, *World Broadcasting System* (California: Wadsworth Publishing Systems, 1985)

50   Louise Bourgault, *Mass Media in Sub-Saharan Africa*, Bloomington, Indiana: Indiana University Press, 1995.

51   Jerry Domatob, 'Sub-Saharan African Broadcasters: Social Influence and Status', *The Third Channel: IBS Journal of International Communication* 5 (1987): 660-675.

52   Ebele Ume-Uwagbo, 'Broadcasting in Nigeria: Its Post-independence Status', *Journalism Quarterly* (1986, Spring): 585.

53   Ikechukwu E. Nwosu, 'Privatising Broadcasting for Rural Mobilization and National Development: A Qualitative and Quantitative Analysis of the Nigerian Situation', *The Third Channel: IBS Journal of International Communication* 5 (1987): 632-643.

54   Abraham Bass, 'Promoting Nationhood Through Television in Africa', *Journal of Broadcasting* 13 (Spring 1969): 165-169.

55   Tony Momoh, 'Nigeria: The Press and Nation-building', *Africa Report* 32 (March/April 1987): 54-57.

56   Jerry Domatob, 'The Status and Influence of Nigerian Media', *The Third Channel: IBS Journal of International Communication* 5 (1987): 632-643.

57   See the example o f Nigeria presented in Osabuohien P. Amienyi, Obstacles to Broadcasting for National Integration in Nigeria, *Gazette*, 45 (1989): 1-15

PART I
COMMUNICATION AND NATIONAL IDENTIFICATION

Introduction

National identification is important to national development in a multiethnic nation-state. Feeling a sense of community is necessary if a pluralistic country is to focus the collective attention of its disparate groups on the attainment of mutually beneficial national goals. National identification is defined as the perception of oneself as a member of the national community.[1] It is seen as people of different ethnic, religious, class, and socio-cultural backgrounds expressing their ties to their national community verbally, symbolically and affectively, thereby differentiating themselves from other national entities. Through this identification, communities ascribe to themselves the basic attributes that form the core of their separate definition of themselves (e.g. language, religion, politics, territories, nationality and cultural norms and values), and define those attributes that should be excluded from that definition.

In the period immediately following World War II, considerable scholarly attention was drawn to the emergent countries in Africa, many of which were struggling for independence and most of which were undergoing rapid and uncertain social change brought on by the multiplicity-effect of modernization, industrialization and urbanization.[2] The majority of these states had been created arbitrarily in the latter half of the nineteenth century 'according to the exigencies of the political situation in Europe'.[3] Their boundaries were drawn with little consideration of the ethnic question and the colonial administrators did little foster their integration. Nigeria, the largest of these countries in terms of population (one out of every four Africans is reportedly a Nigerian), for example, brought under a single colonial administration in 1914 a veritable mosaic of about 250 nationalities.[4]

Between the late 1940s and at least the early 1960s, scholars hypothesized that the ethnic identities of these colonies and the newly independent countries they were now part of would gradually be replaced by 'a sense of territorial nationality which overshadows-or-subordinates parochial loyalties'.[5] This transformation was expected to follow a theoretically logical process that Cornell and Hartmann[6] explain as follows: urbanization would bring members of the various group to cities where they would intermingle, intermarry, exchange ideas and lose touch with their regions of origin. Industrialization would compel managers to be mindless of the origin of workers, treating them indiscriminately as individuals and mixing them in the workplace, thereby equalizing their differences. An expanded and modernized education system would teach the disparate groups a common language, a common body of knowledge and a common culture, fostering a shared and comprehensive national consciousness. New technologies of mass communication would bridge the differences between groups by taking individual experiences beyond the local and parochial. The political processes of nation building would institutionalize a comprehensive new identity that would undermine older parochial ties. The theorists reasoned that all of this might take time, as some groups would surely resist the changes that were to come, but in the end the modernization dynamics would prevail. In Nigeria, for example, the Itsekiris, the Urhobos and the Ijaws and all of the other groups soon would become Nigerians not only by virtue of the formalities of independence and citizenship, but also because of the existence of a comprehensive and newly acquired political and cultural consciousness.

At the dawn of 21st century, it has become apparent that these projections have failed to materialize not just in Africa, but also in Asia, Europe, the Middle East and Latin America. Far from receding into the background, ethnicity or identification by ethnic attachments has defied all efforts to lessen its relevance in social and political life, remaining instead a major force limiting both national integration and national development. As Horowitz[7] concluded in 1985, 'Ethnicity is at the center of politics in country after country, a potent source of challenges to the cohesion of states and of international cohesion.' Thus, Cornell and Hartmann proclaim the 20th century as the 'ethnic century'; a century in which 'conflicts and claims organized at least partly in ethnic or racial terms [were] legion'.[8] They substantiate this claim with a number of poignant examples, including the 1995 genocide in Rwanda, the 1967-1970 Nigerian Civil War, the 1991 disintegration of the Soviet Union, the Tamil rebellion in Sri Lanka, the clamor for separatism by the Quebec region of Canada, and a host of others.

These examples illustrate the disconcerting and destructive power of ethnicity in social settings where ethnic identification is 'thick' and national identification is 'thin'. In Rwanda, for instance, the genocide of 1994 fueled by ethnic hatred and rivalry brought social, political and economic progress to a screeching halt. Even though a few years have passed since that unholy event took place, the recovery of the country has barely begun. The ethnic hatred that motivated the brutal killings remains etched in the souls of thousand of Rwandans, triggering new slaughters of innocent citizens. The economy, which was virtually decimated by the conflict, has been slow to revive, even though more than $2 billion of international relief aid has been injected into it since 1994.[9] In development terms, the real cost of the estimated half-a-million human capital lost in the pogrom may be incalculable, but what is certain is that the contribution that this capital could have made to the development of their country may now have been lost forever. Now, much of Rwanda's arable land lies fallow.

Part I argues that ethnic diversity and identification can be sources of pride, unity and achievement for countries in Africa, if appropriate communications schemes are combined with other strategies to minimize the potential of ethnicity as instigators of conflict and division. It will evaluate the communicative aspects of current identification practices in Africa, and suggest a framework for promoting effectively the three dimensions of national identification: verbal, symbolic and affective. Communication is avowed to be a valuable tool for conflict resolution, diplomacy and understanding. Should it therefore not be an essential strategy for 'thinning' ethnicity and identification and 'thickening' national identification? A 'thick' national identification would ensure that the population's allegiance is first and foremost to their nationality rather than to their ethnicity, and nationality would become the sole basis for organizing social life.

Notes

1   Amos Sawyer, 'Social Stratification and National Orientations: Students and Non-students in Liberia', in *Values, Identities and National Integration*, ed. John Paden, Evanston, Illinois: Northwestern University Press, 1980, 285-303.
2   Stephen Cornell and Douglass Hartmann, *Ethnicity and Race: Making Identities in a Changing World*, Thousand Oaks, California: Pine Forge Press, 1998.
3   Thomas Laughlin, Environment, Political Culture, and National Orientations: A 'Comparison of Settled and Pastoral Masai', in *Values, Identities and National Integration*, ed. John Paden, Evanston, Illinois: Northwestern University Press, 1980, 91-103.
4   Richard Olaniyan, 'Introduction: The Relevance of Nigerian History', in *Nigerian History and Culture*, ed. Richard Olaniyan (London: Longman, 1985): 1-9.
5   Myron Weiner, 'Political Integration and Political Development', *Annals of the American Academy of Political and Social Science* 358 (March 1965): 52-64.
6   Cornell and Hartmann, *Ethnicity and Race*, p. 8-9.
7   Donald Horowitz, *Ethnic Groups in Conflict*, Berkeley, California: University of California Press, 1985.
8   Cornell and Hartmann, *Ethnicity and Race*, p. 1.
9   Anon, 'Rwanda's Aftermath of Genocide', *Macon Telegraph* (1999).

Chapter 2

Communicating
Verbal Identification

Introduction

When we are unsure of the origin of an acquaintance we have just met, who speaks our language with a different accent or who speaks another language entirely, who wears foreign attire, who exhibits different customs and values, or whose physical characteristics suggest a different racial or ethnic affiliation, we are apt to ask him or her, 'Where are you from?' An answer to this question allows us to situate such persons within the context of their in-group or out-group ascribed labels or names if we have prior familiarity with such context. Or it inspires us to seek more information when we have no residual knowledge about the named context. The answer to this question, 'Where are you from', lies at the heart of verbal identification, defined here simply as 'an individual or group's articulated statement of belongingness to a national, racial or ethnic entity.'

Throughout Africa, researchers or policy makers have never considered it a priority to explore patterns of verbal identification across the continent or to evaluate its role in national development. It was always assumed that the mere facts of independence and citizenship were sufficient, in and of themselves, to stimulate the population's identification with their nation-state. The theory was that the opportunities and promises that came with independence and the rights and obligations citizenship bears would make the national identity the only salient one for Africans—one they would gladly articulate when necessary. In reality, however, when confronted with the need for identification in the domestic arena Africans generally tended to verbalize ethnic or tribal identity more often than their national identity. Even when an ethnic identity is not verbalized, it is often easily inferred from names, attires, accents, foods, and so on.

But most people would concede that the way a nation-state perceives itself ought to vary significantly from the way its constituent groups perceive themselves. Although situations abound where a single ethnic community forms the nation and both ethnic and national identities merge into one, it is imperative to separate the national identity from the ethnic identity. This is because when ethnicity is the ubiquitous form of identification within a diverse nation-state, the fulfilment of the aspirations of the nation-state can be potentially jeopardized. It is important therefore to explore the positive and negative implications of conscious promotion of large scale verbal identification in pluralistic African nation-states. Specifically, it is necessary to examine the role that increased verbal identification can play in the development process in Africa, and to determine what communication can do to facilitate increased verbal identification.

Verbal Identification and National Development

The relationship between verbal identification and national development can be illustrated with an Edo[1] proverb that states, 'It's on one's own country that one wishes the rain to fall.' This proverb is used to invoke general patriotism and to remind recalcitrant Edos that each member must act consciously to insulate himself/herself from any threat from other groups. This proverb then links identity with social responsibility, and it is this link that makes it particularly relevant to national development. For to reify 'one's own country', as the proverb admonishes, one must undergo the process of identification, because it is impossible to claim a national community as one's own without feeling any sense of belonging. Furthermore, to aspire to the growth and prosperity of one's nationality, as the proverb's second part implores, one must make oneself available for full citizenship.

There is no question that identity and citizenship are both elemental to the achievement of national development. Identity breeds social responsibility, which must operate in the public domain to gain legitimacy and receive appreciation. Identity is a cultural value that has social, political and economic relevance.[2] When we articulate an identity verbally, symbolically or affectively, we reveal an important part of our self-concept, the part that contains the traits or attributes that shape and organize our lives and actions.[3] We define the boundary separating our group members from nonmembers, the perceived position of our group within our society and the meaning attached to our articulated identity.[4] We define who we are in terms of thought processes, mental dispositions, speech and behavior that circumscribe our relationship with others and our environment. We distinguish 'our' way of life from the lifestyles of others and we establish a contextual difference between our language, our religion, our politics, our culture and those of others. In short, we reveal unwittingly to whom we owe our ultimate loyalty.

The demonstration of our loyalty through identification can be seen as an inadvertent consequential expression of citizenship. Waters defines citizenship as the 'set of normative expectations that specify the relationship between a nation-state and its individual members which procedurally establish the rights and obligations of members and the practices by which these expectations are realized'.[5] Citizenship may be displayed in many ways, but 'ethnic' and 'state' are two forms of behavior that can affect developmental planning and accomplishment in a pluralistic nation-state. As Ndegwa[6] explains, 'ethnic citizenship' requires individuals to participate in an ethnic public and submit to ethnic authorities. Conversely, 'nation-state citizenship' requires participation within the national community and submission to national authorities. The ethnic public derives from the 'social customs, social practices, and non-bureaucratic structures that define and uphold citizenship in ethnic groups', while the national public comprises a 'Weberian legal, rational, and bureaucratic framework that uphold identity, legitimacy and authority in the nation-state'. Nation-states maintain and validate their identities in the public fora with legal and bureaucratic means, such as identity cards, voter registration cards, social security cards and passports. Ethnic identity, on the other hand, is validated and maintained by a socially constructed definition of belonging that accrues from 'birth, marriage or adoption into a family and kin, who consider themselves, and are considered by others, to belong a community that believes in a shared history and values'.[7]

This duality of identities and citizenship produces divided loyalty in individuals, a situation that prevails throughout Africa. On almost every occasion, Africans must choose between competing ethnic and national loyalties. The reason for choosing one over the other is explained by Giles and Johnson,[8] who note 'that individuals are motivated to maintain a positive self-regard, such that when confronted with alternative courses of action, they will choose one that enhances self-presentation given the particular context'. Unlike their European or Asian counterparts, African nation-states are not known for demonstrating competence in meeting their substantive obligations to their citizens. African leaders eschew their responsibilities for good governance and social welfare indiscriminately by capitulating to greed, opportunism and corruption. As a result, in times of personal or communal difficulties, ordinary Africans (i.e. people at the grassroots) discount any reliance on national institutions and structures, and look only to themselves, their jobs, their families, and their ethnic groups for salvation. Logically, it is also to these sub-national groups that he/she feels obligated when his/her loyalty is called into question.

African nation-states need social, political and economic stability to achieve national development. As already noted in Chapter 1, instabilities of any kind or proportion divert the human and material resources needed to improve a population's physical quality of life to coping with the centrifugal forces ethnic and regional disaffections and rebellions. Some believe that democracy would solve this problem in Africa. While there is no doubt that democratization is necessary for the empowerment of the grassroots population, it is also obvious that the redistribution of power and resources that tend to follow democracy can increase plurality in a diverse nation-state and further polarize the political system. For example, in Mali, Kenya, Liberia, Nigeria and other African countries where multiparty democracy has been instituted in recent years, incidences of 'ethno-linguistic vitality' have increased greatly, possibly to the detriment of the good governance.

Sociologists use the construct, 'ethno-linguistic vitality', to describe the socio-structural forces that facilitate a particular ethnic group's continued existence 'as a separate and active collective entity within heterogenous societies'.[9] These forces include the status of the group in the larger society, demographic variables, and institutional support for the group. A group's status is determined by economic and social power, socio-historical prestige and linguistic status. Demographic variables are also an important force because the size and distribution of the group are proportional to its representation in the larger society. A group's proportional representation includes not only the total number of group members in relation to other groups, but also the group's birth rate and patterns of immigration and emigration. Institutional support relates to the extent of the group's formal and informal participation in the institutions of the society, region, or state. Institutional support also includes the use of the group's language in the educational system, churches, the government, and the economic sector.

Ethno-linguistic vitality (real or imagined) is an inherited influence on individual attitudes and behavior in pluralistic nation-states.[10] This is because, as noted earlier, social identity shapes individual attitudes and behaviors. A person's social identity comprises three main internalized elements: the person's awareness of his/her membership in a social or ethnic group, and the valuation of, and emotional attachment, to that membership. These, in turn, form the person's self-concept. Giles and Johnson[11] note that the quest for positive social identity is the unwitting source of competition among disparate groups. This competition, in turn, leads social and ethnic groups to form negative attitudes and behavior toward out-group members. Negative attitudes and behavior emanate from unfavorable social comparisons with other group traits valued by the larger society, 'such as power, economic and political resources, and intellectual attributes'.[12] Since the spatial impact of development is naturally unevenly distributed within a social system, it is virtually impossible to prevent the occurrence of conflict-oriented inter-group comparisons.

In 1997, Bornman and Appelgryn[13] conducted an experiment in South Africa to explore the relevance of ethno-linguistic vitality in societies such as those in Africa undergoing rapid and large-scale social, political and economic changes. The results of the experiment showed that stronger ethnic identification is correlated with negative attitudes and behavior toward out-group members. Afrikaans-speaking whites, English-speaking whites and blacks who felt a strong sense of identity with their own ethnic groups were more likely to express negative views and opinions about other groups. The authors found also that the fear of losing one's ethnic identification breeds in people a strong desire to work to protect it. This explains why ethnic loyalty continues to undermine national stability[14] throughout Africa.

The link between ethnic protection and national survival reveals a significant (even if implied) relationship between verbal identification and national development. Aside from being an avenue through which citizens are mobilized, verbal identification is in part the essence of a nation-state's existence, for we cannot speak of national development in the absence of a national entity. People make up a nation. A nation-state exists only when people assert their control over a certain territory and acclaim their association with it publicly and with regularity. This avowal of belongingness to a nation-state establishes the shared rights, privileges and responsibilities that embody the group member's citizenship. As noted earlier, citizenship is instrumental to both social and political stability in Africa. Without it, African countries may find it difficult to institutionalize the continuities of policies, programs and actions required for long-range developmental planning and achievement. All over Africa, buildings, machinery and projects, purchased by one administration, are readily abandoned by another because no one wants to assume responsibility for failure. Such discontinuities of policies and planning are both a failure of civic responsibility and a waste of public resources that create a contentious atmosphere among people who expect the benefits of growth rather than the despair of delapidation. The brain drain that emanates from this deplorable state deprives African countries of the most productive sector of the human capital available for national development.

Factors Affecting Verbal Identification

International Image of the Nation

One factor that determines the extent to which people identify verbally with their nationality is the image of the nationality in the international community. Countries gain a favorable international image from the positive perceptions of governments and peoples of other nations. These perceptions may be gained from cordial contacts with members of the country, fate or national accomplishments in sports, medicine, technology or diplomacy. Whatever its source, positive perceptions generate recognition and goodwill for a country, which produces a sense of national pride. National pride enhances individual and collective self-concept and self-worth in a national population. The positive feelings derived from an enhanced self-concept encourage people to assert their national or ethnic affiliations to others in public or private circumstances. In this vein, a South African who feels good about his/ her nation or country's accomplishments might exclaim, 'I am proud to be a South African.'

Throughout the Western world, the public perception of Africa is generally poor. In most of the Western countries, and perhaps in Asia and Latin America as well, Africa is viewed only with limited interest.[15] As Dawkins[16] argues, most Westerners do not receive much information about Africa. Consequently, they have very little knowledge about how African societies really work. Ungar and Gergen[17] agree and write that most Westerners know little of the people, the politics, or current events in Africa. They observe that Americans, for example, 'often clump together all of Sub-Saharan Africa, also know as 'black Africa', as an undifferentiated mass'. They add that American public image of Africa is generally negative and characterized by AIDS, starvation, corruption, dictatorships or, as one African-American scholar sums it up, 'a continent of poverty and flies'.[18] They conclude that Americans have a broad ignorance of the complexities of Africa and its importance on the world stage.

Africa's poor image abroad derives mainly from 'European attitudes and assumptions in support of slavery'.[19] During the slavery period, Europeans created specifically degrading and dehumanizing concepts about Africans to enslave them. African societies and peoples were maliciously misrepresented in an effort 'to support the enormous profitability of slavery upon which the entire American colonial economy, and a great deal of European economy, depended'.[20] Harris notes that hard stereotypes were disseminated about black intelligence and ways of life, in order to promote a total negation of African humanity and culture. Unfortunately, these stereotypes continue to dominate the perspectives with which outsiders frame the African continent. Thus, it is not uncommon to find the continent still being referred to today as the 'Dark Continent', albeit this euphemism was created early in the 19th century to describe the notion the continent's enigma was beyond the comprehension of early European explorers.

Africans themselves have been hopelessly wanting in their efforts to reverse these negative perceptions. African leaders and peoples have consistently shown in their policies and actions a lack of true 'commitment to indigenize what is foreign, idealize what is indigenous, nationalize what is sectional and emphasize what is African'.[21] This universally demonstrated lack of commitment has left Africa with an unwieldy and irreconcilable triple heritage in religion, politics and social affairs.[22] In this state of confusion, Africa countries have been consigned to an inferior status within the hierarchy of nations. This has happened so much that Africans have come to believe that they are second-class citizens to Europeans. In this atmosphere of self-deprecation, some Africans see little pride in verbalizing their association with their own national heritage. For example, in the 1980s and 1990s, Nigeria's image was severely battered in the US, through media coverage of the nefarious activities of a small number of unscrupulous Nigerians, who were portrayed in major Western media as drug pushers and crooks.[23] Nigeria's autocratic leaders, particularly the despot Sani Abacha, have been frequently ostracized by the international community. Within this context, moral Nigerians, particularly those living abroad, felt ashamed of their national heritage, and would frequently claim other African countries, or even Caribbean countries, as their national origin when their nationality was in question. By the same token, when Nigeria showed a lot of promise immediately after the end of the Civil War in the 1970s, it was not uncommon to find Cameroonians, Ghanaians, Sierra Leonans, Nigers, and other West African nationals claiming to be Nigerians. The point is that people will more readily identify with their geopolitical entity, when it has a good external image. As it is expressed in another Edo proverb, 'a thief is not as ashamed as his/her relatives.'

Patriotism

A second factor that promotes verbal identification is patriotism. Patriotism is what John F. Kennedy alluded to when he told Americans in the early 1960s to 'ask not what the country can do for you, but what you can do for your country'. In many ways, patriotism is why the promotion of verbal identification must be considered paramount in Africa. Patriotism denotes devotion, love and support for one's country and the willingness to defend that country against all foes. This national loyalty is dependent upon an initial acknowledgment, to oneself and to others, that the existence of the nation is consequent upon the recognition of one's belongingness to the nation. One way this recognition is expressed is verbal identification.

The degree to which Africans have a sense of patriotism varies from country to country, and within different ethnic groups in each country. However, it can be concluded that patriotism is generally low in Africa. The reason for this is explained partly by professor Etienne Le Roy,[24] a legal anthropologist who has written extensively on Africa. Le Roy argues that the very notion of state is alien to Africa. He writes that the 'state' was a political instrument that the colonizers hoped to use to transform Africa and to make it compliant with the Western view of the world. He explains that in 1956 the French formally introduced the experience of state to Africans. The French had adopted the idea in the 14th century, when people began to show a devoted attachment to the idea that it was 'right to die for one's country'. But it took four hundred years for the idea to become institutionalized in France, and it was not until 1792 when the declaration was made that the 'motherland was in danger' that people really began to accede to the state's power.

Even though several decades have passed, the idea of 'state' has still not taken a firm hold in Africa. Consequently, patriotism has not been fully entrenched. Le Roy explains that 'the African view of the world is completely different and individualistic'.[25] According to him, Africans do not view the world through the Judaeo/Christian perspectives of unity and centrality. Rather, traditional African societies are organized along the principle of the complementarity of differences, in which the world is viewed as a series of interactions and connections between diverse constituencies. In the African view of the world, exchanges are concerned not only with relationships between humans themselves, but also 'with everything that surrounds them, be it visible or invisible'.[26]

African complementarity of differences is rooted in the clan or ethnic group as the basic form of social organization. This is the direct opposite of the principles of equality and uniformity that characterize Western notions of a modern nation-state. Constrained by about three centuries of slavery and 150 years of colonization, African societies are attempting to operate a principle of social/political organization not in keeping with the way their indigenous social and political systems functioned. By their very nature, traditional African societies are pluralistic, separational and segmented. Centralized power is dispersed to achieve a balance between the realities of division and the ethic of complementarity of differences. Yet neither the colonizers nor their neo-colonizing counterparts (African elites) have attempted to accommodate Africa's own realities within the Western model of the state and its institutions. This is why successive generations of Africans have focused their allegiance inward towards themselves or their ethnic group rather than outward toward their nation-state.

In terms of verbal identification, the absence of patriotism parallels infidelity in a marriage. Just as a disloyal spouse might forgo the disclosure of his/her part in promiscuous endeavors, so also does an unpatriotic individual tend to conceal his/her national attachment from public knowledge. This concealment is often aided by the individual's distortion of his/her normative values. The distorted values provide justification for the individual's disloyalty towards his country of origin and any precipitous actions that the disloyalty may bring, including the lack of identification. Such distortion of values appears to account for the wanton veneration of money and power in Africa, which has many public officials willing to sell their souls for material acquisitions. For patriotism to develop and lead to verbal identification, African institutions must be operated on a modified version of the Kennedy principle in which the question can be restated: 'ask not what you can do for your country, but what your country can do for you'.

Ideology

Still another crucial factor that aids verbal identification is a national ideology. Ideology is vital to verbal identification because it summarizes the normative values that a nation-state holds as its guiding principles. A nation-state without an ideology is like a house without a foundation, a living organism without a soul, or a machine without an engine. Ideology is the political tool used to promote a common objective among citizens of a nation-state. It establishes the moral barometer of the nation-state. Thus, ideology can be describes as an essential part of a nation-state's identity.

Good Governance

Perhaps the most important factor that determines the extent to which people will verbally identify with their nation-state is good governance. Good governance here refers not merely to the stability of the system, but to openness, accountability, popular participation and efficiency in leadership. Openness presupposes that the affairs of state will be conducted in a transparent manner so that people will understand the reasons behind the major decisions taken by those in power and the manner in which these decisions were made. Accountability means that political leaders will exercise their duty to answer to the public for any or all of their decisions. Popular participation suggests that the public is involved in the implementation and evaluation of the decisions made by their leaders. Efficiency indicates that leaders will gain the public's trust by taking decisions that 'are not just beneficial but essential for social progress and the political and economic development of the countries whose destinies lie in their hands'.[27]

Together, these characteristics of good governance promote both vertical and horizontal identification. Vertical identification is identification between the ruler and the ruled.[28] Where there is vertical identification, rulers fully understand the problems facing people in the larger society to the extent that they are willing to do something concrete about it, and people in turn truly understand the decisions made by the rulers to the extent that they are willing to give them their unequivocal support. There is a lack of vertical identifications when rulers act only in their own self-interest, and citizens, who have no recourse to extricate themselves from deplorable economic conditions, are left to their own devices.

An example of a lack of vertical identification is the following exchange between a newspaper reporter and a former minister of finance in Nigeria's second Republic, which took place at a press conference in the early 1980s:

> *Reporter*: Mr. Minister, are you aware that most people cannot afford to buy food in this country, and have to eat from the garbage in the streets?
> *Minister*: I have never seen anyone eating from the garbage.

This minister's response to the reporter suggested that he was not in touch with the plight of ordinary citizens in his country, even though they are the ones to whom he was ultimately responsible. The minister lived on the posh side of town, where no one was eating from the garbage. However, the minister was remiss in his public duty for failing to travel to the poor parts of town and across the blighted communities throughout the country. If he had, he might not have been surprised to find that there were people indeed who were rummaging through the dumps for their daily meals. Such a visit would have established vertical integration between the minister and the people, for the minister might have developed empathy for the plight of the downtrodden. In turn, the people might have more appreciated the minister's role in the government.

Horizontal identification is identification between citizens and groups. This is achieved when individuals and groups perceive commonality in their problems, prospects and causes. The perception of this commonality promotes trust between the groups and compels them to put aside their difference in order to work for common purposes.

Communicating Verbal Identification

Verbal identification is by its nature a communicative act. The expression of one's identity in an oral, written or visual disclosure serves both the rhetorical and relational functions of communication. Rhetorical communication is about influence. Rhetoricians attempt to get others to do what they want or need them to do and/or to think the way they want or need them to think. In other words, the purpose of rhetoric is to persuade.[29] Verbal identification fulfils the rhetorical function by establishing the mode by which one person sees and evaluates another. For example, a person who tells another person that he/she is from such and such a nationality expects acceptance or rejection. This acceptance or rejection depends on how the nationality is perceived or judged. The perception or judgment may be positive or negative depending on the hearer's existing knowledge or stereotypes. If one person said to another, I am a Nigerian and the hearer has a positive image of Nigerians, then it could foster acceptance. On the other hand, if the hearer's image of Nigeria is negative, then it could foster rejection. Therefore, verbal identification will influence the relational outcome of verbal identification by either strengthening or weakening the ties that exist between the former and the latter.

Relational communication is concerned primarily about fostering relationships. The essence of this form of communication is transaction or co-orientation, meaning the use of interaction to promote the well-being of a relationship between people. This is achieved when people coordinate 'their communication to reach a shared perspective satisfactory to all'.[30] Verbal identification is relational communication because it fosters the development of understanding between different people. The revelation of an identity casts out any illusion that may exist regarding place of origin that may obfuscate people's willingness to develop mutual ties. In this process, the boundaries of commonality and/or differences are established, the seed of friendship is planted, and empathy is developed from the possible agreement and/or consonance of thought. In this vein, verbal identification yields not only appreciation, but also tolerance of diversity and pluralism.

The combined rhetorical and relational function of verbal identification compels leaders and development planners in Africa to assess the unique effects that the classical elements of sender, message, channel, receiver and feedback can have on outcomes in this form of human transaction. The issue relating to sender deals with motivation. What motivates the expression of verbal identification beyond the mere fact of someone else's query? Generally, the expression of verbal identification is meant to fulfil one of three self-serving motives: altruism, deception, or deflection. For the majority of people, verbal identification is expressed mainly as a show of fervent national pride or altruism. The communicator is often so self-fulfilled with his or her identity that he or she wishes to share it with others.

Others, however, express identification verbally merely for the sake of expediency. If it is in their personal interest to do so or when external circumstances dictate, they state their national identity authoritatively even when it is apparent that their true reverence is for an ethnic or other sub-national identity. Others identify verbally with a nationality to conceal their true national identity. For example, a person may claim to originate from one country in order to deflect attention from their true nation of origin. I once met a Sierra Leonean who claimed a Nigerian origin because he did not want people to know that he was actually Sierra Leonean. Similarly, some Nigerians have been known to claim the 'islands' as their land of origin when they wish to conceal their true national identity. This game of deception usually occurs when the nation to be identified with has a perceived negative local or global image.

This deception also speaks to the unintended effects of communication channels, which can adversely affect verbal identification by distorting the reasoning behind it, obfuscating its meaning and possibly negating its final relationship outcomes. Adverse channel effect can occur in interpersonal verbal identification when non-verbal cues clearly negate an oral disclosure. For example, a person may dress in attire associated with one ethnic identity, but claim another identity verbally. The dress becomes a confounding factor in the person's identity. If it were not for speech, an observer might wrongly associate the person with the identity suggested by the dress. The fact that people may intentionally mask their identity by their actions or behavioral choices suggests that avenues for promoting national identification must be considered carefully.

How credible then is verbal identification in Africa? In short, how genuine are people's verbal claim to their nationality on the continent? It is commonly known that the identities of African nation-states are essentially a social construction. It is no secret that the majority of the countries in Africa were created and named arbitrarily by colonial administrators or by events surrounding colonization. In many cases, the names of these countries were indiscriminately imposed upon people. In this light, African national identities have been veritably subject to people's acceptance, resistance, rejection, redefinition, specification, manipulation, invention, and so on. Thus, verbal identification in Africa can imply an active 'we' or a passive 'they', depending on situations and circumstances. We connote association and involvement, both of which are inspirational for achieving national development. They, on the other hand, imply dissociation, aloofness, and distrust, which are contrary to the cohesion required for achieving development. There is therefore an inherent perpetual conflict between the 'we' and 'they' modes of thinking, which invariably engenders an 'us' versus 'them' attitude.

This is the attitude that appears to undergird most of the inter-tribal and inter-regional transactions in Africa, including the estranged relationship between the state, leaders and the grassroots population in most African countries. Intentionally or unintentionally, this attitude convolutes the verbal identification message. As such, someone who says publicly that he/she belongs to a country or nation may contradict this proclamation through behaviors, acts and actions. For example, a person may claim verbally to be a Kenyan, but convey the opposing Masai, Kikuyu or other ethnic identity through dress, inflection and mannerisms. Conflicting identification is misleading. The meaning of the main message in any verbal identification is a simple 'my body, heart and soul belongs to such and such a country'. When a communicator's non-verbal identification cues are contrary to his/her speech, meaning can be subsequently altered to 'my body belongs to such and such a country, but my heart and soul belongs to such and such ethnic group or cause'.

The patriotic and developmental implication of this contradiction seems to be submerged in the prevailing belief in Africa that being 'ethnic' equals being 'national', that is to say that being Kikuyu and Masai is considered tantamount to being Kenyan. But this is an erroneous belief. The identity of a nation-state may be the product of the sum of its parts or an arbitrary creation neutral to all parts, but it is not tantamount to the characteristics of each of its parts. Geertz[31] noted this when he wrote that at the beginning of nationalism, it is necessary to grasp the cultural issue that confronts each of the myriad of racial, tribal, regional symbols, as well as the attitudes created by past eras and to substitute for them a new phenomenon that is essentially abstract, artificial and self-conscious: a new political citizenship that changes all notions held by everyone about who he is and what he is not.

Many African countries, (particularly those in sub-Saharan Africa) have not yet taken the necessary step towards the creation of a national identity, even after more than four decades of independence. The apparent elusiveness of these national identities has been aided by the narrow definition that national governments have applied to the political philosophy and colonial legacy of 'unity in diversity'. Rather than viewing this principle as the agglomeration of common elements in diverse ethnic cultures into an independent national culture, national governments see it only in terms of political unity. Thus, they define it merely as the existence of a unified political system within a heterogenous cultural and linguistic environment.[32] This narrow definition limits attainable unity to a mere fragile tolerance. Fragile tolerance among disparate ethnic entities may have been sufficient for the colonial administrators to accomplish their imperialistic goals in Africa, but it has lacked the substance to promote meaningful nationality after independence. The stronger linkages among diverse national communities must therefore be extrapolated and transformed into a sense of national identity, which must be inculcated into the psyche of every sub-national population of African nation-states in order to make them perpetually aware of their common 'systemness'. Such inculcation should ultimately strengthen the verbal identification message, such as when people say they are from a country they will mean it with their body, mind and soul.

Correspondence exists between the inherent system of social organization in Africa and the need to imbue national populations with their national identity, be it derived or ascribed. Innate to Africa's system of social organization is a collective orientation that stresses group-think, continuity, harmony, and balance. Group-think compels individuals to situate the locus of their identification within the larger social grouping.[33] According to Chernoff, the locus of individual identity is derived from important attachments to the group. He notes that Africans face a marked existential dilemma when they are unable to establish group ties or can no longer find meaning within social networks. Tempels explains that 'a key feature of the conception of human nature [for the African] is that the person is not an entity separate from others, but rather participates in other beings (including persons) and is in part constituted by other beings'.[34] Wright[35] adds that the question 'Who are you?' is meaningless in Africa without the additional question 'Of where and of whom are you born?' For an African there can be no self without one's group, and one who does not avow a group is considered as 'lost'.

Concomitant with group-think is the highly valued sense of balance and social harmony, which requires individuals to negotiate their personal needs into the framework of their groups.[36] The African world is one where individuals continually balance pluralistic forces and demands to maintain social harmony. Happiness and success is defined as one's ability to meet the needs of kinsmen, age-graders, ancestors, gods, and ethnic group. When harmony is perceived within the group, the social status and self-concept of the African is heightened. Thus, it can be argued that the chaos in Africa since independence is in part due to the lack of people's identification with and selfless service to the nation-state.

Africans place a tremendous importance on continuity. Inbred in Africans is the 'need to regularly reify his or her membership in the group through the continued performance of rituals whose form was maintained through tradition'.[37] Each tribe or group has distinctive marriage, burial, and circumcision rituals, which are sacrosanct. Rituals are vital to identification. Aside from demarcating group boundaries, they are vital avenue through which the integrity of the group is maintained. Children are socialized to the rituals of group at an early age so as to maintain the continuity of the group. National rituals must replace ethnic rituals in the quest to bind citizens psychologically to their nation-state.

The collective orientation of African peoples presents promoters of national identity with an effective rational appeal for persuading them to see themselves as their nation-state. Africans have not fully embraced their national identity because they have not been shown how doing so can promote social harmony, balance and continuity. Compelling evidence has not been used to show that the legitimacy and independence of ethnic nations are foregone, having been lost in the colonial period. Nowadays, the ethnic group or tribe is an intrinsic unit of the nation-state, as is the self, family, and schools. It is the nation-state that bears all of the distributive economic, political and technological powers. This puts the nation-state at the apex of the hierarchy of African social organizations. In this regard, Africans must come to realize and accept the fact there can be no ethnic group without the nation-state, which means that the nation-state must come first in their thoughts and behavior.

Notes

1   Edo is an ethnic nationality in the southwestern part of Nigeria. This ethnic group is called Benin in English.
2   John Paden, *Values, Identities and National Integration*, Evanston, Illinois: Northwestern University Press, 1980.
3   Stephen Cornell and Douglass Hartmann, *Ethnicity and Race: Making Identities in a Changing World*, Thousand Oaks, California: Pine Forge Press, 1998.
4   Cornell and Hartmann, *Ethnicity and Race*, p. 81.
5   Malcolm Waters, 'Citizenship and the Constitution of Structures and Social Inequality', *International Journal of Comparative Sociology* 30 (December 1989): 159-180.
6   Stephen N. Ndegwa, 'Citizenship and Ethnicity: An examination of two transition moments in Kenyan Politics', *The American Political Science Review* 91 (September 1997): 599-616.
7   Ibid., p. 603.
8   H. Giles and P. Johnson, 'The Role of Language on Ethnic Group Relations', in *Intergroup Behavior*, ed. J. C. Turner and H. Giles, Oxford: Basil, 1981: 199-243.
9   R. Y. Bourghis, H. Giles, and D. Rosenthal, 'Notes on the construction of a "Subjective Vitality Questionnaire" for Ethnic Groups', *Journal of Multilingual and Multicultural Development* 2 (1981): 145-155.

10   P. R. Grant, 'Ethnocentrism Between Groups of Unequal Power in Response to Perceived Threat to Social Identity and Valued Resources', *Canadian Journal of Behavioural Science* 24 (1992): 348-370. See also P. R. Grant, 'Ethnocentrism in Response to a Threat to Social Identity', *Journal of Social Behavior and Personality* 8 (1993): 143-154.

11   Giles and Johnson, 'The Role of Language on Ethnic Group Relations', 199-243.

12   Ibid., p. 201.

13   Elirea Bornman and Ans E. M. Applegryn, 'Ethno-linguistic vitality under a new political dispensation in South Africa', *The Journal of Social Psychology* 137 (1997): 690-707.

14   Ndegwa, 'Citizenship and Ethnicity: An examination of two transition moments in Kenyan Politics', pp. 599-616.

15   Osabuohien P. Amienyi and Gilbert T. Abraham, 'An Experimental Investigation of the Influence of Photographs on College Student Perceptions of Africans', *Southwestern Mass Communication Journal* 11 (1995): 67-80.

16   Kristin Dawkins, 'Food Self Reliance and the Concept of Subsidiarity: Alternative Approaches to Trade and International Democracy', Paper presented at the Tenth Annual Pan-African Studies Conference, Indiana State University, Terre Haute, Indiana, April 15-16, 1993.

17   Stanley Ungar and David Gergen, 'Africa and the American Media', *Occasional Paper No. 9*, The Freedom Forum Media Studies Center: New York: Columbia University (November 1991).

18   Ungar and Gergen, 'Africa and the American Media', 4.

19   Michael D. Harris, 'African-American Baseline Essays: An Excerpt,' *Editorial Research Reports* (November 30, 1990): 690-694.

20   Harris, 'African-American Baseline Essays', 690.

21   Ali Mazrui, *Cultural Engineering and Nation-building in East Africa*, Evanston, Illinois: Northwestern University Press, 1972).

22   See Ali Mazrui's highly acclaimed documentary for PBS, *The Africans*, for a full discussion of this concept.

23   In the Unites States, for example, major newspapers and television networks have presented newsports and features linking Nigerians to drug trafficking, identity theft and securities fraud.

24   Interview with Professor Etienne Le Roy, 'Rethinking the State in Africa', *The Courier* 171 (September-October, 1998): 53-56.

25   Ibid., p. 53.

26   Ibid., p. 54.

27   Adboulaye Niandou Souley, 'Sub-Saharan African Under pressure from the West', *The Courier* 171 (September-October, 1998): 48.

28   Alan P. L. Liu, *Communication and National Integration in China*, New York: Holmes & Meier Publishers, Inc., 1977.

29   James C. McCroskey, 'Human Communication Theory and Research: Traditions and Models', in *An Integrated Approach to Communication Theory and Research*, ed. Micheal B. Salwen and Don W. Stacks, Mahwah, New Jersey: Lawrence Erlbaum Associates, Publishers, Holmes & Meier Publishers, Inc., 1996.

30   Ibid., p. 234.

31   Clifford Geertz, *The Interpretation of Cultures*, New York: Basic Books, 1973: 234-243.

32 Osabuohien P. Amienyi, 'The Problem of Broadcasting for National Integration in Nigeria', *International Third World Studies Journal and Review* 1 (1989): 196.
33 Louise M. Bourgault, *Mass Media in Sub-Saharan Africa*, Bloomington: Indiana University Press, 1995, pp. 4-5.
34 Placide Tempels, *Bantu Philosophy*. Trans. A. Rubbens (Paris: Presence Africaine, 1959). Cited in Bourgault, *Mass Media in Sub-Saharan Africa*, 5.
35 Bonnnie Wright, 'The Power of Articulation', In Creativity of Power: Cosmology and Action in African Socities, ed. W. Arens and Ivan Karp, Washington, D.C.: Smithsonian Institution Press, 1989, pp. 39-59.
36 Bourgault, *Mass Media in Sub-Saharan Africa*, 5.
37 Ibid, p. 5.

Chapter 3

Communicating With
Salient National Symbols

Symbolic Identification in Africa

Identifying with salient symbols of nationhood is an important part of the expression of national integration. Symbols of nationhood constitute a crucial component of the national identity of a social system. They are the emblematic repository of a country's history and the aspirations of its peoples. Thus, they make meaningful the political notions of sovereignty, self-reliance, self-determination and ideology. By identifying with national symbols, the people of a social system participate in national rituals that form part of the collective identity of the nationality. This participation expresses the willingness to exhibit common norms, values and behavior, and the desire to fervently demonstrate a communal spirit of national consciousness.

There are many symbols used to construct socially the identity of a social system, as well as to reaffirm its integrity and legitimacy. Among these are the national flag, national anthem, sports, national leaders and the use of the names of national heroes for streets, airports or seaports, constitutions, laws and the like. In general, these symbols can be evaluated in two complementary ways: first, as an assessment of the communicative effectiveness of the symbols; and second, as an analysis of the extent to which each symbol can promote national identification and integrative behavior within the context of Africa's teeming social problems. This chapter assesses the integrative messages that African national symbols communicate within the context of their ability to reflect identity, deepen national values, and generate national pride; all of which are elemental to imbuing a national population with integrative behavior.

The National Flag

Although the date of the first flag is unknown, flags have existed for at least 5,000 years. Flag-like objects, made of metal or wood, have been traced to ancient Indian and Egyptian civilizations,[1] and flags have been used to represent families, tribes, cities, monarchs, or religions. The earliest historical record of flags is said to be of a Chinese emperor in 1122 B.C., who had a white banner carried before him everywhere he went. The oldest flag in existence is a small metallic version of the national flag used today by Iran. It dates back to 3000 B.C. and the ancient city of Khabis in eastern Iran. In ancient Egypt, Greece and Rome, soldiers went to war carrying flag-like emblems bearing the representations of the revered national deities, such as eagles, owls, bulls, tortoises or the legendary Pegasus.[2]

However, the use of a flag as a national symbol is relatively new. It began in 1606 with the creation of the flag of Great Britain. Today, every nation (including those in Africa) is represented by a national flag. While the majority of these were created by nationalists and revolutionaries in the 18th and 19th centuries, some of those in Africa were created in the early to mid 20th century by colonialists as a way of formalizing the partition of the continent into distinguishable nation-states.

Most flag designs are intentionally steeped in history. But this does not mean that they are either archaic or relics. Flag designs are modified periodically, as the need arises, to reflect new government philosophies, expanding territories or even the whims of rulers. In the United States, for example, the state of Georgia made two changes in recent years to eliminate racially offensive symbols from its flag. When South Africa became a multi-racial democracy with the election of Nelson Mandela as president in 1992, the national flag was changed to reflect the emergence from the apartheid era of intolerance to the new political dispensation of racial accommodation. Similarly, following the 1994 genocide, Rwanda replaced its red, yellow and green flag, with a capital R in its center, with a red, white and green flag with a new coat of arm showing an ear of sorghum, a wreath and a bird in its center. Rwanda's Local Government Minister Desire Nyandwi gave the reason for the change. He told Reuters that '... we judged it necessary to change the national flag, the anthem and the coat of arms to bury the divisive past and foster national reconciliation'.[3] Many of the remaining national flags in Africa were adopted in the last 50 years.

National flags are more than just colorful pieces of cloth. They are representations of a country's history, culture, philosophy, geography and hopes for the future. They can represent the unity of a nation, as well as the divisiveness and oppressive policies of a ruling majority. That is why they can communicate joy, sorrow, courage or bravery.[4] Each aspect of a flag, its symbols, colors and shapes, tells a story about a nation and its people. Therefore, the flag is an important instrument of communication.

Flag symbols have evolved in many ways, with familiar symbols meaning different things to different countries. For example, each of the 50 stars on the U.S. flag represents a state in the Union. Five of the stars on the Australian flag represent simply stars, and are arranged in the shape of the Southern Cross, a constellation visible from Australia. Stars on the Brazilian flag have both spatial and galactic connotations, and are arranged in the form of actual constellations, with each star also representing a state. The lone black star at the center of Ghana's flag symbolizes African freedom, while the three green stars on Iraq's flag represent the aspiration to find common solutions to Arab problems.

The colors of national flags are more than just fashion statements. They are a vital part of the story a flag tells about the country it represents. Here are a few examples of the common messages flag colors send. *Red* often symbolizes revolution or resistance. It can signify blood shed in defense of the country or its principles, and has also come to represent the political doctrine of communism or socialism. *White* commonly signifies peace and tranquility. It can also mean purity as in the flags of Greece and Thailand, or more singular meanings as it is used in the flags of Peru and Chile. In the flag of Peru, the white and red stripes come from a group of flamingos that appeared during an attempt to liberate Peru from Spanish domination. The white rectangle on Chile's flag represents the snow of the Andes mountain. Traditionally, *blue* means freedom, the sky or the sea. But on the North Korean flag and Burma's flags, blue is seen as a commitment to peace. On the flag of Laos, blue represents prosperity. *Green* means fertility, vegetation or agriculture. Other meanings are hope (Burundi, Nigeria) and independence (Mexico). Green is also recognized as the traditional Muslim color. *Yellow* has a variety of meanings including wealth (Brazil), the fruits of labor (Guinea-Bissau), justice (Guinea), copper (Cyprus) and sunshine (Uganda). *Black* often reflects the ethnic heritage of a people, but it can also signify the defeat of enemies, as in Kuwait's flag, or determination, as in the flag of the Bahamas.[5]

Countries may use the same combination of colors in the design of their national flags, but the flags may communicate entirely different meanings. The most common flag design is the tricolor, which was made popular by the French revolution. Similar designs are seen today throughout Africa and Europe. The red, white and blue of the French and American flags symbolize revolution and freedom. The red, yellow and green used throughout Africa represent freedom and the desire for African unity. These are seen as Pan-African colors. Red, white, black and green appear in the flags of many of the Persian Gulf nations, and are seen as Pan-Arab colors.

African national flags are more than simple representations of political philosophies or national ideologies. They are the embodiment of the innate desires of disparate groups, with different politics, customs and languages, to find a way to sing, pray and cry with one voice. They are the poignant reminders of the fact that national cohesion is a necessity and not a luxury in pluralistic societies, where the need to frame the problems of the nation and the solutions to them within a national rather than tribal or regional perspectives is often greater.

Yet, in spite of the vital role they can play in fostering social cohesion, national flags have been limited in their ability to affect social and political behavior in Africa. There are many reasons for this failure, but the most important is that the majority of Africans (particularly those at the grassroots) are simply oblivious to the integrative messages that are implicit in their national flags. Even though countries take prudent measures to explain the nature and meaning of their flags in official publications, gazettes and even on the internet, there is still a general ignorance of the symbolic importance of flags on the African continent. This ignorance stems from poverty and illiteracy, which makes national flags insignificant among the daily concerns of most Africans. There are no known statistics on the percentage of the population who possess a national flag or who display it on ceremonial occasions in Africa, but it is apparent that flags are not among the important daily preoccupations of ordinary Africans. The basic unimportance of national flags is reflected in a pidgin English expression in Nigeria that goes: 'na flag we go chop?' (meaning 'is it the flag that we'll eat?'). This expression suggests that achieving the basic needs of life (food, clothes, shelter), as stipulated in Maslow[6] hierarchy, is the primary preoccupation of a majority of the African population. Teeming social problems preclude many Africans from expending energies on reveling in flags as a symbol of nationhood, particularly when the nations the flags are supposed to represent are a shadow of themselves, unable to address the needs of ordinary citizens.

The National Anthem

Every country has patriotic hymns that express the people's love for their country. Some are derived from existing folk songs. Others are composed in times of war or revolution to express hope, salvation or future expectations. Many countries have selected one of their patriotic songs as a national anthem, to be played and sung on ceremonial occasions. A national anthem usually expresses religious feelings, as well as feelings of pride in one's country. It is customary to stand in reverence, while one's national anthem is being played or sung.[7]

Excerpts from the national anthems of Ghana, Kenya, Malawi, Nigeria, Uganda, Zambia, and Zimbabwe suggest that African national anthems are purposeful and powerful integrative messages. That is to say they are ebullient articulations of each country's history as well as the aspiration of its peoples, inspirational expressions of hope that the spirit of togetherness will guide the process of nation-building, and fervent advocates for the creation and maintenance of national unity. For example, the opening lines of the Ugandan national anthem are a testimonial to the inextricable bond that should exist between citizen and country. The lines articulate the fervent sentiment that the subsumption of individual destiny into the destiny of the country is the surest way for both sides to realize their full potential:

> Oh Uganda! May God uphold thee,
> We lay our future in thy hands.
> United, free, for liberty.
> Together we'll always stand.

The lines make clear the choices that most African populations must make: to stand united and build a formidable and virile country, or to stand divided and sow the seeds of the demise of both national and individual aspirations.

Individual sacrifice for the sake of nation-building is also the main theme of the Kenyan national anthem. The anthem enjoins disparate groups to put aside their differences and face the task of nation-building with common purpose and determination:

Let all with one accord
In common bond united
Build this our nation together
And the glory of Kenya
The fruit our labor
Fill every heart with thanksgiving.

In Africa, the task of nation-building has not been consensual among disparate groups. While some groups have worked for the universal interest of nation-building, other groups have worked against it. In such a counterproductive environment, national anthems like Kenya's, if properly promoted, understood and adhered to, can become the means for motivating everyone to become a servant to the nation, instead of to themselves or their ethnicity or region.

Each time Ghanaians sing their national anthem they pledge to work for national unity with determination and fortitude, and to be a servant to their nation. The inclusive tone that the anthem bears add immensely to its persuasive power:

Hail to thy name, O Ghana
To thee we make our solemn vow
Steadfast to build together
A nation strong in unity;
With our gifts of mind and strength of arm,
Whether night or day, in mist or storm,
In ev'ry need, whate'er the call may be,
To serve thee, O Ghana, now and evermore.

While it is doubtful that Ghanaians recall this pledge during the course of carrying out their daily activities, it is noteworthy that Ghana is one of the few African countries where acts of inter-ethnic rivalry rarely occur. This absence of irredentism has been largely responsible for the economic and political strides that the country has made in recent years.

The absence of irredentism in a social system suggests the presence of elite integration. Elite integration (which will be discussed more fully in chapter 6) is vital to national integration because elites control the instrument of power that they use to spread their shared values and goals among 'illiterate and tradition-bound peasantry'.[8] Thus, elites have the responsibility for synthesizing 'the cultural issues that confront the myriad of racial, tribal, [and] regional symbols, as well as attitudes created by past eras', and supplanting them with 'a new phenomenon which is essentially abstract, artificial and self-conscious: a new political citizenship which changes all notions held by every individual about who he is and what he is not'.[9] Elites facilitate national and symbolic identification across the various sub-parts of the national system by promoting the sharing of common values, defining the nature of community inclusion, and agreeing to the decision-making process within the system.[10] By so doing, they mobilize the rest of a national population towards social cohesion or anarchy.

In Ghana and other African countries, elites are seen rightly as the driving force behind integration or disintegration. This is because what is readily observed as integration in many cohesive states is actually the general population's acceptance and co-option of elite integrative behavior. When elites are perceived as a united group, working towards a monolithic national goal, the feeling of stability permeates the general population of the social system. This perception provides ethnic communities with a frame of reference to reflect on national issues through universal lenses. It also presents a model of integrative behavior that the rest of the population emulates.

One of the main tools elites use to mobilize the rest of the population is the national anthem. Elites see national anthems as persuasive instruments for eliciting social cohesion and positive collective action. Throughout Africa, national anthems are intentionally ladened with integrative verses. A common presumption is that these inspirational verses will imbue diverse populations with the motivation to cultivate the spirit of oneness and to apply this spirit to the goal of nation-building. It is hoped that, at the very least, elite integration might result that would gravitate the entire population toward national integration.

But for all the integrative potential that national anthems may possess, there is a crucial barrier to their effectiveness as a communication avenue. This barrier is language. Except for a handful of countries, African national anthems are written and sung in a language that differs from that which most Africans use in their everyday lives. The majority of the anthems are in the language of the colonial countries: English, French and Portuguese. However, only a tiny fraction of the population, mostly educated elites, civil servants, academics and business people, use the lingua francas for everyday purposes in their homes. In many cases, teachers who are supposed to teach these foreign languages can barely manage a conversation in them. This barrier precludes people from feeling the intensity of involvement in national affairs that these anthems elicit.[11]

Sports

In his *More than a game: Sports and politics*, Martin Barry Vinokur quotes J. H. Strayer, who says 'the tools men use or the food they eat may determine the chances for survival of a people; the games they play or the stories they read may establish the character of a nation'.[12] Amidst the divisiveness that plagues many African countries, 'sports' has become a metaphor for unity. When athletes from African countries are participating in a sporting event, be it at the international or domestic levels, they bear the hopes and aspirations of the entire population of their countries upon their shoulders. Those watching them at home or elsewhere put aside their differences for the moment to share in the 'joy of victory' or 'agony of defeat' experienced by their national sports teams, who are inadvertently turned into heroes. Thus, sports transform diverse populations into a oneness of mind, body and spirit, at least for the short duration of the sporting event.

Such was the case when South Africa won the 1996 version of the African Nations Cup, the continent's premier soccer tournament. The significance of the victory was not lost on the South African press, which saw the implications as more than winning a trophy. South Africa's *Sunday Times* said in an editorial that the victory could lead to the unification of an erstwhile racially divided nation, and that the victory 'has made us one'.[13] In agreement, Mutume[14] opined, 'perhaps that is what we need all the time. Our country's success in sports field seems to translate into a dose of enthusiasm, optimism and togetherness'.

Mngerem[15] writes that football (soccer) has a similar integrative effect on divided Nigeria. When watching football, 'Nigerians become human beings. They are no longer Tiv, Ijaw or Urhobo. They are no longer Sango worshippers, Gani Adamas, sat Guruans, Zamfarans, Olumbans or Hari Krishnas. They are just people'. He adds that although he does not like the game, he has a good feeling when football season is in the air:

> Truth be told, the unity you see in our faces, the hope you feel in the air, the oneness of spirit which is so thick you can't cut with a knife is so beautiful...There is this festive air and you can see a spring in the walk of the Nigerian. There is the pride in being Nigerian and he looks at you and feels proud that you are his fellow Nigerian, you can feel the embrace and warmth in his look, especially when Nigeria has just beat those troublesome North Africans or heaven help them - Brazilians.

Somberly he adds, when football is over people go back to their divisive ways, becoming more concerned with where one is from than the substance of one's character. Facetiously, he advises that government could integrate football into the national policy and do so in such a way that before a Nigerian takes any action or says anything, images of the country's soccer exploits could be flashed before his/her eyes. According to him, maybe there could be peace and the proverbial 'Where is he from?' will be erased from Nigerian minds.

The integrative efficacity of sports derives from the innate socio-cultural and political roles sports plays in the life of a social system. In many countries (including those in Africa), sports are viewed as a vital means for maintaining public health and improving human character. Sport or physical activity is touted as a logical path to physical, psychological and emotional well-being among the young and the old. The belief is that the healthy person is more civil, productive and better able to fulfil his/her citizenship obligations. According to a 1997 article in World Health[16], poor health can undermine economic performance and the resulting poverty can mean fewer resources for addressing the needs of the population. Vinokur[17] supports this contention with his assertion that sports aid in fighting against sedentarism, and is a 'precious means in the multi-sided growing up of the younger generation'. The 'theatrical qualities of sports and the mystical sentiments they inspire'[18] help people dissipate excess energies. This produces improved mental health in the population, which produces a multiplicity effect of increased productivity in both public and private endeavors.

Sports serve four main political functions in a social system. First, sports are an effective means of marketing and reinforcing specific political ideologies. Allison notes that success in sports are seen by association as success for a political system. Said he:

> ...Whatever the preoccupation with the bodies and souls, governments in modern times have habitually seen sport as an important agent of political socialization: it is an expression of British values; a metaphor for American imperialism and [a beacon] at the forefront of modernizing nationalism in Africa.[19]

He writes that politicians universally use sport venues as settings for disseminating ideological messages to specific groups, 'drafting in international sportsmen to lend credence to their arguments'. This tactic has become more ubiquitous in recent years as sport spectators and participants who are potential ideological adherents, are held inadvertently in the captive environment of huge stadiums and subjected to forceful or subtle political indoctrination, especially through the use of nationalistic symbols.

Sports as a Means to Gain Prestige

Second, sports are an avenue through which national leaders can garner prestige. Allison notes that for generations American presidents have associated themselves with the youthful image of sports. Presidents and heads of states further exploit the opportunity to use sports for political advantage when they make congratulatory phone calls to victorious athletes. The athletes are often told how proud their entire nation is of their success, and how much the success means for the nation's existence. For example, president Nixon often called victorious teams in their locker-room during presidential campaigns. Ford, Carter, Reagan and Bush followed suit during their presidencies. President Clinton extended this policy a step further when he gave the victorious American women's soccer team a tour of the white house, following their victory in the 1998 women's world cup, hosted by the United States. The American media portrayed the team as 'America's team,' and by so doing, made the team a symbol for successful and peaceful multiracial coexistence.

African leaders have learned from their foreign counterparts how sports can be used for personal political gain. President Jomo Kenyatta of Kenya was the first African leader to use sports for this purpose, frequently exploiting the enormous political capital that association with an international sporting hero can bring. In 1968 he welcomed home the highly successful Olympic team from the Mexico games. He displayed political guile, when he reminisced that of one of his senior Ministers had praised the national team on its return from the Tokyo Olympics four years earlier for 'showing the rest of the world that there was a country called Kenya in which lived people with the ability, energy and potential to be reckoned with'.[20]

Soon, other African Heads of State began adopting this policy, as increased international media coverage of sports became an unwitting ally in nations' quests for international recognition, which is one of the main ways through which countries promote national identification and pride. Ghanaian leader, Flight Lieutenant Jerry Rawlings, who seized power in a coup in December 1981, personally welcomed home the Ghanaian national soccer team, *The Black Stars*, after the team won the thirteenth Africa Cup of Nations tournament in Libya in January 1982. He told the returning players, 'What you have won without expectation of any promised material reward is tribute to your revolutionary strength. The revolution thrives on women and men who fight without any expectation of any reward, but for the glory of their people'.[21] This comment was a sequel to a statement a month earlier, in which he declared the success of the coup 'a tribute to the Revolution, which had raised the hopes of all Ghanaians'.[22] Rawlings saw sports as an avenue for improving diplomatic relations between estranged nations. Immediately prior to his 'December revolution,' the then Head of State, President Limann, had barred the Ghanaian team from attending the games hosted by Libya. Limann's refusal to grant the team permission was in protest of Colonel Muammar Ghaddafi's perceived interference in the domestic affairs of other Africa states, which Linmann felt was destabilizing the entire continent. Upon his rise to power, Rawlings immediately reversed Limann's policy 'to further cordial relationship between two revolutionary governments'. In pragmatic terms, this reversal meant Libya would supply Ghana with food, drugs and oil. The rioting which followed Ghana's soccer success over Libya brought momentary fear that the budding friendship between the two nations would be jeopardized.[23]

Later that year, the Ghanaian Secretary for Youth and Sports re-emphasized the role of sports in international relations when he announced that Ghana would attend the Commonwealth Games in Brisbane 'to foster international relations and understanding through sporting activities'. Rawlings appeared on the sporting platform once again in the following year, this time as the leader of a host nation magnanimous in defeat when he presented the trophy to an Egyptian team who had won the final of the African Cup Winners Cup, hosted by Ghana. In March 1985, Rawlings again reveled in sporting success when he welcomed home the newly-crowned world featherweight champion, Azuma Nelson. His most recent attempt to exploit the political benefits of sport was in January 2000, when he attended the opening game of the African Cup of Nations tournament which Ghana co-hosted with Nigeria. This occasion presented Rawlings an opportunity to showcase the relative economic success Ghana had made in recent years, in contrast with Nigeria where the economy was still in a deplorable condition.

Prime Minister Mundia of Zambia used similar opportunities to gain political recognition. In October 1984, he encouraged the expression of national pride in the achievement of the national athletic contingent, which returned home victorious from the Central African Senior Challenge Cup Final. President Kaunda seized the same opportunity, albeit in a less overt fashion, when he sent a congratulatory telegram to the successful team.

Nigerian leaders have also use sports for political benefit. In 1985, the then Nigerian Head of State, General Mohamadu Buhari, personally welcomed home the victorious national youth soccer team, the *Golden Eaglets*, who won the inaugural under-17 soccer world cup in China. Buhari declared a public holiday to involve the citizens of Nigeria in recognizing the importance of the team's success. Since then, it has appeared as if welcoming home victorious athletes is part of the official function of Nigerian leaders.

Sports Heightens National Consciousness

Sports have proved a magnificent way to stimulate national consciousness. Allison[24] notes that sports can generate a collective emotion unrivaled by art, politics or religion. Sports sociologist Harry Edwards says that sports are a 'value receptacle' for society's dominant social values. Political scientist Richard Lipsky[25] explains that sports' dramatic appeal helps people escape everyday life by compelling us to form bonds that transcend our traditional parochial loyalties. The nationalistic or patriotic intent is obvious in flag raising events at the opening ceremonies of international sporting competitions like the Olympics or Soccer's World Cups, or the national anthem prior to the start of an event. National flags, banners emblazoned with nationalistic slogans, or chants of patriotic cheers during contests are all demonstrations of national identity, pride and consciousness. Nicolae Ceausescu's government in Romania and the Communist government in the former East Germany made huge investments to ensure their nation's success at international events. How seriously the Romanian government viewed sport investment compelled an American Embassy official in Bucharest to remark: 'The Romanians are trying to prove their national identity through excellence in sports, and they play only to win'.[26]

The former leader of Zaire (now Democratic Republic of Congo), the late Mobutu Sese Seko, also understood the role of sport in promoting a sense of nationhood. Most now believe Mobutu staged the now-famous Ali-Foreman world heavyweight championship fight (elegantly dubbed the 'Rumble in the Jungle') to enhance his political status. However, the event unwittingly became a vehicle for national identification and reconciliation. Mobutu took the boxers on a nation-wide tour that injected a sense of national cohesion in some 200 ethnic groups. Leaders of the ethnic groups were brought together to watch the fight live 'in an effort to develop the sense of national unity'.[27]

Sports as Tools of National Policies

Sport is an effective instrument of national policy. President Jimmy Carter used the United States boycott of the 1980 Moscow Olympics to demonstrate American opposition to Soviet policies in Afghanistan and Soviet human rights practices. In

1984, the Soviets retaliated by boycotting the summer games held in the United States. In Africa, Sani Abacha's government precluded the Nigerian national soccer team, *The Super Eagles*, from taking part in the 1988 Africa Cup of Nations tournament held in South Africa, in protest about South African foreign policy regarding Nigeria. In 1972, Palestinian guerrillas sought to use the Olympic games to gain publicity for their cause, with fatal consequences. These boycotts, engineered by political disaffections and considerations, and the patriotic fervor that the U.S. ice hockey team generated at the 1984 Winter Olympics, leave little doubt that sport is an intrinsic aspect of a country's political-economic system,[28] and a potent instrument of foreign diplomacy.

Sports social and political functions make it a formidable tool for achieving national, social and political integration. By identifying with a sports team, people identify with larger political entities that the team represents—city, provinces, region or country. Sports also socialize youths to possess team spirit, leadership and character; qualities that are essential for maintaining social integration. The identification and integrative behavior that sports participants and spectators display usually lasts well past the completion of competition.[29] This furthers the goals of nation-building and political integration. Furthermore, the success of a national team in international competitions generates international recognition for the nation. This enhances personal pride, which increases individual and collective self-worth, intensifies interest in national affairs and manifests active citizenship. Thus, through its many social and political functions, sports act as a unifying force that may counteract other divisive elements like economic conditions, racial differences, class inequalities, or religious hatred.[30]

But for every apparent integrative success achieved through sports, there are many opportunities for social dislocation or political disintegration, which are counterproductive in the seemingly futile struggle for nationhood in many African countries. Africa has not been spared the ubiquitous problem of violence associated with domestic and international football, both on and off the field. Although ethnicity has not been the sole cause of violence in African football, it has played a part for many years in setting back national unity. Ethnicity-aided football violence is particularly divisive because football matches offer ethnic groups in large cities an opportunity to 'ventilate the educational, occupational, or residential antagonisms that they experience towards each other'.[31] The more the clubs unite people at the sub-national level of ethnicity, the more competition between them heightens fan and player hostility. Football is undisputedly Africa's most popular spectator and participant sport. Therefore, any violence associated with the game 'is well reported'[32] and produces new cleavages, which distract members from allegiance to the nation.[33]

There are many examples. In Nigeria, bitter ethnic and religious rivalries have often manifested violent confrontations at football matches in the domestic league. In 2000, several clashes were reported.[34] The clashes left vast destruction of property and personal injuries. In one such fracas between supporters of the Plateau United Club of Jos and Jigawa United, more than 234 people were injured amidst large scale destruction and/or illegal seizure of property.[35] An earlier incident in 1981 resulted in violent rioting which left 13 spectators dead. Nigeria's eastern neighbor, Cameroon, also experiences the problem of inter-ethnic rivalry on the football field. In their analysis of the modernization taking place in Cameroonian football, Clignet and Stark[36] note that inter-ethnic rivalry is a prominent feature of football in Cameroon.

In Tanzania, football violence originated from a disconnection between urban and rural communities. Although sport was seen as a means of integrating urban and rural communities, football has widened the gap to the detriment of national integration. Football clubs based in Tanzania's largest cities (particularly Dar es Salaam—the capital city) have access to more resources and better facilities. This gives them dominance and virtually guarantees them supremacy over their impoverished rural counterparts, which often precipitates an angry rural-based backlash.[37]

Football has also exacerbated micro-nationalism in Tanzania. Tanzania was created from the amalgamation of the island of Zanzibar and the mainland Tanganyika. Sports were thought to be an ideal avenue for cultivating mutual understanding and unity between the peoples. But as Fair[38] points out, football became a vital arena for highlighting the differences between disparate communities within Zanzibar and with the mainland. She writes: 'In football Zanzibari men found a new venue for expressing class and neighborhood rivalries and for strengthening communal identities'.[39] Football competitions produced sub-national identification and rivalry that seriously damaged the intended unifying function of the sport.

The disintegrative consequences of football violence can also be felt at the international level. Football violence has severely limited sport's role in aiding supra-national integration.[40] Violence at international football matches has often exposed antagonism between estranged nations. Even where nations are in discord, the pressures of regional or continental cup competitions have produced the violence, giving rise to tension between nations. The African Nations Cup, Champions Cup and Cup Winners Cup competitions have often been the venue for expressing animosities. The semifinals of the African Champions Club tournament in Abidjan between Asec Mimosa of Cote d'Ivoire and Asante Kotoko of Ghana ended with more than 3000 Ghanaians to take refuge in police stations, churches and diplomatic missions. Angry Ivorian youths went on a beating and looting rampage that left about 50 Ghanaians dead and over 400 injured. The rampage was supposedly to avenge an earlier alleged assault on Ivorian soccer fans in the first-leg match between the two clubs in Kumasi.[41] The thirteenth African Cup of Nations final in March 1982 between Ghana and Libya ended in clashes between players and supporters, and the flags of both countries were ceremoniously burned.

In 1979 both Sierra Leone and Liberia repeatedly claimed the victimization of their respective nationals living in the other country. When their teams met in Sierra Leone in November, the game became a tinder-box and crowd trouble soon followed. Visiting ministers of the Liberian government were given rough treatment and subsequently removed from the stadium by gun-wielding soldiers. A formal protest was lodged with the Confederation of African Football, and the return leg was cancelled. The incident also resulted of the heads of state of both nations to publish a joint communique. Two years later, a similar incident occurred at a match between the national teams of Gabon and Cameroon. The resulting rioting left two dead and more than 4000 Cameroonians were airlifted to safety.

When Nigeria brutally expelled Ghanaians in February 1983, the expulsion led to increased tension. In November, the planned match between the Super Eagles of Nigeria and the Black Stars of Ghana could not take place. A date or venue could not be arranged for the fixture as protracted negotiations failed to yield agreement on the safety of both players and supporters. The Nigerians, in particular, feared violent reprisals from Ghanaians for the wanton deportation.[42]

All of this illustrates that the application of sports to the goal of generating inter-ethnic ties and fostering intra-national and supra-national integration is fraught with uncertainties. Nevertheless, African countries are in desperate political situations that call for desperate measures. The least desperate measure is the exploitation of sports for national integration. The inefficiency of sports vis a vis their integrative task in Africa derives mainly from improper administration that leads to the occurrence of violence at football matches. Western countries show that prudent administration is vital to the competitiveness and success of national participants at international sports competitions. Still, the management of African sporting organizations remains poor and unprofessional, tarnished by a lack of vision, corruption and bureaucratic wrangling. Because it is well understood that only the expansion of sporting success at all levels of competition can bring the full political benefits of sports, sport administrators must realize that they have a crucial role to play in the struggle for national and continental integration. Success in domestic and international competitions brings pride and joy that integrates a nation's people. Such success will be more frequent and more meaningful when the selection of teams and administrators is devoid of ethnic politics, and both the teams and administrators display skill, professionalism and patriotism in their service.

National Heroes, Landmarks and National Integration

The building of national monuments, the creation and observance of national holidays, and the naming of streets, airports, seaports and other landmarks for national heroes are essential tools for promoting national integration. Rosenberg[43] affirms this in his description of the central role that monuments and holidays have played in the construction of national identity in the southern kingdom of Lesotho. Lesotho, a small land-locked country, has lived under the constant fear of annexation into South Africa, which surrounds it. This fear galvanized the country's inhabitants to develop a strong sense of national consciousness. In constructing their national identity, the people of Lesotho have looked to King Moshoeshoe I and the Thaba-Bosiu (or 'mountain of the night'). King Moshoeshoe I built the nation now known as Lesotho, and the Thaba-Bosiu was where he began to build it. Legend says the walls of the mountain rose at night to form an impenetrable fortress, making any breech attempt impossible. Under the protection of this natural fortress, the king had time to successfully amalgamate those fleeing white tyranny in South Africa with the Basotho already living in the valley. To commemorate this birth of a nation, statues have been erected in Maseru (the capital of Lesotho) in honor of Moshoeshoe I and Makaanyane, his trusted counsellor and military commander[44] and March 11th has been declared the national or Moshoeshoe Day.

National monuments give self-representation to a nation, and objectify the ideals for which the nation is supposed to stand. But Mosse[45] notes that this was not always so. Before the nineteenth century, he notes, monuments were mainly erected to honor kings or generals. At the beginning of the nineteenth century, they began to include poets and writers, adding a cultural dimension to the political and military ones. Mosse says that the early monument's symbolism lay in facial expressions or attires. They were plain at first, but were soon surrounded by other symbols to add to their meaning. For example, a hero was set on a horse led by the mythical representations of the goddesses of Peace or War, or one was crowned with laurels, or the pedestal on which a man stood was decorated with ornaments to demonstrate his deed or worth. The early monuments always had symbolic meaning, but this meaning became far more pronounced at the beginning of the nineteenth century as symbolic representations of nationhood began to replace the more simplistic and purely dynastic symbolism of earlier times.[46]

As national monuments became more elaborate, designers began to place space in front of them for national festivals. Mosse[47] writes that the sacred space for national worship and the use to which it was put determined the difference between a living and a dead monument. To keep national monuments alive, people make periodic pilgrimages to them. Such visits render monuments inseparable from national festivals, so that they become the focus of national celebrations. Monuments, holidays and heroes act as the inanimate corollary of the oral tradition by communicating to successive generations the people, places and events that have shaped the existence and character of the nation-state. They deepen people's awareness and appreciation of their past, while laying a historical foundation for the future.

The observance of national holidays and periodic visits to national monuments are ways to build new inter-cultural relationships or rekindle faded kinships and ties. Children and adults use the moments to learn about their country's history, founding fathers and patriots, as well as its prevailing norms and values. This socialization is important to preserve the normative traditions of the nation-state. It instills the foundation or ideals for the nation, thereby forcing a re-commitment to its integrity and growth. Such commitment is necessary for the survival of the social system, because no nation can guarantee its existence without the entrenchment of its culture and traditions in successive generations.

National Leaders

Liu[48] labels identification between rulers and the ruled 'vertical integration'. Vertical integration implies that the rulers and the ruled share a common vision, values and purpose. This sharing of these socio-cultural attributes cultivates the perception of a sense of community in a diverse political unit. This perception increases and strengthens communal bonds, which means a pluralistic society is able to enjoy the benefit of lasting social harmony and political stability. Logic says that vertical identification constitutes a crucial component of national integration.

Many good examples of vertical identification exist. It is perhaps best exemplified by the relationship between former president Bill Clinton and many American people. According to Minor,[49] 'it is beyond dispute that many of us (Americans) related to Clinton in an unprecedented way'. He says Clinton seemed to invoke a deeply favorable personal reaction. This favorable reaction, he argues, arose mainly from feelings of simple loyalty ('he's done well for us') and political pragmatism ('he'll keep doing well for us'). But he adds that the reaction also reflected substantively the established nature of the American community and the advanced state of its politics. In the United States, as in other Western countries, a strong sense of national community is established by the preexistence of '... a well formed national ideology, a national elite, national institutions and national pride'.[50] This sense of community produces strong feelings of public support for a leader and his/ her policies, which is used to weld the polity together in time of polarization. Vertical identification does not allow disaffected interest groups, even if motivated by latent parochial loyalties, to gain momentum to the point where they can destabilize the social system. However, in the developing countries, where no such sense of territorial nationality overshadows—or subordinates—parochial loyalties, it is often difficult to cultivate vertical identification. Where vertical integration exists, it is never strong enough to keep small dissensions with the leadership and national policies from undermining the integrity of the whole system.

Yet, it is not true that vertical identification has not existed or does not exist in Africa. African leaders such as Kwame Nkrumah, Julius Nyerere, Kenneth Kaunda, Mu'ammah Al-Qadhafi, Murtala Mohammed and many others have enjoyed the admiration and support of their people. When their motivation was to improve the social, economic and political situations of ordinary people, these leaders and their policies received unwavering support. For example, Kwame Nkrumah was swept into office as prime minister of Ghana on March 6, 1956, in a political wave described as 'a true expression of the Ghanaian population'.[51] Although he embarked on an unambiguously ambitious social development program, Ghanaian peoples were fervently united behind their leader, harmonized by his ebullient oratory, glib rhetoric and zeal. Everything indicated his projects could be successfully undertaken on a sustained basis. Ghanaians were filled with 'a vibrant national passion for development and self-reliance. Throughout the nation, in every region, every chiefdom, the population enthusiastically and earnestly embraced his sponsored and supported self help schemes'.[52]

In Tanzania, Julius Nyerere also instituted and benefitted from vertical identification. His desire to liberate the Tanzanian masses from poverty and pestilence endeared him to the country. Contrary to some other African leaders, he was recognized as an astute, pious and honest leader. People had faith in his leadership and were willing to make personal sacrifice to achieve his presidential aspirations. However, his political ideas were often elusive, even to elites in his society. Meisler[53] says that few of Nyerere's people understood his ideas well enough to implement them. Consequently, Nyerere's government failed to produce his envisioned development. Nevertheless, he is still considered one of Africa's visionary leaders. His ability to understand the plight of the common people and his attempts to remedy imbalances and injustices in Tanzanian society are still seen as a model of leadership for other African nations.

During Kenneth Kaunda's presidency, Zambians felt a certain degree of kinship with the ruling class. This arose ostensibly from a perception that Kaunda desired to emancipate his people from poverty, pestilence and illiteracy. Brody[54] notes that Kaunda wanted what subsequent Zambian leaders have not had: His people and his country to achieve a standard of living not defined by Western norms, 'but simply by their having the opportunity to develop a future; a real future of hope and possibility'. Kaunda was a good, humble, sincere and caring person, whose popularity was spread throughout the nation and not just restricted to his ethnic group.[55]

Thus, effective leadership can be said to be a precondition for vertical integration. In research spanning more than 70 years, it has been found that effective leadership is driven by leadership behavior, leadership characteristics and the ability to build organizational culture.[56] Leaders are said to be effective when, by their behavior, they:

- Provide a clear focus on key issues and concerns;
- Get everyone to understand this focus through effective organizational communication practices;
- Act consistently, over time, so as to develop trust;
- Demonstrate through actions that they care for and respect the organization's members; and
- Create empowering opportunities that involve the organization's members the right things their own priority.[57]

Effective leaders also exhibit many of other leadership characteristics, including the development of 'self-confidence,' 'need for power' and 'long time span'. Although it is developed through experience, 'self-confidence' is grounded in an innate belief that one can make a difference. 'Self-confidence' is a sense of assurance that what one does can have a real and meaningful effect. Similarly, the 'need for power' derives from one's desire to be in control of the situation of others, as well as self. Thus, power can be intoxicating and corrupting' 'Absolute power corrupts absolutely'. Consequently, not all 'need for power' translates into effective leadership.   Effective leaders use power and influence to benefit the organization and its members, not just to satisfy their own desires or to benefit themselves. 'Long time' span relates to the duration and complexity of tasks that one can plan and think through. Effective leaders often have a vision span of more than a decade. They can plan and think about multi-faceted projects spanning over many years. It is important to note that these characteristics are not fixed but can be developed, thus negating the dominant wisdom in the 1920s that effective leaders were born, not made.[58]

Effective leaders also display an ability to build organizational cultures. They exhibit the ability to imbue organizational members with widely shared assumptions, values and beliefs. This ability is targeted towards the achievement of four organizational functions: coordinating team work; achieving goals; managing change; and maintaining a strong organizational culture.

Anecdotal evidence suggests that not many African leaders exhibit these effective leadership traits. In Africa, news reports are plentiful detailing the managerial shortcomings of national, state and regional leaders or managers. Diurnal reports of misappropriation of public funds, nepotism in the distribution of public resources and other corrupt practices in government are far too many to enumerate here. Even those who were brought to office by universal suffrage have not been immune from such reprehensible behavior; they have often tended to forget the masses who elected them. They live in extraordinary opulence on ill-gotten wealth, while the population they were supposed to serve lives in poverty.

This corruption is exacerbated by the largely exclusionary nature of African politics. African politicians achieve legitimacy by pandering to ethnic aspirations. This ethnicization of politics excludes others who share a different ethnic heritage or different point of view. It rids leaders of their people's trust. Lack of trust constrains the development of vertical integration. The absence of vertical integration limits the extent to which leaders can describe their actions or themselves in national terms.

Thus, the development of vertical integration in Africa impinges on the ability and willingness of leaders to increase:

- the extent to which they display effective leadership behaviors;
- the degree to which they possess the personal characteristics required of effective leaders; and
- the extent to which they have (or could have) a positive effect on their national culture.

Communicating Symbolic Identification

In the Western world, the importance of national landmarks, national holidays and national heroes in maintaining national identification and cohesion is articulated through the planned analysis and publicity of spectacular rituals, such independence celebrations. These ritual ceremonies and celebrations form part of the social system's cultural inventory, and are staged at rural areas especially and urban settings simultaneously to foster the shared feeling of nationhood.

In Africa acceptance of the cultural relevance of national symbols has yet to be institutionalized. It is not that African countries have insufficient useful symbols for promoting common identification or purpose among diverse national populations. Anyone who has traveled to Africa can attest to the plethora of national representations with which everybody should identify: 'flags, anthems, national days, national leaders, national stadiums, national heroes, national airlines and other symbols'.[59] Many of these symbols are presented on government-owned media on an almost daily basis.

Rather, it is the lack of uniformity in perceiving the unifying tendencies of these symbols among various ethnic nations comprising each African country. This lack of uniform perception derives from the complex nature of intercultural communication. In intercultural communication, perception of a shared phenomenon is shaped by the system of symbols and meanings participants bring with them.[60] This semantic system is influenced by differences in norms, values, beliefs, attitudes and frames of reference, and each culture teaches the patterns of thought that are most appropriate for assessing universal objects or situations.[61] Thus, most people in all nations see national symbols as sacred objects of reverence and obeisance, but some people perceive them as alien intrusions or wanton representations of oppression and hegemony.

This then is the communication problem related to symbolic identification in Africa: how to create common perception among diverse entities so that everyone can adhere equally to the unifying tendencies of national symbols. The key to solving this problem lies in inspirational communication. At every opportune moment, the language used to describe or present national symbols in promotional messages must evoke unparalleled passion so that any interaction with national symbols can lift people's souls and spirits in time of pain, offer them hope in times of hopelessness, solace in times of abandonment, and unity in times of division. That is to say the symbols must be promoted in such a way that they generate feeling, emotion and patriotism. This type of promotion will enable these symbols to tap into that 'universal desire to display the intangible values that distinguish nations and cultures from one another'.[62] This yearning will become the catalyst for producing the unity of thought, action and purpose that will pull diverse populations together in an organized or spontaneous celebration of their national heritage.

Presently, national celebrations revolving around national symbols occur in urban areas (usually at state and provincial headquarters, and national capitals). That is where many of the national symbols are also found. Thus, the majority of African populations who live in the rural areas are expected to travel to the urban areas to experience the national spirit (which scarce resources prevents many doing), or to co-opt it from television (which many of them do not have). Is it surprising then that the national spirit is thinner in the rural areas than in the urban areas? In order to unify the meaning and significance of the national symbols among the masses, publicity and promotional efforts must focus on the village, small towns and then individuals. Relaying examples of national behavior in urban areas to rural areas may facilitate imitation or replication of these behaviors by opinion leaders and individuals in villages and small towns. As Ghandi notes, 'If a few individuals in a village are influenced by the example set by the leader, they are converted to the new way of life, and regeneration of the locality is facilitated'.[63]

The extrapolation and promotion of the unifying tendencies of national symbols should be undertaken by national leaders, community leaders, opinion leaders, sports heroes, teachers and inspired commoners who have some measure of influence at the grassroots. As Verma[64] suggests, these contemporary propagandists must be expert psychologists, adepts at symbol-making, phrase-coining, and demagoguery 'who can by subtle suggestions and mass hypnosis evoke in people the desired emotional effect and behavior'. They must be people who possess charisma and oratory, which can deeply touch the minds of the masses. They must be learners who learn not just from others but also themselves, and who understand that persuasion begins with the self. They are visionaries, who recognize the wisdom in Ghandi's belief that 'the appeal of reason is more to the head, but penetration of the heart comes from suffering'.[65]

Africa can boast a small number of such leaders who put the national interest above his own and who through personal example promotes a national symbol worthy of emulation by the masses. There is Leopold Senghor, Kwame Nkrumah, Sekou Toure, Jomo Kenyatta and, of course, Nelson Mandela. Mandela is especially notable for his personal sacrifice for the ideal of a genuinely democratic South Africa. Having spent 27 years of his life for the ideal of a racially integrated democracy, his leadership reconciled white fears with black aspirations. He talked to his enemies and negotiated them out of power. He supported the creation and execution of Archbishop Desmond Tutu's Truth and Reconciliation Commission, and accepted its report in October, 1999, even though the report indicted both Apartheid and ANC members guilty of human rights abuse.[66] Wherever Mandela goes in South Africa or Europe, he is seen a symbol of the South African nation, not of his tribe or ethnic group. Whereas other African leaders sit in press boxes as spectators during national celebrations, Mandela led his divided population in celebration of every national event. He attended soccer games involving the national team, wearing the national jersey rather than a custom-made suit. He was committed to justice, equality, reconciliation and moral integrity. Through his example, Mandela reminds us that diverse political constituencies can be united by a national symbol if ample opportunities are provided for interaction.

Official and unofficial channels of communication should be used to facilitate this interaction between people and their national symbols: interpersonal and traditional channels that include folk media, rallies, parades, radio, television programs, news, commercials, documentary film, newspaper articles, posters, books, newsletters, leaflets, pamphlets, stickers, and messages on T-shirts, bowls, plastic bags, etc. Spreading messages about the national symbols across several media in accordance with the synergism principle will intensify the effect. The intensified message should complement what education is already doing. Because children are already learning about their national flag, singing their national anthem, and observing national holidays at schools, mass media promotions can stimulate visits to national monuments. Such visits will help to make concrete the experiences and events that the symbols represent.

Notes

1   Maria Elena Fernandez, 'Grand Old Flags: Symbols of Our Unity, Our Purpose, Ourselves,' *Los Angeles Times* (Sunday, June 11, 2000): 1.
2   This information was obtained from the America's Best Product's home page. Http://www.niceflag.com/history.htm. April 11, 2000.
3   Jean Baptiste Kayigamba, 'Rwanda to change flag in effort to bury past,' *Reuters* (May 18, 1999).
4   Joe Tersigni, 'Taking pride in our National Flag,' *The Toronto Star* (February 15, 1999).
5   This information was obtained from the America's Best Product's home page. Http://www.niceflag.com/history.htm. April 11, 2000.
6   Abraham Maslow, Toward a Psychology of Being, D. Van Nostrand Company, 1968.
7   Anon, 'The National Anthem,' *Compton's Encyclopedia Online* (1999). Http://www.optonline.com/comptons/ceo/03358_A.html April 13, 2000.
8   George W. Shepherd, Jr., 'National Integration and Southern Sudan,' *The Journal of Modern African Studies* 4, 2 (1996): 194.
9   Clifford Geertz, 'The Integrative Revolution, Primordial Sentiments and Civil Politics in the New States,' in *Old Societies and New States*, ed. Clifford Geertz, New York: Basic Books, 1973.
10 John Paden, ed., *Values, Identities and National Integration: Empirical Studies in Africa*, Evanston: Northwestern University Press, 1980.
11 This perspective is consistent with the views expressed by Anon, 'A new Strategy to Empower people in Africa,' *World Health* 6 (November-December, 1997): 4.
12 Martin Barry Vinokur, *More than a game: Sports and Politics*, New York: Greenwood Press, 1988, 1.
13 Quoted in Gumisai, Mutume, 'South Africa-Sports: More Than Just a Soccer Victory,' *Inter Press Service English News Wire* (February 6, 1996).
14 Ibid.
15 Mngerem, Suleyol, 'Football as Metaphor for Nigeria's Unity,' *The Guardian* (February 5, 2000).
16 Anon., 'A New Strategy to Empower People in Africa,' *World Health* 6 (November-December, 1997): 4.
17 Vinokur, *'More than a game,'* 35.
18 John Hoberman, The Olympic Crisis: Sports, Politics and the Moral Order, New Rochelle, New York: Aristide D. Caratas, Publisher, 1986
19 Lincoln Allison, *The Politics of Sports*, Manchester, England: Manchester University Press, 1986, 13.
20 Ibid., 156
21 West Africa (London, April 1982).
22 West Africa (London, March 1982).
23 West Africa (London, April 1982). See also Allison, *The Politics of Sports*, 156.

24 Allison, *The Politics of Sports*, 152.
25 Richard Lipsky, 'Towards a Political Theory of American Sports Symbolism'. *American Behavioral Scientist* 21 (January/February 1978): 348.
26 Vinokur, *'More than a game,'* 33.
27 Allison, *The Politics of Sports*, 158.
28 Vinokur, *'More than a game,'* 17.
29 Ibid., p. 18.
30 Ibid.
31 Remi Clignet and Maureen Stark, 'Modernization and Football in Cameroun,' *Journal of Modern African Studies* 12, 3 (1974): 409-421.
32 Allison, *The Politics of Sports*, 159.
33 Dean E. McHenry, Jr., 'The Use of Sports in Policy Implementation: The Case of Tanzania,' *Journal of Modern African Studies* 18, 2 (1980): 237-256.
34 Duro Ikhazuagbe, 'Riot Act for Clubs: Referees Threaten to Boycott the League: Pepsi League Fall-out,' *Post Express* (May 18, 2000). In the following matches: Kwara United versus Plateau United in Ilorin, Berger versus Gabros in Abeokuta, Ebonyi Angels versus Rovers in Calabar, NITEL versus Eagle Cement in Lagos, and Sharks versus Enyimba in Port Harcourt, violence took on an ethnic dimension. Many lives were lost.
35 Stephen Oboh, 'Fans on Rampage in Jos,' *Post Express* (May 1, 2000).
36 Clignet and Stark, 'Modernization and Football in Cameroun,' 417.
37 McHenry, Jr., 'The Use of Sports in Policy Implementation,' 237-256.
38 Laura Fair, 'Kickin' it: Leisure, Politics and Football in colonial Zanzibar, 1900s-1950s,' *Africa* 67, 2 (1997): 224-251.
39 Ibid, p. 225.
40 Supra-national integration is the agglomeration of independent nation-states into a functional regional and continental political, economic, technological, and military community.
41 Anon, 'Football violence Takes its Toll,' Inter Press Service (November 5, 1993).
42 Allison, *The Politics of Sports*, 158.
43 Scott Rosenberg, 'Monuments, Holidays, and Remembering Moshoeshoe: The Emergence of National identity in Lesotho, 1902-1966,' *African Affairs* (Winter 1999): 49-74.
44 Richard P. Weisfelder, 'The Basotho nation State: What Legacy for the Future?' *Journal of Modern African Studies* 19, 2 (1981): 221-256.
45 George L. Mosse, *The Nationalizatioon of the Masses: Political Symbolism and the Mass Movements in Germany from the Napoleonic Wars Through the Third Reich* (New York: Howard Festig, 1975): 47.
46 Mosse, *The Nationalizatioon of the Masses*, 47.
47 Ibid., p. 63.
48 Alan P. Liu, *Communication and National Integration in Communist China*, Berkeley, California: University of California Press, 1971.
49 J. Douglas Minor, 'The Moral Cost of Political Unity' (A New Visions Commentary Paper, National Center for Policy Research, September 1998).
50 R. Jahan, *Pakistan; Failure in national integration*, New York: Columbia University Press 1972.
51 Anon, 'Kwame Nkrumah, His Rise and Fall, 7 march 1957 - 24 February 1966: Part III,' *Great Epic Newsletter* 2, 1 (January, 1998).

52   Ibid.
53   Stanley Meisler, ''Saints and Presidents:' A Commentary on Julius Nyerere,' *One world News Service* (December 19, 1996).
54   Paula Rae Brody, 'Zambian Reflections,' *Great Epics Newsletter* 3, 3 (March, 1999).
55   Ibid.
56   Vuli Cuba, 'Developing Visionary Leaders - An African Imperative,' (Vuli Cuba Safika Investment Holdings Ltd, 1997): 3.
57   Ibid., p. 3.
58   Cuba, 'Developing Visionary Leaders,' 3.
59   Tawana Kupe, 'Comment: New Forms of Cultural Identity in an African Society,' in *Media and the Transition of Collective Identities*, ed. Tore Slatta, Oslo: University of Oslo Press, 1996: 118.
60   Devorah K. Lieberman, 'Ethnocogniotivism and Problem Solving,' in *Intercultural Communication: A Reader*, eds. Larry A. Samovar and Richard E. Porter, Belmont, California: Wadsworth Publishing Company, 1991, 229.
61   L. Kohls, *Survival Kit for Overseas Living*, Yarmouth, ME.: Intercultural Press, 1984.
62   Fernandez, 'Grand Old Flags:,' 1.
63   Quoted in M. M. Verma, *Ghandi's Technique of Mass Mobilization*, New Delhi: R. K. Gupta & Co, 1990: 117.
64   Ibid., p117.
65   Ibid., p117.
66   John Battersby, 'Nelson Mandela's Moral Legacy,' *The Christian Science Monitor* (May 10, 1999), p. 9.

Chapter 4

Communicating
Affective Identification

Introduction

A universal custom among immigrants is to send their offspring to their homelands for education. It is believed these children should have knowledge of their cultural roots and a full understanding of life in the land of their parents' birth, particularly its culture and traditions. As Mangaliman[1] points out, 'most immigrants retain a strong connection to their homeland' and work to pass this connection to their children. Contrary to the myth of assimilation, he says, immigrants do not work hard to become part of the national identity of their host countries. Rather, they hold tenaciously to their culture and heritage through their attires, mores, dance, religion and food.[2] That is why cultural enclaves, such as the 'Little Havana' in Miami, 'Little Italy' in New York, and 'China Town' in Chicago, flourish in many major American cities. Immigrants living in these enclaves usually put forth concerted effort to maintain or replicate homeland structures in architectural designs, social relationships and interpersonal networks. For this reason, Winland has challenged the previous research premise 'that assumes a permanent rupture between immigrants and their countries of origin'.[3]

The existence of a strong passion for the homeland among immigrants is a poignant testimony to the importance of this emotional attachment in the life of a nation. Nations emerge, survive and prosper on the abiding and horizontal comradeship that forms among their members, regardless of any actual inequality and exploitation they may exist. It is this fraternity that places the physical and psychological well-being of the nation at the apex of the hierarchy of individual and community needs and priorities, and that empowers patriots to think and act assiduously in the interest of the common good, rather than succumbing to the selfish need for personal gratification. It is this fraternity that breeds the passionate and blind devotion to one's country, and that motivates so many millions of people to be willing to kill and die for their nation.[4] This fraternity is nurtured and sustained by the emotional disposition that political scientists label 'affective identification'.[5]

Although it is a vital ingredient for national cohesion, affective identification does not accrue to a nation simply by default and its intensity varies from one nation to another. Nations that are blessed with linguistic, cultural and religious homogeneity or are founded on concrete political and moral principles, may enjoy a strong national feeling almost as a divine endowment. But others with a plurality of socio-cultural conditions that tend to subjugate national feeling to ethnic passion must cultivate affective identification as part of a comprehensive nation-building strategy. Africa is a prime example of this. African nations were carved out of more than one cultural or ethnic or political homogenous group. Thus, African leaders have had to devote an enormous effort towards making viable and functional nation-states from the 'veritable mosaic of nationalities' that constitutes each state. They have had to confront head-on the reality that nationhood is a new phenomenon that cannot be taken for granted and must be built.[6]

While it has been self-evident that African countries must devise strategies to supplant the seemingly intractable inherent parochial loyalties with a stronger and more resilient sense of national attachment, complacent African leaders have not gone beyond the tactics of political demagoguery in addressing this important objective. Many believe that national feeling is generated internally and independently in each citizen. They believe that linkage by ancestry or by birth is sufficient in-and-of-itself to imbue people with an abiding, even self-sacrificing, love for their nations. They assume that national love is eternal, that once a person falls in love with his/her nation, he/she remains in love until death. However, the arbitrary origin of many African nations and the ephemeral nature of passions about arbitrary creations have combined to contest these beliefs. Therefore, it is essential to evaluate affective identification practices in Africa, its role in national development, and its relationship with communication. As a prelude to this evaluation, this discourse begins with an explanation of how affective identification is manifested in a social system.

Expression of Affective Identification

Affective identification is expressed through language, thought or action. Its linguistic expressions are found in numerous vocabularies of kinship, such as 'homeland,' 'motherland' or 'fatherland'. For Africans, these idioms of emotional attachment conjure images of an ancestral linkage between members of a nation, regardless of any obvious diversity in the ethnic origins of these members.[7] They suggest an unassailable bond between them and the land where their ancestors lived, worked, and eventually lay buried, even if this is not the land of their birth. By so doing, they give meaning to the expression that 'home is where the heart is' in times of crises and of peace.

Cognitive expressions of affective identification are found in various cultural products of nationalism. Poetry, prose, music and art are often used to convey four main beliefs that form the deepest cognitive expressions of affective identification. These are the beliefs that:

- One's country needs one's service;
- the main way for one to gain self-esteem is through the status and prestige of

one's country;

- one would feel ashamed if any of one's country's leaders did something disgraceful; and
- an outstanding accomplishment by one's country would give one a feeling of pride.

Measurements of these beliefs tend to indicate the nation's morale. Where there is a preponderance of these feelings, there is usually a strong spiritual and cultural bond among people and the nation is integrated. Conversely, where few people share these beliefs, there is generally little faith in the survival of the nation.

The following examples from Kenya and Mozambique illustrate cognitive expressions of affective identification in Africa. First is a song by the Kenyan-born German musician, Kelly Brown, in which he expressed his passion for his homeland:

Kenya nchi yetu ni nzuri (Kenya our country is good)
tupendane sisi kwa sisi (Let's love one another)

Kenya nchi yetu ni nzuri (Kenya our country is good)
tusaidiane sisi kwa sisi (Let's help each other)

The second example is another song, which appeared just before Kenya's independence. It was used to arouse support for the nationalist struggle to gain independence for the country. The song, which is in Kiswahili, is translated into English thus:

Kenya is on 'fire' brothers
Leaders are working hard, don't blame them

When we get independence, let us be peaceful
We should welcome visitors from all over the world

We should assist each other so that we can all be rich
We should forget tribalism so that we can develop our Nation

In Mozambique, the Companhia Nacional de Canto e Danca (Song and Dance Company or CNCD) 'collect, preserve and value the major expressive art forms of the various peoples of country'.[8] Playwright David Abilio, the company's director, notes these collections are blended into national productions that help to unify the people and provide a boost for the economy.[9] Evaluating the contributions of the company to Mozambican national feeling, *The Courier* writes:

In a country that has suffered so much, and which still confronts many economic and social problems, it is encouraging to find such a successful example in the field of cultural endeavor. The spirit of the CNCD - perhaps of the nation itself in these days of renewal - is probably best encapsulated in one of the company's most spectacular shows, appropriately entitled Em Mocambique, o Sol Nasceu (the sun has risen in Mozambique).[10]

Although patriotic songs play an important role in generating emotional support for the nation, they generate mixed reactions from Africans. The reaction varies by ethnic, political and economic vicissitudes. For example, immediately after independence most Kenyans showed a deep sense of emotional attachment to their country by reacting positively to patriotic songs. The songs inspired them to believe that political freedom from the colonial administration would translate into economic empowerment for each citizen. Five years after independence, the feeling of optimism was replaced with a feeling of pessimism, when it became clear that the indigenous government would continue to neglect the ordinary Kenyan. With this perception, patriotic songs became less influential in evoking a strong national feeling.

Following the political assassination of Tom Mboya, the diminishing influence of Kenyan patriotic songs became stratified by ethnicity. Jaramogi Oginga Odinga, who was a former vice president, had formed a rival political party to KANU (the current ruling party). Mboya and Jaramogi ethnic group, The 'Luos,' could not bear listening to patriotic songs of the time. Many of their leaders would turn off their radios deliberately during news time, when the Voice of Kenya (VOK) played its news signature tune, a patriotic song titled 'KANU Ya Jenga Nchi' (KANU Builds the Nation). On the other hand, the 'Kikuyus' remained subject to the emotional appeal of these patriotic songs because one of their members, J. M. Kariuki, occupied the presidency. But when Kariuki was assassinated in 1975, their loyalty dwindled.

The reign of former president, Daniel Arap Moi, saw the gross misuse of patriotic songs, which seemed directed towards entrenching Moi in power. The VoK devoted half of its airtime to playing patriotic songs in praise of Moi. Songs like 'Tawala Kenya' (Rule Kenya) and many others are played repeatedly, but they repulse listeners. This was because of the repressive stance taken by the Moi government in the late 1980s and descent of the Kenyan economy into the 'Intensive Care Unit' (as one minister put it). The mass disillusion that followed has kept Kenyans from playing patriotic songs. Today, Kenyans generally abhor patriotic songs. The exception was the few members of the Kalenjin tribe (Moi's ethnic group), who derived their sense of patriotism from the fact that a member of their ethnic group was president of Kenya.[11]

Behavioral evidence of affective identification can be seen in the various activities used to express overt love for one's nation. For example, homes are adorned with flags and firework displays are set off on national days. Visits to national monuments, museums, and historical sites, which are used to connect with ancestors or events, which have helped to shape the nation, are also illustrative. So also are the waving of national flags, banners and signs inscribed with nationalistic slogans, and the chanting of patriotic cheers at international sporting events. Others sing national anthems with deeper feeling or stop to rekindle their attachment to the past on national day celebrations.

In African and East European countries, affective identification behavior includes several thousand members of the armed forces, labor unions and students taking part in national day parades, dressed in new uniforms. Streets are decorated with bunting and banners, and singers and dancers entertain crowds at various venues.

Immigrants also demonstrate public displays of their ties to their homelands as well. For example, they maintain links with family through overseas communication or taking periodic trips back home. They send monies to family members or invest in business enterprises in the homeland. Some take active interest (and sometimes are directly involved) in political affairs in the homeland.[12] With these physical, intellectual and social capital investments[13], immigrants provide ideological, financial and political support to national movements aimed at the renewal of the homeland.[14] This support aids individual wellbeing, as well as the macro-economic situation. It is no surprise therefore that commitment to country of origin is of immense importance to the immigrants themselves, their 'relatives and friends back home, development planners, and national policy makers in both the home country and the country of residence'.[15]

Affective Identification and National Development

As early as the late 1960s, Seton-Watson,[16] a respected historiographer, social scientist, and author of the most extensive English-language text on nationalism suggested that nations were basically social constructions. He wrote, 'All that I can find to say is that a nation exists when a significant number of people in a community consider themselves to form a nation, or behave as if they formed one'.[17] Nearly three and half decades later, Anderson[18] restated this assertion. He described nations as 'imagined communities'. He pointed out that even though members of a nation will never become acquainted with most of their fellow members, meet them, or even hear of them, the image of their communion will live nonetheless in the mind of each.[19]

If, as these authors suggest, nations are the product of the human mind, then the life of a nation will surely be determined by the concerted effort of people who consider the survival of the nation their fullest and highest form of obligation. Dutiful commitment to the preservation of one's nation requires thinking and acting with purpose and determination, regardless of any exacting situation that may be faced along the way. This is an expression of solid passion, and it is this link between emotion and a nation's destiny that makes affective identification a crucial requirement for national development.

Development requires action. Emotion lies logically at the base of all action. Oatley[20] notes that emotion is a 'mental state of readiness for action, or a change of readiness'. He notes that as we undertake an evaluation of something happening that affects important concerns (sometimes unconsciously), emotions predispose our behavioral choices by specifying a range of options. He described the process in the following examples:

When frightened, we evaluate a situation in relation to a concern for safety and become ready to freeze, fight, or flee. We stop what we're doing and check for signs of danger. In an emotional state we are pressed towards a small range of actions in a compulsive way. In fear, it may seem impossible to act except in ways to make ourselves feel safer. When angry, we are prompted to attack. When sad, we may not feel able to do anything very much.[21]

Emotion is thus essential for positive social change in a society. Social change cannot occur in a social system unless citizens have the passion to focus their collective consciousness on a sustained achievement of national goals. As is readily evident in industrialized societies, individuals and groups who feel a deep sense of national attachment are usually most likely to be empowered and emboldened by their resolve to make sacrifices for the national cause. Gray[22] illustrated this point in an opinion letter to the *Saturday Evening Post* in 1943, during World War. Cognizant that emotion is vital to social mobilization, he urged using effective emotional appeals to strengthen American's resolve to win the war. He wrote: 'The will to sacrifice; the will to prepare; the will to die for principles-these must be geared to the proper emotional pitch if we must win'.[23] If Gray's sentiment is to be applied to the African situation, it would be expressed thus: The will to act solely in the national interest; the will to forsake greed and opportunism; the will to defend national principles; the will to operate efficient political and economic institutions—these must be geared to the proper emotional level if African nations are to win their wars for cohesion and development.

Unfortunately, few African countries can boast that their names mean anything more to their citizens than being just a distinctive appellation for distinguishing those who live within the boundary of one country from another. Ethnic identification remains sine qua non in many countries and people's hearts remain closer to their ethnic groups than to their nations. Mazrui had anticipated a quick reversal of this trend when he observed in 1982 that:

> In term of loyalties, for the time being a Kikuyu laborer in Nairobi is probably a Kikuyu first and a laborer second 'when the chips are down'. In terms of identifying his ultimate interests, a Kikuyu businessman sees his future in the survival of Kikuyu preeminence in Kenya much more than he sees his future in terms of a shared destiny with a Luo businessman.

But this statement appears truer today that it has ever been. Throughout sub-Saharan Africa, the primacy of the ethnic attachment is such that everyone is allowed to get away with a personal or ethnic focus. Leaders seldom have the interest of the nation or its entire population at heart. They abuse their powers by diverting public funds to personal fortunes, or to enrich members of their kin or ethnic groups. They show little concern about the adverse effects on the trusting and unsuspecting poor. As long as they or 'one of their own' is not adversely affected, the unscrupulous leaders sacrifice the aspirations of their nations for personal or ethnic gain. Nyamnjoh[24] notes that it is typical for a president, minister, director or general manager in Africa to fly his pregnant wife to France,

Switzerland or the United States to have their baby in order to gain French, Swiss or American citizenship, or to feel prestigious and superior. Quizzically, he wonders whether such a person believes that his country has a future? He asks, 'Does he feel for his country? Does he have a vision for his fatherland?' Grimly, he concludes that none of them gives any reason to think of patriotism as a virtue.

But what is really odd is that no ordinary African citizen sees such reprehensible behavior as aberrant and abhorrent. In fact, it has become normative for the general public in most parts of Africa to see such conduct as appropriate, or a divine bequest. It is curious then how Africans can speak of achieving national development, when elites who should lead the necessary social, economic and political transformations persistently bring their nations to disrepute? Is it any wonder that Africa continues to lose its brightest citizens with alarming regularity?

According to a recent World Bank study[25], brain drain is Africa's greatest development problem. Since the middle of the 20th century, hundreds of thousands of African managerial staff have worked outside the continent. Africa has lost one-third of its management personnel between 1960 and 1987. An average of 23,000 academics and 50,000 other professionals leave the continent each year. Forty thousand Africans with doctorate degrees do not live in their home countries. For instance, 120 Ghanaian doctors left the country in 1998 and 700 others reside in the United States alone, which represents 50 percent of the total number of Ghanaian doctors. More than 100,000 Nigerians are working in the United States and South Africa alone. Sixty four percent of Nigerians in America with a bachelors degree are between the ages of 18 and 25. Three hundred and sixty-nine doctors have left South Africa since 1994. The situation is similar in Zimbabwe where more than 1,000 management staff emigrated in 1997. The bank notes further that these figures generally do not reflect the actual situation because many professionals emigrate unofficially.

In the early 1990s, democratic reforms were instituted in a number of countries in the hopes that its attendant empowerment of different political interests would heighten the importance of a strong national sentiment above all others. To date, this expectation has not materialized. In countries that have embraced democratic governance (e.g. the Democratic Republic of Congo, Kenya, Liberia, Nigeria, and South Africa), the practice of distributive and re-distributive politics are further exacerbating parochialism and divisiveness. Nepotism remains rampant. The satisfaction of personal interest lies at the apex of the collective consciousness. Rather than apply universal criteria to public job placement, performance and evaluation, decisions are based on ethnic, religious and familial considerations. Self or ethnic-centered individuals entrench a 'culture of mediocrity' in the management of public resources. Public institutions wallow in the failure to meet people's needs, as constituent ethnic groups are left with little choice but bitter competition for scant national resources. In this depth of recurrent despair over broken promises and unfulfilled hopes, persuading the population to feel sincerely passionate about their nations has been akin to asking a couple to marry purely for convenience. Oblige they may, but not with their hearts.

Affective Identification in Africa

The majority of African nations were created in the late 19th century according to the exigencies of the political situation in Europe.[26]   But the colonial authorities did little to weld the diverse peoples of their arbitrary creations into a functioning political whole. The policies of indirect rule or assimilation they implemented in many countries intensified existing cultural affinities. As these affinities have deepened through the years, they have left the political climate restive and the economy in ruins in many countries. This has made it extremely difficult for these countries to transcend their status as mere 'geographic expressions'[27] and for their citizens to supplant entrenched ethnic passions with a strong national feeling.

There are no statistics to show the absolute level of affective identification among the African general populace. But the realities of the cruel conditions and hardships that endure throughout the continent present a formidable obstacle against which Africans are asked to love their countries unconditionally. It is not uncommon to hear some people say that if they had the means they would emigrate in search of the favorable social, economic and political conditions they cannot find in their homelands. And many who can frequently do. The prevalent feeling is that it is better to be free in a strange land than to be a slave at home. Some are so disgusted that they work against their homelands.   History is replete with accounts of unscrupulous African nationals who salt away ill-gotten wealth in foreign banks, where it cannot help the economies of their countries. On a flight from Nigeria to the United States once, a British national told this writer that the wealth of five Nigerians in Britain was sufficient to lift the economy of Nigeria from the doldrums.

Family and ethnic ties appear to be the most compelling reason to explain African immigrant's desire to return to homelands, not love of nation. During the despotic regime of Idi Amin, for example, hordes of Ugandans fled to Kenya for safety. When calm was restored to Uganda, many returned but not because they loved Uganda. They opted against permanent residence in Kenya because they missed their families and friends, and the situation in Kenya was not much better than in Uganda. That seems to be the case throughout Africa.

Nevertheless, it would be inaccurate to suggest that all African nations have not enjoyed or do not enjoy some measure of affective identification. To do so would discount the sacrifices made by those who have seen their nations as something worth dying for.   Examples are such illustrious sons as Patrice Lumumba of Congo, Amilcar Cabral of Cape Verde, Murtala Mohammed of Nigeria, Steve Biko of South Africa and many more. Lumumba loved *The Congo*, so much that he wanted to see it independent in deed as well as in name. Following his death at the hands of agents of the Portuguese colonial administration, Cabral was honored as 'Founder of the Nationality' for leading the struggle to create the legal and political basis for Cape Verdean independence.[28] Mohammed's affection for Nigeria was revealed in his determination to bring efficiency to the country's civil service to better the lives of ordinary citizens. Although his rule lasted only six months, he was a dynamic personality who left 'an indelible mark on the sand of time that no other Nigerian leader living or dead has ever achieved'.[29] Biko paid the ultimate price for preaching the gospel of racial equality in apartheid South Africa. His belief that political freedom could only be achieved if blacks stopped feeling inferior to whites is believed to be the turning point in apartheid's demise. For this, he is widely acclaimed as 'the greatest martyr of the anti-apartheid movement'.[30]

Among the living, Nelson Mandela sacrificed 27 years of his life to achieve a non-racial South Africa. Mandela was at the prime of his life and painfully aware of the grim realities of apartheid, when he was imprisoned for his struggle to gain equal rights and justice for all South Africans. Upon his release, he showed his love for his country by leading a 'remarkable transition from tyranny to democracy'.[31] Undoubtedly, it was his unwavering commitment to reconciliation that saved the country from a bloodbath.

To these patriots, self and nation were as closely knit as biological families bound together by blood. No matter the circumstances or situations, they placed the aspirations of the nation above their own. They understood that a nation must enjoy the same degree of 'togetherness' as that of a biological family if it is to reach its fullest potential. And they worked tirelessly toward this end—the development of geopolitical entities impervious to the ravages of tenuous political situations and persisting social problems. Like many at the grassroots whose aspiration they had hoped to fulfil, these patriots bore no illusion about the importance of their nations to their lives. Their nations were the land where they were born, weaned and raised. There was no other home or family to cherish or to behold.

Affective Identification Predictors

External or Internal Threat

One impetus for the expression of a strong national feeling is the presence of external or internal threat. Writing at the beginning of the 1980s, political scientist Arendt Lijphart[32] described the inherent nature of the potential for external or internal threat to the life of a nation. He wrote:

> Men and women have always been social creatures, ready to band together to form clubs, clans, tribes, nations. But just as in science, every action must have an equal and opposite reaction. The formation of social groups or communities, based on common characteristics or interests, implies the exclusion of those who do not share those same characteristics or interests. Thus are the potential lines of dispute drawn.[33]

Horner notes that at the dawn of the 21st century mankind has found others ways of 'satisfying its inherent 'group reflex' without the accompanying mistrust of other groups that so often spills over into conflict'.[34] He notes that battles are now more likely to be fought as diplomatic negotiations. He says human rights have been declared and accepted, and people of different cultures can communicate with each other in ways previously unimaginable.[35] But these seemingly more rational methods have not entirely displaced aggression by one nation-state against another or the acquisition of rights by conquest.

In 2003, there were many trouble spots across the globe. Palestinians were battling Israel over the reconstitution of Palestine. Pakistan and India were fighting over the disputed Punjab region. Algeria, Armenia, Azerbaijan, Bosnia, Macedonia, Sri Lanka, and Russia were dealing with ethnic separatists seeking self-determination. Internal conflicts were also ongoing in Angola, The Democratic Republic of Congo, Somalia, Southern Sudan, Sierra Leone, and Liberia. These struggles illustrate vividly that the human race still had a lot to do to achieve the goal of peaceful coexistence.[36]

Ross[37] points out that the spirit of loyalty lies at the heart of all social relations. He speaks of not just loyalty to individuals, but also loyalty to ideals. One ideal to which loyalty is crucial is the nation. From birth, people are socialized to perceive their nation as a sacrosanct or inviolable entity. Because of this socialization, threat to a nation's survival is generally regarded with considerable disfavor and viewed as a potentially traumatic experience. Because national threat presents people with the possibilities of spatial dislocation, economic disruption or political upheaval, contemplation of these possibilities lead to the development of a 'we' feeling among disparate residents of a social system. As this feeling grows, the residents 'gain the capacity of mutual sympathy from their identity and the early impressions from their physical environment'.[38] This is subsequently expressed as a perception of feeling alike both physically and psychologically.

Through such perception, individuals and groups attach interest to their common possessions. Ross notes that the interest attached to group possessions is a means of upholding national feeling. He says that a community of interest socializes, whereas a collision of interest leads to coolness and ill-will. Accordingly, when people perceive their nation to be vulnerable to external or internal threat, they develop strong positive emotions to protect national objectives and strong negative reactions to resist the potential sources of threat. This is what makes external or internal threat a vital source of affective identification: the propensity to galvanize the population of a pluralistic geo-political system to act together, for the preservation of the common possessions and satisfaction of the common good.

Desecration of National Symbols

National feeling is also greatly aroused by the desecration of national symbols. People desecrate national symbols for a variety of reasons. Some do it to express their freedom of speech; others to show their anger and frustration with governments, national institutions and divergent community or interests. Still others do so for the enjoyment of being deviant. No matter the motivation, the verbal and/or physical assault on a national symbol evokes unparalleled emotions among patriots. This is because national symbols embody the collective identity of a national population; their vision of themselves, their purpose, and their unity.

They display those intangible values that distinguish one nation and culture from another. They lift people's souls in time of distress.

However, just as they have the power to inspire and unite, so also they can provoke and divide. For example, when four men burned the Stars and Stripes of the United States on the Capitol steps in 1969 to protest American involvement in the Vietnam War, the demonstration inspired endless campaigns. Several members of Congress sought constitutional amendments that would allow states to ban such occurrence. None has been enacted, but flag burning amendments have become a recurrent item on the U.S. legislative agenda.[39]

Similarly, when California introduced Proposition 187 (the measure to deny public assistance to illegal immigrants) in 1984, polls showed that it would be defeated. It passed after protesters hoisted the red, green and white flag of Mexico during several demonstrations. This result may not have been the protesters' intent, but many believe that the flags exacerbated anti-immigrant sentiment. Also, when a video store owner in Orange County's Little Saigon displayed the Communist Vietnam flag and a poster of Communist leader Ho Chi Minh in 1999, it sparked 53 days of demonstrations by crowds of as many as 15,000 people.[40] From these and other similar events not recounted here, it is clear that desecration of a national symbol will arouse intense emotions in citizens, and that these emotions can be the basis for integrative or polarizing behavior.

National Image

Another powerful predictor of the amount of passion people will have for their nation is national image. National image comprises the collective impressions that indigenes and foreigners form about a political system. These impressions derive from a formal or informal (quasi-statistical) appraisal of a country's domestic and international performance. Periodically, citizens take stock of the state of their country's social relations, politics, economy, athletics, health, military, and technology. When these assessments yield positive and/or encouraging impressions, the citizens experience a general sense of wellbeing and a morale boost. This enhances individual and collective self-worth, fostering feelings about the country.

Africans rarely have a good image of their countries. To many Africans, the poor state of social relations, political organization and economic performance in their countries are simply metaphors for hopelessness. Etieyibo[41] cites Nigeria as illustration. He points out that rampant corruption, rising crime, zero power supply, poor roads and pitiable employment opportunities are all Nigeria can show for its four decades of existence. He notes that since Nigeria's independence, the country's has had little progress. Its leadership has lacked direction, purpose and efficiency. Some critics have dubbed the country's 40 years of existence as 'the wilderness years'. But Nigeria is hardly an exception. Throughout Africa, people long for a return to pre-colonial times, when peace, unity and order reigned, particularly those living south of the Sahara.

Browne[42] notes that African societies are handicapped by both a 'lack of means' and a 'deprivation of capability'. He writes that many Africans are unable to participate fully in society, are economically inactive and marginalized by conflict or discrimination. In short, he notes, they are unable to exert much control over their lives.

Communicating Affective Identification

Like verbal identification, affective identification is inherently a communication phenomenon. As Oatley and Johnson-Laird[43] note, emotions are themselves communication. Emotions communicate both within the self and to others in a social system. Internally, they communicate among the different parts of the cognitive system. In a social system, they communicate among individuals and groups,[44] imbuing the society's cognitive system with empathy and humanity, without which a society has difficulty insulating itself against potential threats from systemic dislocation. Emotions therefore constitute an essential component of the human transactions that a social system uses to mobilize its population, and to stimulate popular participation in development and integrative programs. For this reason, absence of emotion can have far reaching consequences beyond political discord for a nation. Its absence can lead to economic stagnation, social disruption and retarded cultural progress.

In Africa, the communication challenge underlying the absence of affective identification epitomizes the concept of 'communicative distance'. This is the intercultural communication concept that describes the way speech is used to establish different feelings of distance or avoidance between persons.[45] Peng notes that communicative distance is invisible and difficult to measure directly. He says that our awareness of its presence in a conversation depends greatly on certain linguistic cues. These cues, he says 'serve, from the speaker's point of view, to set up the communicative distance, or from the hearer's point of view, to let the hearer know that it has already been set up by the speaker'.[46]

Lukens[47] adds to Peng's discussion the notion of ethnocentric speech, which he defines as speech used to generate different feelings of closeness between us, and those with whom or about whom we are communicating. He notes that ethnocentric speech produces three specific types of distances: The Distance of Indifference, The Distance of Avoidance, and The Distance of Disparagement. Individuals may use ethnocentric speech to demonstrate a lack of concern for persons of other cultures and show insensitivity to cultural differences (the distance of indifference), avoid or limit the amount of interaction with out-groups (the distance of avoidance), or demonstrate feelings of hostility towards out-groups and to deride or belittle them (the distance of disparagement).[48]

In Africa where disparate peoples perceive each other as out-groups, communicative distances created by ethnocentric speech are abundant and apparent. These distances have often been called the centrifugal forces of division and polarization among groups, which have threatened to jeopardize the nation's integrity. However, the communicative distances created by ethnocentric speech should not be confused with the type of speech being discussed here. The speech in reference here is that used to express feelings of closeness between 'us', and the geographical entities about which 'we' speak. Africans, like their world counterparts, may often express verbal or written disaffections about what they call their countries, while at the same time expressing profound love for their compatriots. This type of expression is more appropriately termed 'alienation speech', described simply as speech used to reveal different levels of psychological attachment to the nation.

Alienation speech produces the same three communicative distances as ethnocentric speech. The distance of indifference results when speech is used to show a lack of concern for national issues, and to demonstrate mass political and social apathy. People may say, 'I'm not voting in this election', or 'I don't care about politics or the economy'. The distance of avoidance occurs when speech is used to discourage performance of a civic responsibility or to discourage acts of patriotism. A more recent trend has been the call by national governments for African immigrants to invest in their homelands. To this request, some Africans have retorted, 'I'm not investing in that country', or 'What has that country done for me?' Sometimes, speech may be used to arouse feelings of hostility towards the nation, it symbols and its representatives, to deride or belittle them. This creates the distance of disparagement. An example of this is the speech defectors usually give when denouncing their homelands. This writer has heard many Africans describe their countries as 'worthless places to live'.

Nations that exhibit low levels of alienation speech, tend to have leaders who keenly understand the art of impression management. Impression management encompasses putting the best face of their nations forward at every opportunity. With regards to their manner, setting, appearance, face-to-face and mediated (electronic) communications, leaders skilled in impression management take nothing for granted. They chose their words and actions carefully when making public or private speeches, taking great pains to articulate the interest and emotion of the larger majority. They dress in a neutral manner in deference to the multiplicity of identities in their nation-state. Their political platforms tend to reflect the popular will of the people. They work tirelessly to provide efficient, affordable and generalized social services (good roads, clean water, clean environment, etc), so as to make everyday life relatively easy for the population of their nations. They do all of this because they understand that a poor public image is a serious handicap to the developmental ambitions of a nation. As the saying goes, 'It is impression that counts'. When a country has a bad public image, it is unworthy of a high level of affective identification. Its citizens may act like a woman scorned; it may engage in acts, destructive both to itself and to the nation.

Thus, the objective of impression management is the creation of empathy, for empathy is an important avenue for communicating affective identification. U.S. President Bush illustrated this when he gave a passionate speech following destruction of the World Trade Towers by terrorists on September 11, 2001. Although the dastardly act itself was capable of arousing affective identification, it was Bush's speech that crystallized the feeling of oneness among Americans. It challenged people to consider their unity instead of their division. While Western leaders seem to understand the importance of empathy in arousing emotional attachment to their nations, African leaders tend to display arrogance or stupidity. For example, instead of showing sensitivity and concern for thousands of people displaced by explosions at the Ikeja Army Cantonment in January 2002, President Olusegun Obasanjo of Nigeria snapped at them on his visit to the area. He told them to 'Shut up'. He said:

> I took the opportunity of being here to see what could be done. I don't need to be here. After all, the governor of the state is here, the General Officer Commanding The Two Division and the Brigade Commander as well as the Police Commissioner were all here. These sets of people could between them do what needs to be done. I really don't need to be here.[49]

He later explained that he reacted as such because people were unruly. What should he have expected from people who have just been rendered homeless by explosions they did not anticipate or could not prepare for? His remarks immediately drew strident criticisms from Nigerians who said he should have shown restraint. Although Obasanjo tried to retract his statements, he had unwittingly communicated the distance between his government and the plight of the people. Similar lack of empathy can be found in utterances made by other African leaders, who expect people to have strong feelings for their countries.

Thus, communicating affective identification in Africa should combine words and action. Action should culminate in a nation of which everyone can be proud. This means having a country, where citizens can satisfy their hierarchy of needs openly and without let or hindrance. It means having a country, where the lives and property are highly valued and security is assured. It means having a country where leaders show immense respect for the people and the country they govern. It means having a country where the rule of justice prevails, not where some leaders feel they are above the law. It means having a country that cares for its citizens so that its citizens can care for it in return.

The greatest lesson Africans must learn in communicating affective identification is that love is ephemeral and perpetuated only through sustained effort. In every relationship, the initial passion upon which the relationship is built soon fades. Then the hard work of maintaining love begins. It matters not the kind of love. Every kind of love is liable to wane when the emotional environment is no longer positive or conducive. For example, when sufficient positive emotion is no longer available to sustain their relationships, parents may become estranged from their children; lovers may grow apart emotionally. So goes the love for a nation as well. The emotional bond between a patriot and his/her nation may diminish when it is no longer conducive for such bonds to yield meaningful relationships and benefits. When that happens, a patriot may suddenly become traitor.

Notes

1 Jesse Mangaliman, 'Immigrants Send Kids Back to Homeland to Learn Culture: Indo-American looking to Defy U.S. Assimilation,' *The Mercury News* (October 29, 2000).
2 Ibid.
3 Daphne N. Winland, "Our home and native lands?': Canadian Ethnic and the Challenge of Transnationalism' *The Canadian Review of Sociology and Anthropology* 35, 4 (November 1998): 555-577.
4 Benedict Anderson, *Imagined Communities: Reflections on the Origin and Spread of Nationalism* (London: Verso, 1991), pp.224.
5 see John Paden, *Values, Identities and National Integration*, Evanston, Illinois: Northwestern University Press, 1980.
6 Quoted in George Wedell, 'Radio Broadcstsing in Developing Countries,' *The Courier* 105 (September-October, 1987).
7 Anderson, *Imagined Communities*, p. 224.
8 Dossier, 'Mozambique: Making a Song and Dance About Peace,' *The Courier* 168 (March-April, 1998), p. 27.
9 Ibid., p. 27.
10 Ibid., p. 27.
11 Culled from the text of the author's interview with Dorothy Madahana, a Kenyan national working for the African Council on Communication Education, Nairobi, Kenya, March 22, 2001.
12 Winland, 'Our home and native lands?' p. 560.
13 C. Macpherson, 'Changing Patterns of Commitment to Island Homelands: A Case Study of Western Samoa,' *Pacific Studies* 17, 3 (1994), pp.83-116. See also L. Merkle, and K.F. Zimmermann, 'Savings, Remittances, and Return Migration,' *Economics Letters* 38 (1991), pp.77-81.
14 K. Tololyan, 'The nation and its others: In lieu of a preface'. *Diaspora* 1, 1 (1991): 3-7.
15 Dennis A Ahlburg and Richard P C Brown, 'Migrants' intentions to return home and capital transfers: A study of Tongans and Samoans in Australia,' *The Journal of Development Studies* 35, 2 (December 1998)pp. 125-151.
16 Hugh Seton-Watson, *Nations and States* (London: Longman, 1968), p. 5.
17 Anderson, 'Imagined Community,' p. 5.
18 Ibid., p. 5
19 Ibid., p. 6.
20 Keith Oatley, *Best laid Schemes: The Psychology of Emotions* (New York: Cambridge University Press, 1992).
21 Ibid., p. 20.
22 Weller Gray, 'Letter of Opinion,' *The Saturday Evening Post* (January 1943).
23 Ibid.
24 Francis B. Nyamnjoh, 'Cameroon: A Country United by Ethnic Ambition and Difference,' *African Affairs* 98 (1999), pp. 101-118.
25 Anon, 'Brain Drain: An Endless Stress in Africa,' *African News Service* (April 17, 2000).
26 see Robert Goldman and Wilson Jeyaratnam, eds., *From Independence to Statehood: Managing Ethnic Conflict in Five African and Asian States* (New York: St. Martins Press, 1984).

27 Obafemi Awolowo, *Path to Nigerian Freedom* (London: Oxford Univeristy Press, 1947), pp. 47-48. This author used this expression to describe Nigeria. He wrote: 'There are no 'Nigerians' in the same sense as there are'English,' 'Welsh,' or 'French'. The word 'Nigeria' is merely a distinctive appelation to distinguish those who live within the boundaries of Nigeria from those who do not'. However, the same conclusion can be applied to the majority of the nations in Sub-Saharan Africa.

28 Anna Maria Cabral, 'Amilcar Cabral'. Fundacion Amilcar Cabral (Praia, Cabo Verde).

29 Author Unknown, 'Murtala Mohammed: The Untold Story,'*Africa One Stop Service* (December 17, 1998).

30 Anon., 'Steve Biko: Martyr of the Anti-apartheid Movement,' *BBC News Online*: Background (December 8, 1997).

31 Anon., 'Newsmakers: Nelson Rolihlahla Mandela,' *ABCnews.com*

32 Arendt Lijphart, 'Preface,' in *World Minorities in the Eighties*, ed. Georgina Ashworth, Sunbury, UK: Quartermaine House Ltd, 1980.

33 Simon Horner, 'Dossier: National Minorities,' *The Courier* 140 (July-August, 1993), p. 49.

34 Ibid., p. 49.

35 Ibid., p. 49.

36 Ibid., p. 49.

37 Edward Allsworth Ross, 'Socialization,' *American Journal of Sociology* 24 (1919), pp. 652-671.

38 Ibid., p. 652.

39 Maria Elena Fernandez, 'Grand Old Flag: Symbols of our unity, our purpose, ourselves,' *The Los Angeles Times* (June 11, 2000).

40 Ibid.

41 Edwin E. Etieyibo, 'Opinion: Nigerian at 40: 4 decades of wasted years?,' *African News Service* (October 10, 2000).

42 Stephen Browne, 'Governance and Human Poverty,' *Choices Magazine* 10, 3 (September 2001): 8.

43 Keith Oatley and P. N. Johnson-Laird, 'Towards a Cognitive Theory of Emotions,' *Cognition and Emotion* 1 (1987): 29-30.

44 Keith Oatley, *Best laid Schemes: The Psychology of Emotions*, p. 44.

45 Peng, S. 'Communicative Distance,' *Language Sciences* 31 (1974): 33.

46 Ibid., p. 33.

47 J. Lukens, 'Ethnocentric Speech,' *Ethnic Groups* 2 (1978): 35-53.

48 Deepak Prem Subramony, 'Communicative Distance and Media Stereotyping in an International Context,' Paper presented at the AEJMC conference, Phoenix, Arizona, August 2000.

49 Rotimi Ajayi, Kingsley Omonobi and Kenneth Ehigiator, 'Obasanjo apologizes, cancels US trip,' Vanguard (January 31, 2002).

PART II
COMMUNICATION AND
INTEGRATIVE BEHAVIOR

Introduction

Integrative behavior (also called integrative tendency) is critical to the quest for national integration in pluralistic nation-states. Without an institutionalized display of integrative behavior, a pluralistic social system cannot achieve true, or even functional unity. And its population will have difficulty replacing local or regional symbols with national ones, or focusing on national interests, values and aspirations instead of particularistic identifications and loyalties.

Abernethy[1] defines integrative behavior as the readiness of an individual or group to work in an organized fashion for common purposes and to behave in a manner conducive to the achievement of these common purposes. Deutsch[2] describes it as the psychological state in which groups or individuals interlock their communication habits, share meaning, learn to predict each other's behavior and coordinate each other's action. Through the institutionalization of integrative behavior, a multi-ethnic social system can nationalize its values and norms, build its linkages and structures, and focus the energies of its disparate communities on satisfying the interest of the common good, rather than meeting the challenges of ethnic or religious difference.

Achieving integrative behavior in any given social system is contingent on the availability of adequate facilities for the free mobility of people, goods and services throughout their social systems. This availability is often dependent on the formulation of policies to secure full residence rights for every citizen in all regions of their country, encourage intermarriage among persons of different places of origin, or of different religious, ethnic, or linguistic associations or ties, and to promote associations that cut across ethnic, linguistic, religious, or other sectional barriers. Such policies may exist already or may have to be formulated anew. Regardless of which prevails, the policies must be vigorously promoted so that every segment of the population can be made aware of their national existence.

The mass media are looked upon as the avenue for educating and unifying the masses. To underscore the importance of this integrative function, most governments in Africa include it as a policy objective in the articles of association of their broadcasting stations,[3] and media managers frequently cite it in their public speeches.[4] Generally, it is believed that since the national interest supersedes all other interests, broadcasters have a duty to win, maintain and perpetuate support for national unity in the country.[5] Producers attempt to fulfill this obligation by structuring, producing and disseminating programs that will 'imbue audiences with positive nation-building values'.[6]

But try as they might, African media practitioners find the integrative function a difficult task to perform. To date, the practitioners have been unable to formulate and implement programming strategies that could forge the required sense of nationhood among African audiences. Scholars have given many reasons why the integrative contents have failed to accomplish their assigned task. These include the lack of an ideological orientation in the programs,[7] the ethnic, religious and linguistic diversity and low level of literacy of target populations, Third World media practitioners' misunderstanding of the process of integration and the general dysfunctional use of the electronic media in Third World countries.[8] Added to this is the absence of a model upon which the integrative function could be planned and executed. This has meant that African media officials have had to perform the integrative function on the basis of their whims, rather than on information gleaned from scientific research. For this reason, even though integrative programs have been entertaining and consistently popular among audiences, they have not succeeded in their primary mission of uniting disparate groups.

Part II will argue that African national entities can achieve value and normative congruence if the communication issues related to the promotion of integrative tendencies are carefully considered and addressed. It will suggest strategies for communicating common historical experiences, encouraging social interaction, promoting economic integration, and facilitating political development. Kuo[9] observes that the communicative ability of a society is a determinant of the rate of assimilation or disintegration. Communication therefore can foster a melting-pot environment by encouraging spatial, associational, governmental and linguistic integrative behaviors. Without a sustaining national spirit, values and attitude, African populations cannot expect to truly fulfill their individual and collective aspirations.

Notes

1   David Abernethy, *The Political Dilemma of Popular Education: An African Case*, Stanford, California: Stanford University Press, 1969.

2   Karl Deutsch, *Nationalism and Its Alternatives*, New York: Alfred A. Knopf, Inc., 1969.

3   Ebele Ume-Uwagbo. (1986, Spring). 'Broadcasting in Nigeria: Its Post –independence Status'. *Journalism Quarterly*, P. 585.

4   Abraham Bass, 'Promoting nationhood through television in Africa'. *Journal of Broadcasting* (Spring1969), 13 2, pp. 165-169.

5   Tony Momoh, 'Nigeria: The press and nation-building'. *Africa Report* (1987, March/April), 32, pp. 54-57.

6   Vincent Lowe, 'Some Policy Dilemma in Coping with Malaysia's Multi-ethnic Audience: Their Effects on the Roles and Status of Broadcasters'. *The Third Channel* (1987), 5, pp. 644-659.

7   Adelumola Ogunade, 'Mass Media and National Integration in Nigeria,' In L. Atwood and S. J. Bullion (eds.). *International Perspectives on New*, Carbondale: Southern Illinois University Press, 1982, pp. 22-32.

8   Osabuohien Amienyi, 'Obstacles to broadcasting for national integration in Nigeria'. *Gazette* (1989), 43, pp. 1-15.

9   Eddie Kuo, 'Language, Nationhood and Communication Planning: The case of a multi-lingual society,' in S. A. Rahim and J. Middleton (eds.). *Perspectives in Communication Policy and Planning*, Honolulu, Hawaii: East-West Communication Institute, 1980, pp. 319-335.

Chapter 5

Communicating
Historical Consciousness

I don't known where I'm going, but I know where I've been. I can't say what life
will show me, but I know what I've seen.

Jimmy Cliff, Famed Jamaican Reggae Artist

Introduction

All nations are a product of history. History is how the identity of a nation is
established and differentiated. National identity is created by the perennial
structural context in which it exists, and history is the principal structural context
in which the meaning of national events is generated and realized. As Cooper
illustrates in his acclaimed fictional novel *The Spy*, history can substitute for the
romantic environment and even for the social coherence lacking in many pluralistic
countries.[1] It can provide the context for extrapolating national traits or
characteristics (e.g. culture, language, religion, and politics), enhance the self-
concept of the nation, and deepen public expressions of citizenship and patriotism.
It is important, therefore, to consider the dissemination of common history as a
quintessential part of the process of national integration.[2]

Africans have ample historical experiences to energize their quest for national
solidarity and development. From the tyranny and exploitation of colonization to
the unfulfilled and broken promises of independence and self-rule, African history
is replete with national glories or catastrophes that can expedite consensus and
invoke community. However, these events are seldom considered relevant to
national discourses regarding ways to achieve social cohesion, nor are they
consulted in the quest for effective development policies and programs. It is not
that Africans are inherently anti-history. On the contrary, throughout the continent
various ethnic nationalities and sub-national groups are living the past in everyday
life of the present, through folk songs, dances, rituals and other traditional
practices. As Miller[3] points out, in Africa popular interest in understandings of the
past is quite literally as old as time. Why then are historical wisdoms virtually

ignored in national planning in Africa? Perhaps it is because of the fear that recalling certain historical events can arouse the sensibilities of diverse communities, revive age-old ethnic rivalries, and by so doing undermine progress toward national cohesion.

Such fear is not entirely unfounded because historical origins lie beneath the systemic dislocations that have plagued many African countries in recent years, particularly in Angola, Burundi, Congo, Liberia, Nigeria, and Rwanda. However, it is important to point out that history and historical experiences are neither functional nor dysfunctional, in and of themselves. It is the choice of historical events and the political uses to which they are put that ultimately determines whether positive or negative consequences are received. Countries that have learned this lesson have been quite successful at maximizing the benefits obtained from sharing common history. For example, the United States has adeptly used historical references to consolidate national unity. Programs aired on cable and television networks frequently relate and reinforce the shared aspect of U.S. history, particularly the moral ethic of the country as laid down by the founding fathers and the numerous struggles that the republic has undergone since its founding. By identifying with these references, Americans are able to perceive a sense of commonality in their nationality. They are able to find a general sense of pride in proclaiming their belongingness to, and identifying with the ideals of, the nation. Historicism is so important in the United States that a cable channel is dedicated exclusively to history, appropriately called *The History Channel*. Thus, even though, Schultz and Felter[4] have noted that 'Americans are notoriously ignorant of history—their own and others,' visual and performing artists never miss the opportunity to historicize. As a result, elites (including media elites) and other segments of the American population are generally adept at history and make every effort to ensure that historical consciousness is pervasive.

On the contrary, in Africa national history is rarely an active component of people's cognition. Nevertheless, one should consider the possibility that the promotion of national history can play a role in furthering the integrative and development goals of African countries. Could such disseminations provide the emotional appeal to persuade national populations to place the achievement of cooperation and integration at the top of their individual priorities? Could they facilitate extrapolation and synthesis of the stronger linkages in a country? Could they remind everyone of the moral obligation to consider the survival, stability and growth of the country as sine qua non? This chapter explores these questions. As part of this exploration, the chapter assesses the possible contributions that the broad dissemination of common historical experiences can make to the nation-building project in Africa. Of particular interest is how the communication of history and historical experiences through popular culture, oral tradition, and mass media can facilitate the move towards social harmony, political integration and economic growth. In short, the chapter examines the link between history, communication and national integration.

History and National Integration

In 19th century Europe, the basic objective of nationalism was to construct nations around people who shared the same culture, religion and language.[5] Except in extraordinary cases, the strategy was consistently the same—to glorify the 'oneness' of the nation-state because the nation-state meant a 'united state: One state, one sovereignty, one nation, one motherland, one people, one culture, one language, one history and so on'.[6] There was no tolerance for 'otherness' in the nation-states external manifestation or its public life. In fact, persons who failed to uphold the requirements of the national standard were subject to physical or mental exclusion. Physical exclusion meant mass population movements, expulsions or elimination—the crime of genocide, the solution of choice for many totalitarian states. Mental exclusion involved assimilation or wearing down the solidarity and coherence of minority groups by removing or restricting the possibility of collective expression at school, in the media, in the civil service, in the courts and so on. These were the typical tactics adopted by liberal states where individual rights were seen as superseding all else, even though this affirmation of individualism was really 'an insidious way of imposing the culture and way of life of the majority on the minority'.[7]

In the late 1800s, the Europeans applied this romantic approach to nationalism to the creation of nation-states in Africa, in the firm belief that their civilization was the culmination of all human progress and that the colonies could have no better pattern to emulate and should aim at nothing different.[8] Accordingly, they created nation-states in Africa independently of all ethnic, cultural and religious considerations. It was not long before these new states faced the problems of governing populations that were pluralistic from many points of view, including language, religion, customs and politics.[9] The main challenge was how to ensure that people speaking different languages and having different cultures and traditions embraced the 'oneness' of their arbitrary countries with zeal. The strategy adopted by early African nationalists was to promote the emergent social and political orders by disregarding the very traditions that gave meaning to most African lives. As Ajayi explains, the early African nationalists sought 'to emancipate themselves from the local and the particular and to seek a universal fatherland'.[10] Empowered by the teachings of Christian missionaries, they sought to destroy traditional African culture rather than reform it, 'not by force but by attrition'.[11] But this strategy did not institutionalize national attachment; instead it exacerbated ethnic passion.

Through the years, more and more people have become conscious of their right to self-determination. As a result, minorities and ethnic groups have put up peaceful or violent resistance to the unitary approach to nation-building throughout the world. Using the unitary argument as well, the ethnic nationalists are clamoring for the creation of ethnically pure states. Ironically, the clamor for ethnic purification has been no less than a reification of the European nationalistic model of introspection and rejection of the others. By extolling the virtues of homogeneity (i.e. the exclusion of all else), ethnic nationalists are essentially embracing 'the far from-reality theory of independence and sovereignty' which, according to Guyonvarc'h, is irrational because it ignores the future. As Guyonvarc'h points out, the 'aggressor forgets that today's enemy is tomorrow's neighbor and that ways of cohabitation have to be sought'.[12]

While it cannot be denied that history has robbed African people of the opportunity to build their nations on their own indigenous values, institutions and heritage, Deng[13] advises that it would be foolhardy for the continent to attempt at this late date to return to ancestral identities and meanings as bases for nation-building, for such a move would create many unwieldy and insolvent countries. Yet, on the other hand, African countries cannot deny the reality of the diversity of their ethnic composition, for to do so would be to deny the most salient part of their existence. As the famous Reggae artist, the late Bob Marley noted, 'You can't run away from yourself'. How then can Africans develop nations worthy of their population's passion? Deng suggests consolidating a framework that gives adequate recognition and maximum utility to the component elements of ethnicity, culture, and aspirations for self-determination.[14] Guyonvarc'h calls for a demystifying of frontiers, 'where states are made more relative by the implementation of federal-style types of political organization in which differences are accepted and developed, not exacerbated, and no longer thought of as a handicap, but experienced as an asset'.[15]

The practicality and efficacy of these recommendations are being tested in Ethiopia. An ongoing experiment should provide adequate evidence to assess the efficacy of the federalism principle in Africa. Responding to Ethiopia's longstanding question of ethnicity, the government of Meles Zenawi devolved power to the grassroots through its regionalization policy in the early 1990s.[16] The policy gave indigenous people the rights to use their own language and to administer their own areas. Power was devolved not just to the various regions but also to districts and villages. The government acted in the confidence that devolution of power to the grassroots would directly empower ordinary Ethiopians and make democracy more meaningful to them. As Zenawi puts it, 'When the ordinary Ethiopian is empowered, we feel confident that the country would move in the right direction'.[17] Devolution has eased inherent interregional and inter-ethnic tensions. Everyone seems to be focused now on the singular issue of development. As the president explains, 'When you start talking about development, you start talking about a wider economy, a bigger market and you cannot have bigger markets by dividing up states. That, we believe, even the peasant will understand'.[18]

President Zenawi's assertion appears to corroborate Ross,[19] who notes that when people of a nation-state discover that they share similar historical background, they are pleased and are drawn together. There appears now to be a prevailing presence of perception of resemblance among the Ethiopian population that derives not from physical likeness, but from the recognition and appreciation of likeness in existential qualities, such as national feeling. Today, Ethiopians share a similar national outlook not because they think others look a good deal like them, but because they believe others share their common values, visions, problems and prospects. That is an idea that could resonate within other African countries, which can learn much from the successes and failures of the Ethiopian example.

Historical Consciousness in Africa

If African countries are to truly achieve their desired national integration goals, a pervasive sense of national identification, integrative behavior and political awareness must be commonly sought through the classic 'historicist argument that the present is understood by reference to the past, and interpretations of the past are made to generate the present'.[20] This argument is the essence of the notion presented in the history literature as historical consciousness, defined by Glassberg as a 'sense of belonging to a succession of past and future generations as well as to a present community and society'.[21]

Historical consciousness has long been an intrinsic feature of cultural and religious traditions throughout Africa. As Okigbo explains:

> In the indigenous religion of most parts of Africa south of the Sahara, the cycle of life is continuous: birth, life, death and rebirth form an unbroken chain. Time is therefore continuous in its flow and individuals enter at a particular instant, often to relive the past that may have been lived some time ago for them or by them. At each instant of time, a community contains young and old, living and dying members. At any moment, therefore, the society contains a replica of the complete cycle of time and of life. Its future is already sketched by its past; its history may thus indicate the directions of movement in the future.[22]

This point that historical consciousness exists at the very core of African belief can be further verified by vernacular expressions found among linguistic groups throughout the continent. For example, the Edo people of mid-Western Nigeria say that: 'If you don't know where you've come from, you don't know where you're going'. This expression codifies the African belief that a 'man's fate is determined by his past,' a belief similar to the Western concept of manifest destiny.

Also supporting the reality that historical consciousness is entrenched in Africa is the fact that historicism (or storytelling) is the quintessence of the African version of oral tradition. In most parts of the continent, storytelling is the principal means for transmitting and maintaining the history, traditions, norms and values of a community from generation to generation. The stories are usually told at the community or family level by an elder or sage. An example of this is the griot or Jeli. Among the Manding people of West Africa (spread throughout at least six African countries: Mali, Guinea, Guinea Bissau, Gambia, Senegal and Cote d'Ivoire), 'griots' (or storyteller in French) and Jelis (spiritual adviser and keeper of culture in Mande) recount the history of a tribe, family or community. They tell stories about birth, death, marriage and other significant events in a community, singing or chanting it to the accompaniment of a stringed instrument called the *Kora*, or another called the *balaphone*. Their importance in Manding society has been illustrated by Banning Eyre of World Music Productions, who writes that: 'If the memory of ancient Mali still burns brightly today, that's largely thanks to the work of griots'.[23]   Aside from their function as griots, Jelis also provide the spiritual guidance necessary for holding a tribe, family or community together.[24]

Thus, it is not that historicism and historical consciousness are or have been lacking in Africa, but that their existence has not been applied sufficiently to the national sphere of influence. At the national level in most countries, historicism and historical consciousness is still confined to accounts about tribes as discrete entities and bound mostly by the exigencies of ethnic preservation. This is verified because few stories appear in national or ethnic media that reify national monuments or heroes or that vilify national villains or foes. The assumption, albeit erroneous, is that an environment where the past is intrinsically linked with the present, and individual lives are effectively blended with the life of their community, thrives best when it exists at the grassroots. Yet, what anyone traveling through Africa readily discovers at the grassroots is not national thinking but ethnic consciousness. Even among those who symbolize national existence, the preponderant worldview is usually heavily influenced by loyalty to family, clan, tribe or the village frame of reference.

Defining National History in Africa

However, it would defy logic to believe that ethnic history in a plural society, whether presented discretely or in amalgamated form, can constitute the entire history of the country. That would be analogous to accepting the confounding argument that the identity and history of a salad is the same as that of each ingredient that comprise it. It cannot be denied that the history and identity of the salad ingredients (lettuce, green peppers, tomato, eggs, cucumber, croutons, beets, cheese, onions and salad dressing) were independent until they became part of the salad. However, once the salad was made, its history and identity subsumed the history and identity of each ingredient. Therefore, if asked the salad maker might be unable to say how and when each ingredient was planted, what challenges befell their development, and how each made it to the market. But he or she might be able to describe how and why each was selected and combined into the salad. The salad maker may be familiar with the history of the salad but not the history of its constituent ingredients, except in those rare cases when the ingredients came from the salad maker's garden. Thus, the history of the salad cannot be said to have begun until the salad maker began to contemplate making the salad.

Applied to Africa, this analogy illustrates that while each tribe or ethnic group has a history that is undoubtedly relevant and important to members of that tribe or ethnic group, the country's history as a constituted whole is separate and transcends each ethnic group's history. For most African countries, what constitutes national history did not begin until the colonial administrators began implementing policies that led to the formation of each nation-state. On the date each African country was created, the history of its ethnic group became subsumed by the history of the emergent nation as a pluralistic whole. Since those dates, discussions and writings about the history of each tribe prior to European colonization became useful only when used as a context for understanding the origin and subsequent development of each country. Though a die-hard ethnic nationalist might find this definition of national history difficult to embrace, it is essential to place national history at the heart of people's consciousness. It is necessary to consign ethnic history to the periphery of national cognition so that the national developmental cause is not marginalized. But this does not have to translate to a total obliteration of the ethnic group's heritage. If national planners and ethnic zealots can show mutual respect and understanding, there is no reason why ethnic history cannot thrive under the aegis of national history.

Communicating Historical Consciousness

According to Cornel and Hartmann, historical consciousness is acquired through a unique blending of personal experiences with the diverse and sometimes conflicting traditions, or ways of interpreting experience, encountered among kin and friends, and at work, school and places of religious worship.[25] It is shaped partly by 'public historical imagery that prompt individuals to associate their personal experiences and particular traditions with larger, public historical themes'.[26] Foster notes that public historical imagery is conveyed through many communication channels, including popular arts—fictions, paintings, plays, music, movies and dance; oral tradition and folklore; architectural and material culture; nonfiction literature and school textbooks; civil celebrations and historical reenactments.[27] Foster says these channels extrapolate those 'characteristics or criteria that function simultaneously to primordialize insiders and to exclude outsiders'.[28] By so doing, they create the unique identity that forms the core of a national culture. Foster adds that the challenges associated with building a national culture goes beyond just the issue of forging a national identity. He says planners must routinely consider how that identity can be imbued with the aura of authenticity that would give it realism, put it beyond communal dispute, and make it an intrinsic element of personal identity. He says national culture is an ongoing construction, and only a country that has succeeded in nationalizing its history can have a fixed cultural identity.[29]

That is the challenge facing most African countries: how to make national history an intrinsic part of the consciousness of national populations. This challenge necessitates asking the question: How well do African artists, writers, media and cultural anthropologists make unapologetic use of their countries' national history? Based on the wide cultural variations, the answer is contingent on regional variables. However, it is fair to say that visual artists across the continent have long shown a continuing allegiance to historical education, as demonstrated by the four feature-length films released between 1986 and 1991. By educating their viewers about the common elements in their past, these films helped to facilitate a certain measure of social, cultural and political integration. Three of the films are from Southern Africa while the fourth is from West Africa. The first film, Zdravko Velimrovic's *Time of the Leopards* (1987), is a 90-minute Yugoslavia/ Mozambique/Zimbabwe co-production, which recounts a fictional battle during the armed struggle for the liberation of Mozambique. The film's primary action takes place during the turbulent early 1970s when Portugal's war weariness made Mozambique's victory imminent. The setting is the rich northern plateau, which provided protective cover for the guerilla fighters throughout the struggle. The plot is as follows: A hunt is organized for Pedro, the commander of a FRELIMO detachment, whose courageous actions had begun to worry the Portuguese military in the area. He is captured and killed, but his memory inspires a new generation to continue the struggle and attack the barracks where Pedro lost his life.[30]

The second, Jose Cardoso's *O vento sobra do norte* (*The Winds of the North*, 1987), a 16mm 90-minute feature, documents the revolts of slaves against colonial settlers who, unable to comprehend the reality of the revolt, exhibit an arrogant boldness tinged with a sense of uncertainty. The film is set in northern Mozambique where the liberation struggle had been ongoing for four years. Rumors of sweeping changes in the rest of the country create widespread uneasiness and guilt among colonial settlers, who fear the backlash of blacks coming to reclaim the land taken from them five centuries earlier.[31]

The third film, Mario Borgneth's *Borders of Blood*, a 16mm 90-minute documentary completed in 1986, examines South Africa's destabilization tactics and its subsequent impact on Mozambican reconstruction.

The fourth film is Ghanaian Kwaw Ansah's *Heritage Africa* (1988),[32] which depicts the alienation of Africans from their own values during the colonial era. It is the story of an urbanized, well-educated man from a humble family, who sees everything African as no longer good enough for him. Although indigenous names have significant meanings in Ghana and the rest of sub-Saharan Africa, this man changes his. He was named Kwesi Atta Bosomefi. 'Kwesi' means a male child born on Sunday, 'Atta' means he is a twin, and 'Bosomefi' means an illustrious ancestor is reincarnated. When he goes to school, he believes the name does not sound English enough and decides to Anglicize it: 'Kwesi' becomes 'Quincy,' 'Atta' becomes 'Arthur,' and 'Bosomefi' becomes 'Bosomfield'. He eventually occupies an important post in the colonial administration but loses his African values in the process. As Pfaff notes, he 'succeeds in his mission, but at what price?'[33] Taken together, such films provide some of the historical socialization required to develop and maintain national historical consciousness in African populations.

In the early days of television, productions by indigenous producers were also filled with historical messages. For instance, when television first came to Lusophone Africa (i.e. Angola, and Cape Verde Mozambique) after independence, programs aired included productions by local filmmakers on their countries' stories and folklore. Cine-clubs were formed to ensure, among other objectives stated in their charters, that television served as a vehicle for encouraging active participation in national history. Today, local productions across Africa have largely departed from the historical educational mission; they are driven almost exclusively by financial motives. Producers' priorities have shifted completely from the production of politically, historically and ideologically-oriented materials to entertainment. Local producers are no longer socially oriented and their productions are no longer made from the perspective of historical and cultural revitalization. Andrade-Watkins explains the shift. She writes that Lusophone filmmakers, like their counterparts in other regions of Africa, are 'joined in a common, competitive pursuit of a global audience'. The main concern is for materials that would be profitable not just Africa, but elsewhere. Left out of the equation are cultural, historical and political materials that non-native audiences might not understand.

The result has been cultural and historical deprivation. Kwah Ansah explains the social and political implications of this deprivation:

> We [Africans] don't know our villages anymore. We don't know our countries anymore: African Children going to school are more interested in learning about the stars on Michael Jackson's epaulet than in knowing who the foreign minister of their country is. They don't care to know because film and television media would make them feel that all that matters is the showy things happening in the world of entertainment. Their interest is focused on buying records or T-shirts and is being completely diverted to frivolities. These kids are not really sitting down and thinking seriously about contribution to society. Some of them will be leaders of tomorrow, and you already see how they are being culturally alienated and being manipulated by the forces that be.[34]

The exception is Nigeria, where producers still devote a certain percentage of their productions to historical socialization, be it past or contemporary history. For example, Tunde Kelani's 'popular, allegorical tales of traditional kings mirrors Nigeria's political history'.[35] Other videos have explored the country's history of urban and ethnic violence, economic and political corruption, and the social history of female circumcision, prostitution and witchcraft.[36] Although the videos are similar in form, style and themes, the fact that the majority of them are produced in Yoruba, Igbo, Hausa, Itsekiri, Igala and other local languages[37] limits their ability to exert strong national influence. This is so because the videos fragment their audiences along tribal lines, and produce new modes of social organization along the axes of gender, age and class.[38] The result is a medium 'marked by two simultaneous and contradictory tendencies: towards ethnic cultural assertion, and towards participation in a detribalized, national form at a national (or at least pan-southern) market'.[39] But most analysts would agree that African films and videos have been more effective in propagating insular ethnic history and culture rather than promoting secular national history and culture.

Although the active and continuing participation of various media in historical education is in the national interest, African journalists do not generally perceive historical education as part of their responsibilities. They see their main responsibility as attacking their respective governments regardless of the negative consequences these attacks could have on the growth and stability of their countries. Having grown out of the liberation struggle, a time when the colonial government was clearly the marked enemy to bring down, the practice of adversarial journalism has not given way to altruism. As the Ghanaian-born editor of London's *New African Magazine*, Baffour Ankromah,[40] observes, since independence African media have been stuck in a time warp. It has not made the transition from being the adversary of governments into the 'fourth estate of the realm'. In fact, today the best journalist is the one who attacks the government the most.

That is contrary to the practice in Western countries where journalists are guided by the principle of social responsibility. Whether the country is England, the United States, France or Germany, journalists clearly understand that freedom of the press must be pursued in concert national interest.[41] Baffour Ankromah has resided in London for 10 years. He observed that the British media are guided by a nine-point unwritten code: national interest, national security, government lead, ideological leaning, advertisers and readers' power, Fourth Estate of the Realm role, following the flag, reporting into a box, and patriotism. These codes determine whether a story is printed or rejected, how prominent to play it, what words to use to frame it, etc.

The same can be said of the United States, where this author has resided for the past 26 years. But critics may point out that the Watergate scandal and the Pentagon papers suggest that American journalists do not always act in the national interest. Viewed from an etic perspective, however, it is clear that the very notion of an adversarial government-press relation is one of the cornerstones of the American political system. As such, press scrutiny of government behavior is intrinsically part of the national interest.

But that is not the case in Africa, where journalists see patriotism as demeaning to their profession and ape Western practices without respect for African norms and traditions. So much so that if a London newspaper calls the Prime Minister 'bonkers', journalists in Lagos, Accra, Nairobi and Johannesburg feel they can do the same. The result is that printed stories often lack historical context. Readers are not given a sense of how contemporary events fit into the general evolution of the society. Nor are they educated about the visions and ideals of founding fathers, to provide a direction for present and future behavior.

Conclusion

There is little doubt that Africa is replete with public historical imagery that can serve the cause of national integration. Each African country has a different story to tell about its origins, founding and development. It is an inspiring and pleasant tale for some, and a horrific and painful one for others, such as the Mau-Mau uprising in Kenya, the Boer wars in South Africa or the Algerian resistance against the French in North Africa. But regardless of the emotions it may stir, stories of the origin of the African nation-state must be told to sensitize people to the struggles and strife upon which the nation was built. This sensitivity is crucial for motivating individuals and groups to suspend their differences and build lasting national kinships and community ties.

In African countries, competing ethnic histories have always contested for the available media space. As a result, media managers have to ponder constantly the question of whose history to promote? Some may choose to focus mainly on the extrapolated components of the history of a dominant group. Others may attempt to balance their attention to the history of both the dominant and subordinate groups. Those who subscribe to the former have to decide which components of a dominant culture require the consent of subordinates? These components may include 'values, norms, perceptions, beliefs, sentiments, prejudices that support and define the existing distribution of goods, the institutions that divide how this distribution occurs, and the permissible range of disagreement about those processes'.[42]

As with every aspect of African countries, the diversity of each country's history must be agglomerated into a common narrative, to be recounted through oral tradition and mass media. Merging the knowledge gained from both traditional culture and modern societies will surely bring possible risks, but also certain benefits.

Notes

1   See Emily Miller Buddick, Fiction and Historical Consciousness: The American Romantic Tradition, New Haven: Yale University Press, 1989, pp. 1-240.

2   Christina Drake, *National integration in Indonesia*, Honolulu: University of Hawaii Press, 1989.

3   John Miller, 'History and Africa/ Africa and History,' *The American Historical Review* 104, 1 (February 1999), p. 1-32.

4   Daniel Schultz and Maryanne Felter, 'Reading Historically in a Historically Illiterate Culture,' College Teaching (2002), pp. 142.

5   J. F. Ade Ajayi, 'The Place of African History and Culture in the Process of nation-Building in African South of the Sahara,' *Journal of Negro Education* 30, 3 (Summer, 1961), PP. 206-213.

6   Christian Guyonvarc'h, 'The Basis of Prejudice,' *The Courier* 140 (July-August, 1993), p. 53.

7   Ibid., p. 53.

8   Ajayi, The Place of African History,' 206.

9   Guyonvarc'h, 'The Basis of Prejudice,' 53.

10   Ajayi, The Place of African History, 206.

11   Ibid., p. 207.

12   Guyonvarc'h, 'The Basis of Prejudice,' 53.

13   Francis M. Deng, 'Ethnicity: African Predicament,' *The Brookings Review* 15, 3 (Summer 1997), pp. 28-31.

14   Ibid., p.28.

15   Guyonvarc'h, 'The Basis of Prejudice,' 53.

16   Meles Zenawi, 'Democracy and Development Have to Come from the Grassroots,' *The Courier* 145 (May-June, 1994), p. 23.
17   Ibid., p. 24.
18   Ibid.
19   Edward Alsworth Ross, 'Socialization,' *American Journal of Sociology* 24 (1919), pp. 652-671.
20   Maryon Macdonald, 'Celtic ethnic kinship and the problem of being English,' *Current Anthropology* 27, 4 (August-October, 1986), pp. 333-347.
21   David Glasberg, 'History and the Public Legacies of the Progressive Era,' *The Journal of American History* (1987), pp. 957-980.
22   Pius Okigbo, 'The Future Haunted by the Past,' In Adebayo Adedeji eds., Africa Within the World: Beyond Dispossession and Dependence (London, Zed Books, 1993): 28-38.
23   Banning Eyre, 'The Griot is the elder, the Keeper of Tales, the Tribes Memory,' The Kennedy Center (April, 1998).
24   Lisa Traiger, 'Dancing Their Stories,' *The Washington Post* (February 22, 2002), pp. T28.
25   Ibid., p. 957
26   Ibid., p. 957.
27   Robert J. Foster, 'Making National Cultures in the Global Ecumene,' *Annual Review of Anthropology* 20 (1991), pp. 235-260.
28   Ibid., p. 237.
29   Ibid., p. 238.
30   Claire Andrade-Watkins, 'Portuguese African Cinema: historical and contemporary perspectives – 1969 to 1993,' *Research in African Literatures* 26 (1995), pp. 134 (17).
31   Ibid., p. 134.
32   Francoise Pfaff, 'Conversation with Ghanaian filmmaker Kwaw Ansah,' *Research in African Literature* 26 (1995), pp. 186 (8).
33   Ibid., p. 186.
34   Ibid., p. 186.
35   Stephan Faris, 'Hollywood, Who Really Needs It? Nigeria's homegrown film business is booming, but is this a case of too much of a good thing?', *Time International* (May 20, 2002), p. 39.
36   Danna Harman, 'Nigeria Nips at Hollywood's Heels,' *Christian Science Monitor* (June 26, 2002), p. 1.
37   Jonathan Haynes and Onookome Okome, 'Evolving Popular Media: Nigerian Video Films,' *Research in African Literature* 29 (1998), pp. 106 (23).
38   Ibid., p. 127.
39   Ibid., p. 128.
40   Baffour Ankromah, 'African Media Are Stuck in Time Warp,' *African News Service* (June 19, 2002).
41   Ibid.
42   J. T. Jackson Lears, 'The Concept of Cultural Hegemony: Problems and Possibilities'. *The American Historical Review* (1995), pp. 568-593.

Chapter 6

Promoting Social Interaction

Introduction

Will there come a time in Africa when one tribe can trust another completely, when one religion will not consider another a social aberration, when politics will not bring out the worst aspects of mankind, and when economic necessity will not rid a person of his/her dignity? Africa will have a better prospect of enjoying such a time when national leaders demonstrate appreciation of the important role social mobilization plays in achieving and maintaining a politically stable, economically viable, growth-oriented and post-tribal nation-state. Although national development depends on the interplay of many variables, such as skillful planning, workable policies,[1] good leadership,[2] intelligent resource management and social infrastructure, prudent mobilization and management of human capital are essential to its success. When human capital is effectively mobilized in a social system, individuals are likely to think and act in the interest of the common good. Conversely, when the vast majority of the population is apathetic to the plight of the nation, individuals in a social system are likely to be motivated by selfish or parochial demands and interests.

Since independence, the selfish policies of most African leaders and policy makers have generally been insensitive to the plight of the masses. Leaders have hardly considered that their failure to provide ample social infrastructure challenges individual empowerment and limits the ability of communities to raise their physical quality of life through self-help projects. Leaders have always believed that the tokenism they offered periodically (particularly at election time) was sufficient to focus the collective will on achieving the broader interests and aspirations of the nation-state. The prevailing perception has been that the periodic promises of structural improvements and economic progress can align the goals of the country with those of individuals so that the pursuit of one will mean the pursuit of the other. However, Africans have seen through the false disposition of their leaders and gone about their daily lives oblivious of the needs of the state. It is no surprise that a disconnection between the leader's aspirations and desires and those of the general population exists across Africa.

Most people agree that active involvement of citizens is necessary for a country to fully develop. Although small groups of altruistic individuals may aid national growth, any genuine development can be sustainable only where beneficiaries feel a communal ownership for planning, implementation and evaluation of projects. When development is from the top-down and projects are not supply-driven, passion for social change is low and the chances for developmental success are usually minimal.

As most credible literature suggests, African countries can generate citizen involvement by enabling social interactions among their populations. The term social interaction encompasses all of the 'structural linkages and functional flows (of peoples, goods, services, messages and information)'[3] that take place in a social system. These linkages and structures allow individuals in the social system to undertake meaningful social transactions, and to use interactions to promote the health and vitality of established relationships. This relational status is maintained through shared meaning, 'values and identities'.[4] This requires effective communication techniques.   Social interaction is therefore an intrinsic communication activity. As Porter and Samovar explain, communication is a form of human behavior that derives from the need to interact with other human beings.[5] They point out that the need for social contact with other people is elemental to human existence, and this need is met through communication, which unites otherwise isolated individuals.[6] Engaging in verbal, physical or emotional contact in a social, cultural, political, economic or technological environment allows people   to   accomplish   intended   objectives   through   communication. Communication is thus integrally related to social interaction. No interaction can occur without communication and no communication can take place without interaction.

Because of its close relationship with communication, social interaction is indispensable to the process of national integration. Drake[7] notes this indispensability when she writes that interaction is part of the essence of integration, for 'isolation and interaction are antithetical by definition'. According to Spicer,[8] integration is rooted in the constant interactions of people. This constant interaction leads to a shared knowledge, and shared knowledge leads to more interaction.[9]   Interaction is therefore instrumental to how groups and individuals perceive themselves as members of the same community.   This national identification is essential for individuals in a diverse national population to interlock their communication habits and share meanings, learn to predict each other's behavior and coordinate each other's actions.[10] It is also vital for sharing common historical experiences, socio-cultural attributes and a sense of economic interdependence.   When national identification is sufficiently entrenched in a disparate social system, the population will display a readiness to work together for common purposes and a willingness to behave so as to achieve these purposes.[11] Such cooperative attitude and behavior are vital for sustainable social change and stability in a social system.   It is possible therefore to discern the degree of integration in a system by examining how much social interaction takes place among its population.   In this chapter, a critical assessment is undertaken of the infrastructure available for social interactions in Africa.

Social Interaction Infrastructure in Africa

The infrastructure required to enhance structural linkages and functional flows among people in a social system includes roads, railways, seaports, airports, trade, language and communications.

Roads, Railways, Seaports and Airports

Roads are important to the social and economic health of a country and a region. To the extent that they facilitate the movement of people, goods and services, they are necessary for and beneficial to both to economic vitality and to social integration. Yet, throughout Africa, with the exception of South Africa, the road network—national, provincial and local—is generally inadequate to meet the social and economic needs of a country and the continent. As data provided by Jeffrey Ramsay shows, Nigeria (the most populous country on the continent) has a road system of 194,394 kilometers, but much of it is barely usable.[12] Table 6.1 presents the available data on the road and railway system in Africa. The table appears to substantiate Akukwe's[13] observation that less than 16 percent of Africa's road network is paved. South Africa has the best road system on the continent with a total of 232,000 kilometers, but its rural areas have no access to adequate roads.[14]

Similarly, the condition of the railway infrastructure in Africa is generally poor. Much of the blame for this belongs to 'generations of opportunistic and venal African leaders, who have done little to develop their societies and emancipate their peoples'.[15] Nwana[16] notes, for example, how corruption, politicization and mismanagement of scarce resources have caused the decay of Nigerian railway operations. He writes that the lack of genuine effort by the government has kept the Nigerian railways from rebounding from its operational nightmares, which include owing nine months of staff salaries, one year of pensions, and reckoning with decrepit engines, broken down passenger coaches and rolling stock. He notes that successive governments have filled the Nigerian Railway board and management with politicians, instead of technocrats and professionals. These political appointees, who chaired the Nigerian Railway Corporation in recent years, are more preoccupied with generating money for party functions than for national development. These observations can be confirmed by the personal experience of this writer, who is a Nigerian-American. But the Nigerian situation is the not the exception. Throughout Sub-Saharan Africa, poor rail service is the norm.

The initial development of an African rail system occurred during the colonial era. But the objectives of colonial rule 'were not so much the advancement of African interests, as the maximization of profits for the inhabitants of Europe'.[17] Thus, the different colonial rulers (Britain, France, Germany and Portugal) built separate rail systems in the individual countries they administered. These separate systems were not integrated, except for some countries in the central, eastern and southern portion of Africa. As Ming notes:

Communicating National Integration

A cursory glance at the railway maps of Africa will show that the arterial routes run from inland areas to ports. The exception is south and southeastern Africa where an effort was made to interconnect various industrial areas. On the west, lines run to the coast but are barely connected. A prime example is Angola where three lines run parallel from east to west.[18]

It has taken more than forty years after independence for African leaders to realize that harmonizing the railway lines left by the colonial powers would enhance the achievement of economic development throughout the continent. As part of the World Summit on Sustainable Development held in South Africa in August/September 2002, more than 150 government officials, specialists and business leaders attended a three-day Africa Rail 2002 conference. The conference was organized under the aegis of the newly formed New Partnership for Africa's Development (NEPAD). There, the leaders resolved to 'integrate rail operations across national borders to facilitate trade not only between African states but also between Africa and the rest of the world'.[19] Whether this objective can be achieved in the face of the renowned African corruption and misadministration remains to be seen.

Table 6.1 Road and Railway Systems in Africa

Countries	Railway Total (Km)	Paved (Km)	Highway Unpaved (Km)	Total (Km)
1. Algeria	4,820	71,656	32,344	104,00
2. Angola	2,711	19,156	57,470	76,626
3. Benin	578	1,357	5,430	6,787
4. Botswana	888	5,620	4,597	10,217
5. Burkina Faso	622	2,001	10,505	12,506
6. Burundi	0	1,028	13,452	14,480
7. Cameroon	1,104	4,228	30,012	34,300
8. Cape Verde	0	858	242	1,100
9. Central African Republic	0	429	23,381	23,810
10. Chad	0	450	32,950	33,450
11. Comoros	0	673	207	880
12. Congo	894	1,242	11,558	12,800
13. Cote d'Ivoire	660	4,889	45,511	50,400
14. DR. Congo	5,138	N/A	N/A	157,000
15. Djibouti	100	364	2,526	2,890
16. Egypt	4,955	50,000	14,000	64,000
17. Equatorial Guinea	0	0	2,880	2,880
18. Eritrea	317	810	4,040	3,850
19. Ethiopia	681	3,920	20,855	24,145
20. Gabon	649	629	7,041	7,670
21. Gambia	0	956	1,744	2,700
22. Ghana	953	9,346	29,594	38,940
23. Guinea	1,086	5,033	25,467	30,500
24. Guinea Bissau	0	453	3,947	4,400
25. Kenya	2,778	8,932	54,868	63,800
26. Lesotho	2.6	887	4,068	4,995

27. Liberia	490	657	9,943	10,600
28. Libya	0	6,798	17,686	24,484
29. Madagascar	893	5,781	44,056	49,837
30. Malawi	797	2,773	11,821	14,594
31. Mali	729	1,827	13,273	15,100
32. Mauritania	704	830	6,890	7,720
33. Mauritius	0	1,8786	74	1,860
34. Mayotte	0	72	21	93
35. Morocco	1,907	30,254	27,593	57,847
36. Mozambique	3,131	5,685	24,715	30,400
37. Namibia	2,382	5,378	59,430	64,800
38. Niger	0	798	9,302	10,100
39. Nigeria	3,557	59,892	133,308	193,200
40. Reunion	0	1,300	1,424	2,724
41. Rwanda	0	1,000	11,000	12,000
42. Sao Tome & Principe	0	218	102	320
43. Senegal	906	4,271	10,305	14,576
42. Seychelles	0	176	104	280
45. Sierra Leone	84	936	10,764	10,700
46. Somalia	0	2,608	19,492	22,100
47. South Africa	20,384	59,753	298,843	358,596
48. Sudan	5,995	4,320	7,580	11,900
49. Swaziland	297	1,064	2,736	3,800
50. Tanzania	3,569	4,250	80,750	85,000
51. Togo	525	2,376	5,144	7,520
52. Tunisia	2,168	18,226	4,874	23,100
53. Uganda	1,241	1,800	25,200	27,000
54. Zambia	2,157	N/A	N/A	66,781
55. Zimbabwe	3,077	8,692	9,646	18,338

Source: CIA. *The World Factbook 2002.*
    http://www.cia.gov/cia/publications/factbook/index.html

In the absence of good roads and railways, efficient and affordable air travel is essential to economic and social development. However, as a recent article in *The Economist* reveals, by every conceivable measure, Africa's airlines have been in decline for two decades. The article cited a recent United Nations review of the Yamoussoukro Declaration, an accord signed in 1988 to integrate the continent's air network, which concluded that virtually every aspect of airline operation in Africa was behind schedule, including a common ticketing system. The review added that in many countries, airline companies are simply treated as an extension of public service. They are set up as part of government departments and placed under the control of politicians who allot key positions on the basis of nepotism or as political favors 'without any consideration for merit'.[20] As a result, the majority of the African airlines are unprofitable. The exception is South African airways, one of the few financially strong airlines on the continent.

An article in *The Economist*[21] states reasons to be optimistic. It notes that on the demand side, the World Tourism Organization predicts that the African region will experience the fastest growth in tourism worldwide in the next few years. It notes that external financiers—The World Bank and the International Monetary Fund (IMF) are pushing for liberalization and forcing national airlines in Congo,

Cameroon, and Nigeria to face the prospect of privatization so as to improve their efficiency.[22] As a response to this push, some countries like Kenya have turned over management of their national airways to affiliates of European carriers, to improve their efficiency. South African Airways has begun operating a joint venture with Tanzanian and Ugandan flag-carriers. If these reforms take root across the continent, there is bound to be noticeable improvement on the cost side of airline operations, as well. Moribund national airlines would be able to revive their operations and even make a profit. This would increase social contacts within nations and between African populations, which would be good not only for national economies but also for socio-cultural development. However, it should be noted that history does not favor such optimism.

Language

The importance of language as a measure of social interaction has been previously established. In a study conducted in Ghana, Smock and Bentsi-Enchill[23] found that language was a major factor governing the character of inter-group relations. The results of one survey of university students indicated that people who knew another Ghanaian language were more inclined to consider members of that group similar to themselves. They noted that the spread of English as the lingua franca made it possible for members of different ethnic groups to interact socially, but they cautioned that the kind of relationships individuals maintained through an alien tongue often lacked closeness and emotional satisfaction. They concluded that having a national language was fundamentally important to maintaining a viable and cohesive country. Miller agreed, noting that language is a primary resource for enacting social identity and displaying memberships of social groups.[24] So did Moore and Dunbar[25] who wrote that language is a vehicle for transmitting culture.

These writers suggest that the choice of a national language has crucial implications for the development of education and the mass media. As Kuo[26] put it, language planning is essential to communication planning, which is in turn essential to national development. Implicit is the role of culture in slowing or prohibiting social interaction. Culture tends to isolate people, thus precluding or prohibiting them from developing closeness and trust. A good illustration of this is the history of relationships between whites and blacks in the United States.

It is no surprise that to this day, linguistic diversity remains the most fascinating and challenging feature in the general development of modern social systems in Africa.[27] The exception is North Africa, where the use of a single language (Arabic) matches the global norm and countries with an average population of about 25 million have one or no minority language.[28] In Africa, south of the Sahara, where the population averages about 10 million per country, ethnic complexity soars so that 10, 20, 50 or more languages can be found within the same border.[29] This has necessitated the adoption of a lingua franca in these countries. In many countries, the adopted lingua franca is the same as the language of the colonial rulers: English, French or Portuguese. But using these colonial languages has posed more problems than it has solved. In Uganda, for example, the Report of the Constitutional Committee of 1959 noted that the problem of a *lingua franca* was one of the major factors inhibiting the development of political parties and mass nationalism. In the absence of an alternative language, English remained the Ugandan lingua franca. But English is not widely spoken in Uganda; it is limited to a small group, who has acquired western education.[30] This is true also of other Anglophone countries (including Nigeria and Ghana), as well as the Francophone and Luxophone countries. In east Africa where Kiswahili is used along side English in three countries, education has also been the major factor in English taking a role beside Kiswahili.

Some believe that the best way to mobilize African populations is to speak to them in their indigenous languages. To this end, countries like the Democratic Republic of Congo, Benin, Zambia and South Africa have begun establishing community radio stations. Others like Nigeria make allowances for local language broadcasts on national stations. However, as the late Nnamdi Azikiwe, the president of Nigeria's First Republic, has noted, the language issue poses problems for federalism and harmonious co-existence. He asked: 'How can people who speak diverse tongues and have inherited different cultural traditions cultivate the national spirit of oneness?'[31] Although local language broadcasts might increase grassroots participation, what will it do for vertical and horizontal integration (integration between the ruler and the ruled and other segments of the society)?

Perhaps government officials should be required to learn the languages of their constituencies. But is this really feasible or even practical? Will there be enough motivation on the part of government to provide sufficient resources to make the teaching of dual languages possible? Will people readily learn another language for the sake of unity? It would seem that unless African countries can develop neutral indigenous languages into their lingua franca or accept the European languages left as a colonial legacy, the language issue will remain a thorny issue and a major obstacle to social mobilization for some time to come.

Communications

In the early 1960s, the United Nations Educational, Scientific and Cultural Organization (UNESCO) set minimum media assets to classify developing societies as developing. With this declaration, the international community effectively acknowledged that the extent of a country's communication infrastructure was an appropriate indicator of its national development. True to that postulation, it is apparent that the majority of the economically and politically advanced countries have a vast communications infrastructure. Whether it is the United States, Britain, Canada, France, Italy or Japan, telecommunications and broadcasting facilities saturate the landscape, allowing these societies to have maximum communication. Kuo notes that the communicative ability of a country is a determinant of its rate of assimilation or disintegration.[32]

In the pre-colonial period, Africans communicated using various indigenous methods. Gongs, smoke, talking drums, town criers, folk dances, runners, and or other folk media were used to relay news and information within and between ethnic nationalities. They were used to exchange signals in times of war and peace, to promote cultures and preserve them for posterity, to promote vertical and horizontal integration, and to foster interpersonal and inter-communal harmony. However, these methods had two glaring inadequacies: first, they could not cover great distances, and second, they lacked uniformity in form and content. As a result, they were seriously limited in their ability to influence the social, political and economic empowerment of African citizens.[33]

During colonial period, Europeans introduced modern and technical communication to Africa. Beginning with the printing press, they gradually brought cinema projectors, telephones, broadcast facilities, radio and television transmitters and receivers, and videotape and cassette recorders to the continent. Today, the communications infrastructure in Africa is consistent with, albeit not at par, with those of Europe. It includes wireless cable, satellites, computers, modems, faxes, cell phones, The Internet, and the World Wide Web. At the outset, the modern communication tools in Africa were meant for the exclusive use of Europeans. As Hachten notes, Africans were merely 'an eavesdropping audience'.[34] But as African societies have grown more complex in recent decades through urbanization and social stratification, both the interpersonal and non-technical means of communication have become less dependable ways of generating and disseminating broad information. African societies have had little choice but to embrace the modern communication technology, which is seen today as a main avenue through which the continent can keep pace with a rapidly changing global environment and transform itself to achieve new and desirable social, cultural, political, economic and technological heights.

Africans embraced modern communication tools with great optimism in the pre-independence period. African leaders projected that their economies, which were buoyant at the time, would remain growth-oriented. They hoped that this growth, coupled with enduring political stability, would provide sufficient discretionary funds to allow a quick and broad diffusion of modern communication tools throughout the continent. According to Adedeji,[35] throughout the 1960s and the first half of the 1970s, it was generally believed Africa had a better chance for making rapid and steady progress than Asia and Latin America. Africa was thought to lack Asia and Latin America's oppressive social structures and cultural impediments. On the contrary, in the post-independence period, persistent economic, socio-political and technological difficulties have kept Africa far behind the rest of the world in the general distribution of communication infrastructure.[36]

In the last 40 years many African countries have budgeted less money to the information and communication sector than initially projected. Some countries have made no investments because of the basic needs of citizens (food and shelter) or because ethnic, religious and class division have demanded the greater portion of resources. There has also been the tendency to see investments in modern tools of communication as a waste of resources because the majority of the population still perceives them as a luxury enjoyed only by an affluent section of the population. And no one has explained to the general population that communication tools are vital to individual and collective empowerment. No one has bothered to explain that the information flows, which these tools enable, are essential in 'bringing about the conceptual and organizational changes that are an integral part of a society's development process'.[37]

Table 6.2 World Distribution of Television Receivers: Total and Number per 1,000 inhabitants

| Continents, major areas and groups of countries | Number of television receivers | | | | | | | | | |
| | Total (in millions) | | | | | Number per 1,000 inhabitants | | | | |
	1980	1985	1990	1996	1997	1980	1985	1990	1996	1997
World total	563	749	1092	1366	1396	127	155	208	238	240
Africa	8.2	14	25	41	44	18	27	41	58	60
America	202	259	292	338	342	329	388	404	429	429
Asia	104	198	487	653	672	40	70	153	187	190
Europe	243	268	278	322	325	324	349	385	443	446
Oceania	6.8	8.6	9.9	12	12	300	352	378	425	427
Developing countries	88	202	504	697	720	27	55	124	154	157
Sub-Saharan Africa	4.4	7.1	15	26	29	12	17	30	45	48
Arab States	9.3	16	22	30	31	56	79	100	118	119
Latin America/ Caribbean	35	55	72	100	101	98	138	162	204	205
Eastern Asia and Oceania	26	96	346	449	461	18	62	207	249	253
Southern Asia	6.1	15	34	68	73	6.4	14	29	51	54
Least developed countries	1.4	2.2	6.5	12	14	3.5	5	13	20	23
Developed countries	475	547	588	669	675	424	472	492	545	548

Source: UNESCO. *UNESCO Statistical Yearbook 1999*. Lanham, Maryland: Bernan Press

As a result, while many of the developing countries in Europe, Asia and Latin America were experiencing accelerated growth in information and communication technologies (ICT) in the first half of the 1990s, countries in Africa remained relatively stagnant (see Tables 6.2 to 6.4). According to the 1996 *African*

Telecommunication Indicators, even though African telecommunications infrastructure has increased in absolute terms in recent decades, 'the effect on overall access has been negligible, especially for Sub-Saharan Africa'.[38]   The report notes that the growth rate of telephone lines had not changed in Africa since 1990; in fact, it had declined in nine sub-Saharan countries and grown only slightly in most other nations. This is one reason why vast pockets of Africans still lack adequate capacities for communication and self-expression, the opportunities they need to become full participants in the global information age.

Table 6.3 World Distribution of Radio Receivers: Total and Number per 1,000 inhabitants

Continents, major areas and groups of countries	Number of television receivers									
	Total (in millions)					Number per 1,000 inhabitants				
	1980	1985	1990	1996	1997	1980	1985	1990	1996	1997
World total	1384	1684	2075	2396	2432	312	348	394	417	418
Africa	61	90	116	152	158	131	169	190	213	216
America	566	649	711	802	811	918	971	984	1019	1017
Asia	318	416	748	886	900	123	147	235	254	255
Europe	420	504	474	526	531	560	656	657	723	729
Oceania	20	24	26	30	31	875	974	999	1065	1071
Developing countries	398	543	895	1100	1124	120	148	220	244	245
Sub-Saharan Africa	47	68	86	115	121	125	158	173	198	202
Arab States	29	43	56	69	71	175	209	249	267	269
Latin America/ Caribbean	94	126	153	200	204	259	314	347	410	412
Eastern Asia and Oceania	180	223	490	549	558	126	144	293	305	306
Southern Asia	42	77	102	156	160	45	72	86	117	118
Least developed countries	31	45	57	81	85	79	100	112	138	142
Developed countries	986	1141	1181	1297	1308	880	986	987	1056	1061

Source: UNESCO. *UNESCO Statistical Yearbook 1999*. Lanham, Maryland: Bernan Press

UNESCO statistics published in 1998 present the most recent figures concerning the distribution of mass media infrastructure in Africa for the period

1980 to 1997. In this period, the number of television receivers in Africa grew from 8.2 million to 44 million (see Table 6.2). The average number of television receivers per 1,000 inhabitants was 18 in 1980; in 1997 there were 60 sets per 1,000 inhabitants. This suggests that Africa's share of the world's totals for television grew from approximately 1.5 percent in 1980 to 2.7 in 1996. The largest growth was recorded in Sub-Saharan Africa, where television receivers increased from 4.4 million in 1980 to 29 million in 1997 and the number of sets per 1,000 inhabitants increased from 12 in 1980 to 48 in 1997.

Table 6.4 World Distribution of Daily Newspapers: Number and Circulation

Continents, major areas and groups of countries	Number of dailies				Estimated circulation							
					Total in Millions				Number per 1,000 inhabitants			
	1980	1994	1995	1996	1980	1994	1995	1996	1980	1994	1995	1996
World total	7847	8283	8291	8391	491	538	537	538	111	97	95	96
Africa	169	206	219	224	7.4	11	11	12	16	16	16	16
America	3112	2881	2903	2938	98	103	105	111	158	134	135	141
Asia	2090	2897	2960	3010	149	216	221	229	58	64	64	66
Europe	2371	2188	2101	2115	232	202	194	190	309	278	267	261
Oceania	105	111	108	103	5.9	6.4	6.3	6.4	261	233	232	227
Developing countries	3359	4206	4324	4419	122	257	257	272	37	59	58	60
Sub-Saharan Africa	134	161	164	168	4.7	6	6.2	7.1	13	11	11	12
Arab States	107	127	135	140	4.5	9.3	9.3	9.2	27	38	37	36
Latin America/ Caribbean	1243	1225	1262	1309	30	38	42	49	83	81	88	101
Eastern Asia and Oceania	351	404	412	400	60	98	97	102	35	56	54	56
Southern Asia	1432	2181	2249	2299	17	38	42	44	18	29	32	33
Least developed countries	158	180	182	172	1.8	4	3.6	3.9	5	8.6	7.5	8
Developed countries	4488	4077	3967	3972	370	281	280	276	363	288	230	226

Source: UNESCO. *UNESCO Statistical Yearbook 1999*. Lanham, Maryland: Bernan Press

Table 6.3 shows that the number of radio sets in Africa increased from 61 million in 1980 to 158 million in 1997, an increase of more than 100 percent. There were 131 radio receivers per 1,000 inhabitants in 1980, 158 per 1,000 in 1997. Africa's share of the world's totals for radio receivers grew from approximately 3.8 percent in 1980 to 6.5 in 1996. In Sub-Saharan Africa, the number of radio sets grew from 47 million in 1980 to 121 million in 1997; the number of sets per 1,000 individuals increased from 125 in 1980 to 202 in 1997.

In 1980, Africa had just 169 daily newspapers of the world's 7,847 dailies, just 3.5 percent of the total (see Table 6.4). In 1994, this increased to 226 (i.e. 4.7 percent) within an increased world total of 8,391. Africa's share of world totals for newspapers only increased by approximately 2 percent in the 14 years for which data were available. The distribution for Sub-Saharan Africa was 134 daily newspapers in 1980, 161 in 1994 and 168 in 1996. Worldwide production and consumption of newsprint for 1996 was 34 million tons and 34.3 million tons, respectively. Of these, African totals for both categories were merely 500 thousand tons. Sub-Saharan Africa produced 500 thousand tons of newsprint in 1996, and consumed 400 thousand tons.

Table 6.5 Teledensity Distribution in Africa

Countries	Population		GDP		Main Phone Lines	
	Total (M)	Density (Per Km)	Total (B US$)	Per capita (US$)	Total (K)	Per 100 inhabitants
1. Algeria	29.47	12	41.2 [95]	1,442	1,400.3	4.75
2. Angola	11.57	9	18.1 [95]	1,684	62.3	0.54
3. Benin	5.72	51	2.2	400	36.5	0.64
4. Botswana	1.52	3	4.4	2,942	85.6	5.64
5. Burkina Faso	11.9	40	2.4	218	36.3	0.33
6. Burundi	6.19	222	0.9	150	15.9	0.26
7. Cameroon	13.94	29	8.9	657	75.2	0.54
8. Cape Verde	0.41	101	0.3 [94]	876	33.3	8.19
9. Central African Republic	3.52	5	1.1	319	9.8	0.29
10. Chad	6.70	5	1.1	170	7.5	0.11
11. Comoros	0.65	350	0.2 [95]	382	5.5	0.84
12. Congo	2.75	8	2.4	905	22.0	0.80
13. Cote d'Ivoire	15.25	17	10.7	725	142.3	0.93
14. DR. Congo	48.04	20	---	---	36.0 [96]	0.08
15. Djibouti	0.63	29	0.5	846	8.3	1.31
16. Egypt	52.01	62	67.4	1,112	3,452.7	5.57
17. Equatorial Guinea	0.42	15	0.3	668	3.7 [96]	0.89
18. Eritrea	3.78	40	0.6 [95]	61	21.5	0.57
19. Ethiopia	60.15	49	6.0	102	156.5	0.26
20. Gabon	1.14	4	5.7	5.121	37.3	3.27
21. Gambia	1.17	109	0.3 [94]	284	24.8	2.13
22. Ghana	18.34	77	6.3	356	105.5	0.58
23. Guinea	7.61	31	5.1	677	19.8	0.26
24. Guinea Bissau	1.11	31	0.3 [95]	240	7.6	0.69
25. Kenya	33.14	57	9.2	291	269.8	0.81
26. Lesotho	2.12	70	0.9	414	20.4	0.96
27. Liberia	2.88	26	---	---	6.4	0.22

28. Libya	5.78	3	32.1 [92]	6,579	380.0 [96]	6.79
29. Madagascar	15.85	27	4.0	261	43.2	0.27
30. Malawi	10.44	111	2.3	225	35.5 [96]	0.35
31. Mali	11.48	9	2.6	232	23.5	0.20
32. Mauritania	2.39	2	1.1	455	13.1	0.55
33. Mauritius	1.14	612	4.3	3,799	222.7	19.52
34. Mayotte	0.12	328	---	---	9.3	7.55
35. Morocco	27.52	42	36.7	1,350	1,375.0	5.00
36. Mozambique	18,27	23	1.5 [95]	86	66.1	0.36
37. Namibia	1.61	2	3.2	2,051	100.8	6.25
38. Niger	9.79	8	1.7	178	16.4	0.17
39. NigeriaError! Bookmark not defined.	118.37	128	129.5	1,126	412.8 [96]	0.36
40. Reunion	0.67	268	5.9 [93]	9.270	236.5	35.13
41. Rwanda	5.88	223	1.4	258	15.0 [96]	0.28
42. Sao Tome & Principe	0.14	145	[95]	358	2.5 [95]	1.97
43. Senegal	8.76	45	4.8	561	115.9	1.32
44. Seychelles	0.08	191	0.5	6,679	14.9 [96]	19.56
45. Sierra Leone	4.43	61	0.9 [95]	209	17.4	0.39
46. Somalia	10.22	16	---	---	15.0	0.15
47. South Africa	43.34	37	126.2	2,978	4,645.1	10.72
48. Sudan	27.90	11	8.2	301	112.5	0.40
49. Swaziland	0.91	52	1.2	1,318	25.4	2.81
50. Tanzania	31.51	34	6.5	211	105.1	0.33
51. Togo	4.31	76	1.5	345	25.1	0.58
52. Tunisia	9.32	57	19.6	2,143	654.2	7.02
53. Uganda	20.79	88	6.3	317	51.8	0.25
54. Zambia	8.48	11	3.3	399	77.3	0.91
55. Zimbabwe	12.29	39	8.6	719	212.0	1.72

Source: Adapted from the *UNESCO Statistical Yearbook 1999*. Lanham, Maryland: Bernan Press

Teledensity (i.e. the number of telephone main lines (TML) per 100 inhabitants) is the index used to measure telephone penetration in a society. Between 1986 and 1992, African teledensity held steady at an average of 0.4. In 1993 and 1994, this average increased slightly to 0.5. The teledensity figures for 1997 are presented in Table 6.5. For some countries, the figures presented were for 1992, 1993, 1994, 1995 or 1996, as figures for 1997 were unavailable. The table shows a slight teledensity growth in many African countries. This growth is credited to the rapid restructuring that begun in Africa's telecommunications sector in the 1990s. The cornerstone of this restructuring is privatization. Since 1990, many African countries have formally severed telecommunications operations from the Post Office, established telecommunication operations as joint-stock companies and created regulatory bodies to oversee this new structure. For example, the Guinean national telecommunication operator was privatized in 1996. In 1995, the Cape Verde government relinquished 40 percent of its national operation to private interests. Uganda announced plans in early 1996 to privatize part of its telecommunications operation and introduce a second fixed-link operator.[39] Still, in sub-Saharan Africa, the ratio of phone line to inhabitants is one to 200 (excluding South Africa). Akukwe notes that in 2001, there were more fixed lines in Manhattan, New York, than in all of sub-Saharan Africa.[40]

Ashurst[41] writes that in just over five years, the number of mobile connections in sub-Saharan Africa has surpassed the number of fixed lines installed over four decades: more than 12 million versus 9 million. He says in diamond-rich Botswana, more than one in eight citizens has a cell phone. South Africa boasts more than 9 million cells, compared with just 5 million conventional lines. In just a few years even poor countries like the Republic of Congo, Rwanda and Malawi have installed 100 percent digital networks with thousands of subscribers. He adds that on a continent where half the population survives on less than \$2 a day, African mobile-phone users now spend more time and more money on calls than Europeans do. Though the poor restrict their calls to off-peak periods, premium-rate business users have abandoned less-reliable fixed-line networks, boosting Africa's average monthly mobile bill to \$36 per capita, compared with \$22 for Europe. Even beer sales—long an indicator of average Africans' buying power—are falling as consumers opt to spend their limited disposable income on calls, according to South African Breweries, the continent's largest conglomerate.[42]

The television market is also becoming increasingly diverse. The structure of the market is still predominantly monopolistic, but a host of subscription services now exists to complement free services. As the ITU observes, 'A growing number of viewers are willing to pay for subscription television, even though charges are far higher than for basic telephone service'.[43] In countries like Ghana, Nigeria, Senegal, South Africa and a number of others, subscription television is fast becoming a serious competitor in the video market. In Nigeria for instance, most housing estates in the major cities of Benin, Enugu, Ibadan, Jos, Lagos, Kaduna, Kano and Port Harcourt have been wired and television is now available around the clock.[44] Subscription television services are operated by foreign and media entrepreneurs. South Africa's M-NET, the premier subscription television service in the southern hemisphere, is the dominant African player with about 930,000 subscribers. The dominant foreign players include France's Canal Horizon, a subsidiary of Canal+, and TV5, a francophone television station broadcast by microwave distribution systems (MDS) throughout West Africa. Nigeria has the most active subscription television market with about 15 operators.[45] The social and economic benefit that the growing subscription television market is bringing is still subject to intense speculation. What is clear is that a plurality of voices is beginning to appear in places where the only voice used to be that of the government.

In the mid 1990s Barbacar Fall, the Director-General of the Pan African News Agency, optimistically foresaw a future where Africans could easily exchange information through the Internet.[46] Sub-Saharan African countries began connecting to the Internet in 1994. By the end of 1995, 16 African countries had direct Internet connectivity, but only 11 had local access at the end of 1996.[47] Today, all of the 54 countries and territories in Africa have access to the Internet, with the exception of Congo (Brazzaville), Eritrea and Somalia, 'and both Congo and Eritrea have recently announced plans to establish service'.[48] Twelve countries have a local Internet Service Provider (ISP): Angola, Botswana, Egypt, Ghana, Kenya, Morocco, Namibia, Nigeria, South Africa, Tanzania and Tunisia. Seven other countries have one public access ISP: Algeria, Burkina Faso, Central African Republic, Ethiopia, Mauritius, Niger and Seychelles.[49] Africa, like much of the developing world, has now realized that it has a wide window of opportunity to move directly into the information age, through cellular and satellite technologies, bypassing the wired stage at significantly lower costs.[50]

Overall, Internet penetration is still quite low in Africa. As Akukwe[51] points out, there are more Internet connections in New York City than in Africa as a whole. Access is largely confined to the capital cities, although an increasing number of countries have established POPS in some of their secondary towns, and South Africa has POPS in approximately 70 locations. In Senegal, there were only about 50 out of 11 million people using the Internet in 1996.[52] In April 1999, only 52 of the 232 academic and research institutions in Africa had full Internet access. There was only one Internet user for every 5,000 people in Africa, compared with one user per 38 people worldwide, and one user per every five people in Western countries. South Africa still has the highest densities of Internet users in Africa. Nkrumah estimates that there are approximately one million Internet users in Africa, 80 to 90 percent of who live in South Africa.[53]

The human component of the communications infrastructure has seen some growth in recent decades. Over the last 10 years, the number of people in media-related employment has grown at an annual rate of 25 percent in virtually every African country. A study conducted by the Groupe Multimedia Sud Communication shows that the print media experienced the greatest growth in recruitment, followed by radio.[54] However, staff quality is still a major constraint to the effective use of electronic communication in African development.[55] Recruits for media-related jobs in Africa often do not have the pre-requisite educational or experiential media background. In countries like South Africa and the Democratic Republic of Congo (formerly Zaire), new private community radio stations appear regularly and require employees. These employees require training in almost every aspect of media operation, including technical, production, performance and management.

These failings underscore the importance of access. Those who have access can attest to the indispensability of communication in everyday living. If bad weather is heading our way, we can turn immediately to the electronic media to find out what to do; if we need to get in touch with a distant family member, we could pick up the telephone and call or simply E-mail; if we need to send a business document quickly, we can fax it; if there is mismanagement in government, we can learn about it through the various media outlets. Those who have access agree that information is empowerment; a main avenue through which we maintain interpersonal ties, transact efficient business, relate to our environment and actively participate in the transformation of the social order; a means for creating a better-informed community able to anticipate and adapt to changes.

Concomitantly, the literature is well established on the link between the communicative ability of a nation-state and degree of popular interest or disinterest in the affairs of the nation-state. Nation-states with many ways to seek and process input in its affairs tend to experience lower levels of citizen apathy than those nation-states that ignore seeking popular opinion. Participatory communication can be either verbal (e.g. strikes, town meetings, discussion groups, strategy groups, published opinions, etc) or non-verbal (e.g., general apathy, suffering in silence, etc), but verbal communication appears to have the greatest effect on participation. Those who voice their opinion publicly or take overt actions, even if in the minority, are more readily taken seriously than those with good intention who remain silent or take less visible actions. The behavior of those who act publicly is more likely to generate sympathetic, empathetic or other affective reactions than the actions of those who deal privately. Such overt actions are also more likely to galvanize public officials to act in the best interest of all.

It is necessary therefore to consider access to ICT a basic human right for all Africans. Such a declaration is logical in its entirety and consistent with the '*right to communicate*' doctrine enshrined in the United Nations' Declaration of Human Rights. But how is this access to be defined? Should it be defined as universal access, with focus on the macro-level with the objective of providing ample opportunity for citizens to interact with information tools through service centers provided for the citizens? That would mean 'nationwide availability, non-discriminatory access and widespread affordability'.[56] Should it be defined as individual access, where the target is the micro-level and the goal is to provide the tools of communication to every home, business or school? Should it be defined as supply-side access, which focuses on removal of any 'barriers to entry' that might preclude the broad participation of citizens in the information business sector? Or as demand-side access where the objective is the removal of fundamental structural obstacles that might discourage people from acquiring information?

In Africa, there are no simple answers to these questions. The continent is highly diverse, with varying national issues and conditions. Africa is a paradox of experiences; a kaleidoscope of old and new, of competing economic and political ideologies, of pluralistic cultures and languages, of varying human and material potential and competencies. Thus, the definition of access that one chooses must match the particularities of the African society that one is addressing, and the set of peculiar circumstances that prevail. It may be logical for countries with vast economic and technological potential, such as Nigeria and South Africa, to target individual access. However, universal access may be the more realistic goal for smaller countries like Guinea and Benin with generally low levels of capitalization. At the barest minimum, every African country, regardless of wealth and social status, should aim to provide universal access to ICT. This is the globally recognized least expectation that a country must fulfill to have sustainable human development.

Conclusion

The purpose of this chapter was to review the amenities available for social interaction in Africa. Data have been presented showing the growth or decline of transportation and communication facilities. This review has been in keeping with the recent shift in development communication from emphasis on central development planning to community participation and involvement. The current thinking is that people should be allowed to develop themselves. It is believed that ordinary citizens in rural locales have a better understanding of their development needs than the officials in the urban centers. Essentially this belief grew out of frustrations with government inefficiency in many nations of the South. In several African countries, for example, government officials charged with planning and executing development programs to benefit the masses constantly betray the people's trust. They cater to their own individual needs rather than the general welfare of those they were meant to serve. The result has been a disenfranchised general population in many countries.

Throughout history, social interactions have given the masses (the 'have nots') the courage to gain some measure of control over their individual or collective destinies.[57] It has empowered the masses to acquire their voice in setting priorities and policies for development, and by so doing has enabled them to become an indispensable constituency in planning, execution and evaluation of development projects. As the civil unrest in Malaysia, Singapore, Thailand and East Timor have shown in the 1990s, the unified and vociferous voice of the masses can be extremely powerful for engineering social change. It can compel national governments to rethink implementation of ineffective policies, to seek popular input in all aspect of national affair, and to legitimize public activities by restoring the people's confidence in all actions of their leaders.

Within this context, this chapter has argued that it is essential for African governments to provide adequate and good transportation and communication infrastructure if their citizens are to have meaningful opportunities for cognitive and behavioral inputs in the growth and survival of their countries. The facilitation of the free exchange of ideas between rulers and the ruled, and between different communities comprising the nation-state, will place countries in a better position to understand their capacities, limitations, problems, and prospects for national development. In the absence of such freedom of exchange, critical decisions affecting the nation-state are left to a minority who subsequently arrogate to themselves complete knowledge of the needs and desires of the diverse peoples of the nation-state, and the facilities necessary to satisfy them. In this context, national development is erroneously equated with satisfaction of the aspirations of a minority of individuals or groups, who subsequently acquire for themselves (often by unscrupulous means) a greater share of the economic and political fortunes that otherwise would be used to improve the social system as a whole.[58]

African governments need not fear empowering of their populations, as they now often seem to be. Empowering the masses will not bring an end to their ambitions for power, as many seem to think. If anything, it should earn them 'staying-power' if their performance is well received in society. According to social exchange theory, human interactions are governed by a reciprocity principle that says if we are given something, it should be repaid (in some way). Thus, when a politician caters to the needs of his constituency, voters reciprocate this goodwill by granting the politician the privilege of lengthy service. An African leader who invests in his or her people, therefore, is unwittingly investing in himself/herself.

Notes

1   Botswana is a good example of an African country that has achieved growth-oriented status as a result of implementing workable policies. Rather than copy European models, Botswana reached back into its on customs and traditions in setting policy.

2   Chinua Achebe, *The Trouble with Nigeria*, Enugu, Fourth Dimension Press, 1980.

3   Christine Drake, *National Integration in Indonesia: Patterns and Policies*, Honolulu, University of Hawaii Press, 1989, 103.

4   John Paden, *Values, Identities and National Integration*, Evanston, Illinois: Northwestern University Press, 1980.

5   Richard Porter and Larry Samovar, 'Basic principles of intercultural communication,' in *Intercultural Communication: A Reader*, eds. Larry A. Samovar and Richard E. Porter, Belmont, California: Wadsworth Publishing Company, 1991, p. 7.

6   Ibid., p. 7.

7   Drake, National Integration in Indonesia, 103.

8   Edward H. Spicer, 'Developmental Change and Cultural Integration,' in *Perspectives in Developmental Change*, ed. Art Gallaher, Lexington: University of Kentucky Press, 1968, 1-16.

9   Kathleen Carey, 'A theory of group stability,' *American Sociological Review* 56, 3 (1991): 331-332.

10   Karl Deutsch, *Nationalism and its Alternatives* (New York: Alfred A. Knopf, Inc, 1969). See also Osabuohien P. Amienyi, 'The Association Between Mass Media Exposure and National Identification in Nigeria,' *International Third World Studies Journal and Review*, 2 (1991): 337-346.

11   David B. Abernethy, *The Political Dilemma of Popular Education: An African Case*, Stanford: Stanford University Press, 1969.

12   F. Jeffress Ramsay, *Africa 9th Edition* (Guilford, Connecticut, 2001), p. 1-234.

13   Chinua Akukwe, 'Integration will improve Africa's competitiveness,' *African News Service* (May 21, 2002).

14   Anon, 'South Africa has to build new roads in rural areas,' *Xinhua News Agency* (May 21, 2002).

15   Sunday Dare, 'A continent in crisis,' *Dollars & Sense* (July 1, 2001), p. 12.

16   Henry Nwana, 'The railway I knew,' Vanguard (June 26, 2002).

17   Chen Ming, 'News Analysis: Africa ambitious to harmonize railways lines,' *Xinhua News Agency* (August 12, 2002).

18   Ibid.

19   Ibid.

20   Author not available, 'Troubled skies: airlines in Africa,' *The Economist* 334 (March 4, 1995), p. 69 (1).

21   Ibid., p. 69.

22   Ibid.

23   David Smock and Kwamena Bentsi-Enchill, eds. *The search for national integration in Africa* , New York: Free Press, 1975.

24 Jennifer Miller, 'Language use, identity, and social interaction: Migrant students in Australia,' *Research on Language and Social Interaction* 33, 1 (2001): 69-100.
25 Clark D. Dunbar and Ann Moore, eds., *Africa Yesterday and Today*, New York: Prager Publishers, 1969, 27.
26 Eddie Kuo, 'Language, Nationhood, and Communication Planning: The Case of a Multilingual Society,' in *Perspectives in Communication Policy and Planning*, ed. S. A. Rahim and John Middleton, Honolulu, Hawaii: East-West Communication Institute, 1980: 122-126.
27 Ibid., p. 27.
28 Gwynne Dyer, 'Africa takes a step in the right direction,' *The Toronto Star* (July 10, 2002).
29 Ibid.
30 G. N. Uzoigwe, *Uganda: The Dilemma of Nationhood*, New York: NOK Publishers International, 1982, pp. 227-228.
31 Nnamdi Azikiwe, 'Essentials for Nigerian survival,' *Foreign Affairs* 43 (1965): 457.
32 Eddie Kuo, 'Language and communication planning,' p. 125.
33 Osabuohien P. Amienyi, Technology Transfer and Media Development in Nigeria, *Southwestern Mass Communication Journal*, 9 (1993): 44-53.
34 William A. Hachten, *The Growth of Media in the Third World: African Failures, Asian Successes*, Ames: Iowa State University Press, 1993, 14-15.
35 Adebayo Adedeji, 'introduction-Marginalisation and Marginality: Contexts, Issues, and Viewpoints,' in *Africa Within the World: Beyond Dispossession and Dependence*, ed. Adebayo Adedeji, London: Zed Books, 1993, 3.
36 Hachten, 'The Growth of Media,'; Mocks Shivute, 'The Media in posit-Independecne Namibia,' in *Communication & The Transformation of Society: A Developing Regions Perspective*, ed. Peter Nwosu, Chuka Onwumechili and Ritchard M'Bayo, Lanham, University Press of America, 1995; Louis M. Bourgault, *Broadcasting in Sub-Saharan Africa*, Ames: Iowa University Press, 1995.
37 Richard Ouma-Onyango, *Information Resources and Technology Transfer management in Developing Countries*, London: Routledge, 1997, 9.
38 ITU, *World Telecommunications Development Report: Universal Access: Executive Summary*, Luzanne, ITU, March 1998.
39 ITU, *African telecommunications indicators*, Luzanne: ITU, 1996. Http://www.itu.int/ti/publications/africa/afr96en.htm
40 Akukwe.
41 Mark Ashurst, 'Africa's ringing revolution,' *Newsweek International* (August 27, 2001): 16.
42 Ibid., p. 16.
43 ITU, *African Telecommunications Indicators*, 3.
44 Osabuohien P. Amienyi with Gerard Igyor, 'Sub-Saharan Africa,' in *World broadcasting: A Comparative view*, ed. Allan Wells, Norwood, New Jersey: Ablex Publishing Corporation, 1996.
45 ITU, *African Telecommunications Indicators*, 3
46 Sandhya Rao and Chinna N. Natesan, 'Internet: Threat or opportunity for India?' *Media Asia*, 232 (1996): 96-106.
47 Mike Jensen, 'African Internet Status,' *The World Wide Web* (May 1999).
48 Ibid.
49 Nkrumah, 'The African Connection.'

50   C. Owens, 'The developing leap,' *The Wall Street Journal* (February 11, 1994), R15.

51   Akukwe.

52   Rao and Natesan, 'Internet: Threat or opportunity for India?'

53   Nkrumah, 'TheAfrican Connection.'

54   Abdou L. Coulibaly, 'Media growth poses training challenges,' *InteRadio, 9 (1998)*:2-5.

55   Gupe Makabakayele, 'Radio training still under state monopoly,' *InteRadio, 9* (1998):2-5.

56   ITU, *World Telecommunications Development Report*, 2.

57   See for example studies cited in Andrew A. Moemeka, ed., *Comunicating for Development: A New Pan-disciplinary Perspective*, New York: State University of New York Press, 1994.

58   Osabuohien P. Amienyi, 'Communication and Development Quintessentials: The Focus of Development Agencies and Theorists,' *The Journal of Development Communication* 9 (June, 1998): 1-16.

Chapter 7

Communicating Through Economic Development

Introduction

It is reasonable to expect that the absence of economic development poses a serious threat to the stability and survival of a pluralistic nation-state. Even where economic development has been successful, inability or failure to distribute its generated wealth equitably among regions or communities may produce competition that threatens peaceful coexistence and systemic stability. For this reason, in Africa where diversity is the norm, there has been ongoing scholarly interest in the geopolitical ramifications of economic development. Part of this debate has focused on examining the association between economic progress and national integration. The purpose of this chapter is to contribute to this ongoing debate.

African economies seem to have made significant progress in economic development in the five decades since independence in the 1960s. At that time, many countries anticipated rapid economic and social progress. These expectations were largely realized at first, as production and per capita incomes grew significantly in many countries. But after an initial period of growth, the economic performance of some countries deteriorated in the 1970s and then went into outright decline in the 1980s. In an attempt to stem this decline, the IMF and the World Bank forced a number of far-reaching structural adjustments and reform programs in the 1980s. However, these programs weakened aggregate economic performance even further as per capita incomes fell considerably and poverty increased.[1] Towards the end of the 1980s, the economic prospects for Africa looked bleak.

But by the beginning of the new millennium in 2001, the widespread pessimism about Africa's prospects had been somewhat dispelled by renewed signs of economic progress. This progress was the result of a broader commitment to reform that began in the mid 1990s. This reform 'allowed average income growth rate to exceed the population growth rate for four consecutive years, thereby producing gains in per capita income across the continent for the first time in many years'.[2] Data provided by the United Nations Commission on Trade and Development (UNCTAD) demonstrated this gain. It showed that the Republic of South Africa (RSA) and Nigeria together, which account for approximately 50 percent of the total GDP of the continent, excluding North Africa, grew at a rate averaging 2.2 percent per annum during 1995-1999, while the growth rate of the remaining Sub-Saharan countries averaged an encouraging rate of 4.2 percent per annum over the same period. Towards the end of the decade, however, a generalized state of economic slowdown had returned in all of Africa. By 2000, the growth rate of Sub-Saharan Africa had fallen to 2.7 percent, barely matching the growth rate of the population.[3] In 2001, 37 of the 53 economies on the continent had growth rate of approximately 3 percent.[4] But that was still far from the 7 percent annual growth rate, which many analysts project will be the standard needed to eradicate poverty from the continent by the proposed date of 2015.

Some people believe that Africa must continue to find ways to institutionalize the sustainability of economic development throughout the continent. The general consensus is that economic reform efforts must be sustained and strengthened and urgent steps must be taken to resolve the serious conflicts that threaten the continent.[5] This view is supported in part by the results of a study of armed conflicts around the world released by the University of Maryland's Center for International Development in 2001. The findings indicate that 20 of the 33 countries at high risk of instability are in Africa.[6] The profile of these countries suggested that economic mismanagement and political gangsterism were deeply entrenched. The countries' 'low production costs, poor working conditions, and abundant and easily exploitable resources' enhanced greater susceptibility to international financial control.[7] In other words, they were countries covertly governed by economic policies favored by the Transnational Corporations (TNCs) that facilitate their unscrupulous extraction of mineral resources through the creation and reinforcement of corruption.

Corruption of politicians and businessmen invariably 'put private gains before the welfare of citizens and the economic development of their countries'.[8] As the Vice Chairman of Transparency International (a global non-governmental organization) explains, this corruption denies 'the poor, the marginalized and the least educated members of every society the social, economic and political benefits that should properly accrue to them, benefits that are taken for granted in societies that have managed to shake off the yoke of corruption'.[9] Thus, as poverty, unemployment and insecurity spread, and social services decayed, the countries become more prone to conflict. Their citizens become willing to take up arms and fight oil, diamond and copper wars, as the conflicts in Sierra Leone, Angola, Nigeria, Sudan, Liberia and the Great Lakes region attest.[10]

Because of the persistence of conflict in Africa,[11] efforts to find lasting solutions must go beyond traditional economic initiatives. The complementary role communication can play in sustaining economic reform and resolving conflicts must be considered. This chapter explores the numerous avenues by which communication can aid the struggle for sustainable economic development in Africa, and enhance traditional economic strategies. For example, communication is a proven method for conflict resolution and mediation, so essential for attaining supranational economic integration. Communication can also promote good governance, thereby fostering an atmosphere conducive to reform. It can stimulate popular participation in the national economy and improve regional, sub-regional and interregional economic integration. It can constitute a vital economic sector in itself, thereby making its direct contribution to productivity and real income growth rate.

Communication and Economic Integration

Following the global economic instability of the 1970s, it became apparent that Africa and the rest of the developing world needed greater economic cooperation, at the regional, sub-regional or interregional level in order to achieve collective self-reliance. 'Collective self-reliance' was defined as the developing countries' shared determination 'to develop their economies in accordance with their own needs and problems and on the basis of their national aspirations and experiences'.[12] But it was clearly understood that each country would establish its own development priorities or implement its own strategy. The wide variance in national history, social structures and infrastructure made it apparent that imitating another country's development path would not be the most appropriate solution. Each country had to bear the responsibility of translating the aspirations of its people into reality in consonance with its own creativity or genius.

This view was consonant with the prevailing perception at the time that development was a quintessential imperative throughout the South. Development was defined as:

A social process of change through which a society which is underdeveloped at the beginning of the process achieves, fundamentally through a participative and creative effort of its own people and mobilization of resources at their disposal, the elimination of poverty, social injustice, exploitation, marginalization, internal or external socio-political domination, and a continuous unfolding of human personality through creative self expression.[13]

This definition, which is still appropriate today, puts the well-being and dignity of individuals and groups above all other national development priorities. Proponents believed that development should lead to increased productivity, the building of appropriate social, political and economic structures, and the equitable distribution of gains among all social, economic, and geographic groups.[14] These achievements would be required to satisfy the 'basic needs' of citizens, particularly the needs of the poor and underprivileged. 'Basic needs' referred to the minimum requirements for existence (food, clothes and shelter) and right of access to certain public services.

Many forms of economic integration were proposed, with each form resulting in different degrees of integration. Among them were 'free trade zones', a 'customs union', a 'common market', an 'economic union', and a 'complete economic union'. In free trade zones, tariffs and trade barriers are abolished, but each country retains its tariffs against nonmembers. A customs union involves both suppression of discrimination in the movement of commodities within the union and equalization of trade tariffs with non-member countries. In a common market, trade restrictions and restrictions on goods and services movements are abolished. An economic union combines the removal of restrictions on the movement of goods and services with some degree of harmonization of national economic policies, in order to remove discrimination deriving from policy disparities. Finally, there is complete economic integration, which presumes unification of monetary, fiscal, social, and counter-cyclical policies, and requires the establishment of a supra-national authority whose decisions are binding on member states.[15]

Table 7.1 Schemes for Economic Cooperation in Africa

Scheme and Year of Establishment	Membership
African Groundnut Council, 1964	Nigeria, Senegal, The Gambia, Mali, Niger, Sudan
African Development Bank, 1966	Algeria, Angola, Benin, Botswana, Burkina Faso, Burundi, Cameroon, Cape Verde, Central African Republic, Chad, Comoros, Congo, Cote d'Ivoire, Djibouti, Egypt, Equatorial Guinea, Ethiopia, Gabon, The Gambia, Ghana, Guinea, Guinea-Bissau, Kenya, Lesotho, Liberia, Libya, Madagascar, Malawi, Mali, Mauritania, Mauritius, Morocco, Mozambique, Namibia, Niger, Rwanda, Sao Tome and Principe, Senegal, Seychelles, Sierra Leone, Somalia, South Africa, Sudan, Swaziland, Tanzania, Togo, Tunisia, Uganda, Zaire, Zambia, Zimbabwe There are 26 non-African members.
African Timber Organization, 1976	Angola, Cameroon, Central African Republic, Congo, Cote d' Ivoire, Equatorial Guinea, Gabon, Ghana, Liberia, Sao Tome and Principe, Tanzania, Zaire
African Petroleum Producers' Association, 1986	Algeria, Angola, Benin, Cameroon, Congo, Cote d'Ivoire, Egypt, Gabon, Libya, Nigeria, Zaire
Arab Maghreb Union, 1988	Algeria, Libya, Mauritania, Morocco, Tunisia
Central African Customs and Economic Union, 1964	Cameroon, Central African Republic, Chad, Republic of the Congo, Equatorial Guinea, Gabon
Common Market of Eastern and Southern Africa, 1993	Angola, Burundi, Comoros, Djibouti, Ethiopia, Kenya, Lesotho, Malawi, Mauritius, Mozambique, Namibia, Rwanda, Somalia, Sudan, Swaziland, Tanzania, Uganda, Zaire, Zambia, Zimbabwe
East African Community, 1967	Kenya, Uganda, United Republic of Tanzania
Economic Community of the Great Lakes Countries, 1976	Burundi, Rwanda, Democratic Republic of Congo

Economic Community of Central African States, 1983	Burundi, Rwanda, Democratic Republic of Congo
Economic Community of West African States, 1975	Benin, Burkina Faso, Cape Verde, Cote d'Ivoire, The Gambia, Ghana, Guinea, Guinea-Bissau, Liberia, Mali, Mauritania, Niger, Nigeria, Senegal, Sierra Leone, Togo
Gambia River Basin Development Organization, 1978	Senegal, The Gambia, Guinea and Guinea-Bissau
Indian Ocean Commission, 1982	Comoros, Madagascar, Mauritius, Seychelles, France (representing the French Overseas Department of Reunion)
Intergovernmental Authority on Drought and Development, 1986	Djibouti, Ethiopia, Kenya, Somalia, Sudan, Uganda
Lake Chad Basin Commission, 1964	Cameroon, Chad, Niger, Nigeria
Mano River Union, 1973	Guinea, Liberia, Sierra Leone
Niger Basin Authority, 1964	Benin, Burkina Faso, Cameroon, Chad, Cote d'Ivoire, Guinea, Mali, Niger, Nigeria
Organization of African Unity, 1963 / African Union, African Economic Community, 1994	All 53 independent states of Africa
Southern African Development Community, 1980	Angola, Botswana, Democratic Republic of Congo, Lesotho, Malawi, Mauritius, Mozambique, Namibia, Seychelles, South Africa, Swaziland, Tanzania, Zambia, Zimbabwe
West African Economic and Monetary Union, 1994	Benin, Burkina Faso, Côte d'Ivoire, Guinea-Bissau, Mali, Niger, Senegal, Togo
West African Rice Development Association, 1970	Benin, Burkina Faso, Chad, Cote d' Ivoire, The Gambia, Ghana, Guinea, Guinea-Bisau, Liberia, Mali, Mauritania, Niger, Nigeria, Senegal, Sierra Leone, Togo

Source: Adapted from The Political Science Reference Almanac, 2003.

Through the years, Africa's desire to overcome economic fragmentation has seen the emergence of a plethora of economic cooperation schemes 'that formally seek to integrate markets or to bring into being a wider framework for economic activities in general'[16] (See Table 7.1 above). Although some of these schemes have had limited success, others have failed. For example, the Council of the Entente aspired to become an agent of integration but never established the appropriate mechanisms. However, the cooperation agreements negotiated by members of the Permanent Consultative Committee of the Maghreb were never ratified, and this failure led to the demise of the East African Community (EAC),[17] which was later reestablished in November 1999.

The African Development Bank (ADB) provides 11 reasons why Africa's initial efforts to integrate between 1960 and 1990 failed to yield the expected benefits.[18] These are:

- The lack of political will to establish supranational institutions and to implement treaties and mandates;
- The pursuit of import substitution policies;
- The heavy reliance on tariffs for fiscal revenue;
- Over-ambitious goals;
- Pervasive weakness in regional structures;
- Overlapping membership;
- Inadequate mechanisms for equitable sharing of the costs and benefits of regional arrangements;
- Antipathy to markets;
- Lack of policy credibility;
- Endemic political stability; and
- Lack of rule of law and god governance.

A reduction of these obstacles through political and economic transformations since 1990 has renewed African countries' interest in economic cooperation and integration. The latest effort is the African Economic Community (AEC), which came into being in June 1991.

Communication has been vital to Africa's initial attempt and renewed interest in achieving economic integration. For example, media coverage of public discussions of the rising trends of globalization and the deepening regional integration with demonstrable gains in trade, investment and economic growth in Europe, North America and Asia, made it clear African countries faced increased isolation and marginalization unless they strengthened their resolve to integrate. Furthermore, it is through communication that African nations have in the past, and will continue to conceive, negotiate, sign and implement economic treaties and agreements. Therefore, the pertinent question is not whether communication can play a role in fostering economic cooperation, but what form of communication is most effective?

To answer this question, one must consider the factors that build competence in intercultural communication, regardless of the medium employed or the goal to be accomplished. One must first discuss the reasons why communication so easily breaks down across cultural boundaries. According to LaRay Barna,[19] the frustrations and misunderstandings that frequently accompany intercultural communication are the result of six factors: (1) the assumption of similarity instead of difference; (2) language problems; (3) nonverbal misunderstandings; (4) the presence of preconceptions and stereotypes; (5) the tendency to evaluate and judge; and (6) the high anxiety that often exists in international encounters. Given the presumption of the existence of a 'global village' that undergirds most of today's intercultural relations, it is important to comment on the first factor. The global spread of Western ideas tends to ignore the differing customs and traditions that are part of identity and self-concept. Yet, as Barna points out, the mere existence of common characteristics is not sufficient for the purposes of communication, 'where we need to exchange complex information and/or feelings, solve problems of mutual concern, cement business relationships, or just make the kind of impression we wish to make'.[20] Just because cities look alike, people wear the same type of clothes, and eat the same types of food does not mean that inherent cultural differences will capitulate to agreement or mutual understanding. For instance, when this writer shared an apartment with a Ghanaian colleague during his first semester of graduate education, his experiences quickly verified the statement made by Simon and Phoebe Otenberg[21] that the only thing common among Africans South of the Sahara is the color of their skin. Since then, this writer has learned the poignant truth that anyone desiring success in an intercultural encounter must understand what it takes to be effective in influencing those who are not culturally the same. This realization did not suggest the abandonment of culture. On the contrary, it emphasized that culture was the core of one's identity; without it, our very beings are bulldozed.

In his article 'Intercultural Communication Competence,' Brian H. Spitzberg[22] presents the probable characteristics of the effective intercultural communicator. He suggests a course of action that a communicator could use to enhance his or her competence when faced with an intercultural encounter. Spitzberg says an intercultural communicator can increase competence by:

- Being motivated;
- Being knowledgeable;
- Being credible;
- Possessing interpersonal skills;
- Manifesting trust;
- Reflecting similarities;
- Having access to multiple relationships;
- Meeting the expectations of communication partners;
- Offering social support; and
- Striking a balance between autonomy and independence needs.

Spitzberg warns however that these propositions cannot be taken to extremes. He says, 'Someone can be too motivated, too knowledgeable, use too much expressiveness, be too composed, and so on'.[23]

Communication and Economic Participation

Communication can contribute to economic participation in Africa in a number of ways. First, it can serve as an avenue through which citizens take ownership of the formulation and implementation of national economic policy. Nkomo[24] points out that traditionally economics has been the private domain of economists and financial pundits. The common man usually confronts economics as a subject studied at school for the purpose of passing examinations and few ever perceive a direct linkage between their daily lives and economics. Africa is no exception.

Since the colonial period, Africans, like their counterparts elsewhere in the world, have been passive recipients of 'economic policies forced down their throats without fully understanding their implications'.[25] This is primarily because they have never been given the opportunity to understand basic economic principles governing them and how it affects them. Nor have they been consulted when their governments decide to engage international monetary organizations like the International Monetary Fund (IMF) and the World Bank, whose policies seldom include interests of the general population. But if the economy of a nation is for the benefit of everyone, then economic policy should never be formulated and implemented without adequate consultation with the people who will be affected by those policies. Through communication, this economic dialogue, debate and consultation can be carried out.

To illustrate this point, Wanyeki[26] narrates two stories about the use of participatory video in economic discourse and bad policy reversal. The first story concerns the Mtwara Media Center in Lindi, in the southern region of Tanzania. The center had been using participatory video to educate the traditional fishing communities in the region. The Ministry in charge imposed a ban on traditional fishing methods. At the same time, large scale, dynamite fishing for commercial sale and for export was depleting the fish stock available to traditional fishers. Through portable video equipment, 'villagers documented their experiences, the decrease in real incomes and their inability to continue to survive on fishing, for both men and women, even though the kinds of fish traditionally caught by men and women, the fishing areas and methods were different'.[27] By passing the videos from one village to another, the local communities were able to share their experiences. This sharing opened their eyes and enabled them to decide to challenge the ban collectively. They decided to use participatory video to show how traditional fishing practices 'protect coral, fish eggs and young fish in their environment and compared this protection with the devastation of dynamite fishing'.[28] With help from the center, they shot and edited the videos and sent representatives from different villages to Dar es Salaam, where they managed to get an audience with the Minister. The Minister was persuaded by what he saw and decided to lift the ban on traditional fishing methods.

The second story, also from Tanzania, concerns the Orkonerai Integrated Pastoralists' Survival Programme, a programme initiated by the Maasai people in Terrat, who were being dislocated from their land by wildlife conservation projects, large-scale commercial horticultural farmers, and mining. They established a community resource center and began seeking contact and information exchange with indigenous people worldwide. Based on the experiences shared, they attracted human rights organizations to their cause and put forward a case to challenge their forcible removal from the Mkomozi game reserve. In 1999, they won their precedent-setting case, which acknowledged that their removal was wrong and ordered restitution. They are going back to court to seek restitution in the form of their original communal grazing lands. This case has played a part in 'getting the right to communal land recognized and protected in Tanzania's recent land law review'.[29]

Similarly, the international non-governmental organization (NGO) Worldvision, through its subsidiary Shelter Now, has successfully used community print media to raise social, economic and political consciousness in Kenya. In the Kitale district in the Western region of Kenya, the organization taught community leaders how to design, produce and market a newsletter, specific to the needs of the community. Strategic persons from different departments within the district were trained how to write news and feature stories, what constitutes a good photograph, the skills of photography, and marketing skills, so they could feel a sense of ownership and help promote the community. The trained persons, drawn from the medical department, education, NGOs, and selected religious organizations, collected information from their areas and shared it. Literate members of the community also helped collect stories of interest. Freelance photographers captured good images from the region, which they also shared with everyone in the community.

Stories had to be balanced, so reports included comments from relevant officials. Published stories featured issues of development, opened up deliberations and led to action. The lead story of one publication was on prostitution. The question of whether it should have been exposed generated much interest from the community, and the issue was subsequently picked up by the District Development Committee and discussed further. This brought attention to the link between prostitution and HIV/AIDs, a major issue for the region and the country. Thus, the newsletter raised consciousness. Because the newsletter was written in English and literacy levels are low in the district, one might have thought ordinary people were left out. But somehow the information also stirred the uneducated. A cover photo of roadside prostitutes generated lots of discussion among the illiterates. Those who were able to read shared what was in the text with the illiterates. This vertical flow of information gave the communities an avenue to share information from their perspective. Now some NGOs who purport to support certain initiatives are being questioned about their effectiveness. Government hospitals are also criticized because of the unavailability of drugs.

As these examples from Tanzania and Kenya demonstrate, when experiences are validated through communication, solidarity is built that can lead to organizational change at the local level in ways that can affect the national level. Aside from empowering local communities directly, communication can also cater to the financial interests of individuals, groups and businesses. An example of this is economics and business journalism; a source of regular information, analyses and forecasts on trends and shifts in the economic environment that individuals, groups and businesses can use to make prudent financial decisions. This form of journalism is typical in countries like Britain, France, Germany and the U.S., where private enterprise flourishes. But it has also begun to gain some degree of prominence in Africa. Kariithi[30] notes that economic and business journalism is the fastest growing aspect of African media today. This growth was spurred by the protracted economic stagnation of the late 1970s and early 1980s. With the failure of the World Bank initiated structural adjustment programs and the subsequent search for alternative models, economics became crucial in public discourse in many African countries. Journalists mediated this discourse by presenting the contesting voices, debating the appropriateness of World Bank policies for Africa and alternatives offered by the United Nations Economic Commission for Africa. In the early 1990s, when politics began to undergo transition to democratic governance, 'the still fledging economics media again kept pace, constantly advocating through their coverage the need to open up both the political and economic systems'.[31]

It is important to note however that the prevailing practice of economic and business journalism in Africa still lacks the 'sparkle that draws audiences or triggers public debate'.[32] Most business coverage across different media is disconcertingly similar, shallow and unquestioning reproductions of press releases or technical reports. Kariithi explains that too often business reporters fail to differentiate between issues and personalities. Nor do they perceive links between related macroeconomic events. When government sources withhold data, key issues are left underreported and under-analyzed. In countries with large private sector investment, business pages are dominated by news about the few major companies that are the largest advertisers. In some cases, business journalism is equated with coverage of issues that are of concern to these companies. This leads to prominent attention being devoted to the most mundane event. At the same time, attention to financial journalism, particularly that relating to personal financial issues, is scant or has more to do with assisting significant corporations to maintain their visibility in the press than empowering people to make better financial decisions.

Kariithi outlines the factors responsible for this discouraging profile. They include poor working conditions, unstable media entities with no guaranteed means of economic survival, and the irresistible lure of better paying jobs in corporate communications. Perhaps the most important failure is that journalists assigned to the economic beat have poor economic and financial reporting skills. In fact, African economic editors report their most formidable challenge is finding journalists trained in economic, financial and business writing. In recent years, a number of international banking and media organizations have taken the initiative to assist Africa in overcoming this deficit. For example, the World Bank Institute, Reuters, Standard Bank Group and Financial Times of London have established brief introductory courses in economics reporting. While this is a welcomed development, Africans themselves must endeavor to find long-term strategies to overcome these personnel issues. That would be the only way to ensure substantive progress in this field of economic and business journalism.[33]

Communication as a Vital Economic Sector

In liberal societies, particularly those nations where capitalism is deeply entrenched, the communication sector is a significant aspect of the national economy. In these countries, the communications media are operated as big business and a significant contributor to the gross domestic product. Elaborating on the importance of the communications industry to the U.S. economy, Chan-Olmstead and Albarran (1996) noted that it was the ninth largest industry in terms of revenues. According to the 2001 edition of the Veronis Suhler's *Communication Industry Forecast*, the communications industry was the fastest growing portion of the U.S. economy during the last five years and will continue to be the fastest growing through 2004. In 1999 the total U.S. spending on communication grew 8.1 percent to approximately 525 billion dollars; by 2004, the projected spending is expected to rise 7.3 percent to about 746 billion. Kevin Kelly,[34] author of the insightful book, *New Rules for the Economy: 10 Radical Strategies for a Connected World*, notes that the advent of digital technology and media has moved communications beyond just being a sector of the U.S. economy. He says, communication is now the economy in the United States (Fratrik, 2000). That is also true of other Western countries that have made the transformation from an industrial society to an information society.

Conversely, in Africa broadcasting is yet to become a boon to national economies. Many African governments still perceive broadcasting as a social service, to be funded through taxation of the masses or incomes derived from other public sectors. This view is held even in countries where private stations can now operate. In these countries, public (or government) owned and operated stations still dominate the broadcast marketplace. As a result, the only real contribution that broadcasting makes to the national economy in an African country is that of an employer of labor. Many stations lack a profit motive and cannot therefore generate sufficient corporate revenues to stimulate spending for economic growth. Their overall contribution to the gross domestic product (GDP) and the gross national product (GNP) is, therefore, almost always negligible. It is not surprising that critics of African media would perceive broadcast stations as an economic liability, rather than an asset.

However, in this era of globalization, African broadcasters have many opportunities to become a significant contributor to their national economies. These include advertising, content, and access. Broadcast advertising can become a major area of economic activity in African countries. If advertising revenues can be increased substantially by adding smaller retail businesses to the station's client list and by adopting new methods of selling, the contribution to the gross domestic product can grow. Contrary to popular belief, there are enough retail businesses in most countries to support local advertising. Because many small business owners in Africa do not see the need for advertising, the challenge is how to motivate them to advertise. Living virtually in a sellers market, many African retailers see advertising in philanthropic terms rather than as a business investment. In order to attract them, competitive advertising rates and innovative selling approaches must be developed. The rates must be low enough to stimulate the participation of the small local retailer or market trader. Also, there should be different rates for national, regional and local advertisers, based on the economy of scale.

Selling station availabilities (airtime) would require the services of competently trained account executives. In the U.S., broadcast sales people are often recruited from other areas of sales and generally have previous sales experience. For example, it is not uncommon to find a former car salesman selling radio or television times as spots or sponsorship.   Spots are individual advertisements, while sponsorship requires a single business or small group of businesses to pay to make a program available. The success of these measures will depend on the efficient management of the station's marketing department.

Content is another area of broadcasting that is being underutilized as a revenue source in Africa. In general, few produced programs are marketed between African countries. There are two principal reasons for this. First is the dearth of entertainment programs that can be marketed across intercultural and international borders. As Bourgault[35] notes, the programming schedules of most African stations are dominated by imported entertainment content.   Radio is dominated by mostly western music, and television offerings are dominated by dramas, movies and sitcoms imported from Western Europe and the U.S. Local productions are generally meant for a local audience, and seldom appeal beyond the primary target audience.

The export of media programs is generally low in Africa because of the lack of private participation in program production.   In many countries, media production is the sole responsibility of the stations themselves or ancillary organizations set up by governments (e.g. The Egyptian Media Production Company or the Nigerian Television Production Company).   The programs produced by these civil service entities often cannot be syndicated, meaning they cannot be distributed to private outlets or stations in other countries. But, as independent producers in Western countries know, profits from off-network syndication (including sales to African countries) can run into several millions. Knowing this, U.S. independent producers practice *deficit financing;* they pay more to produce programs than the networks will pay in licensing fees. The loss taken from the network affiliation is made up in off-network syndication, when the programs are sold to individual stations in selected markets throughout the world.

The second reason is the inaccessibility of lucrative Western markets to African productions. National program distributors and local station program managers in Western countries do not seriously consider African productions for their markets. The quality of African-made programs is often not considered good enough to attract sizeable Western audiences. Furthermore, the productions are generally in local languages, with most state stations having a special mandate to serve their local communities. As a result, they do not appeal to the least common denominator, or the greatest available audience, domestically or internationally. Some programs should be made specifically for the international market. Such programs would be produced in a way to appeal to a culturally diverse audience.

But ultimately it is the question of access that will determine whether broadcasting is an index of development in Africa. The issue of access has been discussed extensively in the previous chapter and will be mentioned only in passing here.   In the last four decades, public and private investments in information and communication infrastructure have not kept pace with initial projections or expectations. In Africa during the last four decades, public and private investments had to be delayed, as allocations were diverted to address more basic needs of citizens (food and shelter) or to deal with the centrifugal forces of ethnic, religious and class division, more dire. Increased investments must be made to provide both individual and universal access if communication is to become a major contributor to economic growth in Africa. This can be achieved through regional and international cooperation in the fields of production and marketing.

Conclusion

There is little doubt that communication is indispensable to economic vitality in a country, a region or a continent. This is further demonstrated by the ITU's 1998 *World Telecommunication Development Report*, which notes that communication is increasingly a critical component of economic growth and an engine of the evolving global information society. The reports notes that even though the communication sector does not yet constitute a significant percentage of Africa's GDP and GNP, its benefits are becoming more noticeable. Today, businesses in rural areas of Africa can place orders with their suppliers by phone when previously they could only do so by traveling to the capital cities. In 1997, a business in Zimbabwe reportedly generated 15 million dollars by advertising on the Internet. In South Africa, Nigeria and other nations, strategically placed community pay phones save dozens of lives each day because citizens can call the police immediately when their lives or property are threatened.

When African states were created, they found themselves part of an already established international economic system over which they had little or no control. Surviving within this system has presented daunting challenges, as the international system has continued to evolve and successive changes have seemed to move African states further away from the center of influence. The product of the most recent evolution is what has come to be known as the information society, which is characterized by:

- The ascension of communication and information service occupations to a preeminent position among industrial occupations;
- The fundamental changes in the relations among the various sectors of the communication industry;
- Significant changes in how people respond to and use mass mediated communication products; and
- Increased interaction among disparate world populations, a situation summarized by the 'global village' concept.[36]

The center of economic activity in today's world is information acquisition and management. It is no longer industrial production. More information is available in today's human environment because there is increased need and demand for it, and because of increased sophistication in the methods of information production and dissemination.   It seems that industrial production now exists to enable improvements in communication.   Although Africa must not abandon industrial production altogether, it must quickly come to grips with the reality that communication is the heart of global economics today.   Coming to terms with this reality would be the surest way for African countries to ensure the success of their development goals.   Conversely, failure to realize the importance of information in global economics might mean uncertain futures for many African countries, particularly those in sub-Saharan Africa.

Notes

1   Evangelos A. Calamistsis, 'Adjustment and growth in Sub-Saharan Africa: The unfinished agenda,' *Finance & Development* (March, 1999), p. 6.

2   UNCTAD, *Economic development in Africa: Performance, prospects and policy issues*, New York and Geneva: United Nations, 2001, p. 5.

3   Ibid., p. 6-7.

4   Author Unknown, 'Finance and economics: A look on the brighter side: Africa's economies,' *The Economist* (July 20, 2002), p. 69.

5   Calamistsis, p. 6.

6   Cited in Sunday Dare, 'A continent in crisis,' *Dollars & Sense* (July 1, 2002), p. 12.

7   Ibid. p. 12.

8   Author Unknown, 'Corrupt political elites and businessmen kill economic development: Transparency International Says,' *www.Arabicnews.com* (September 23, 2002).

9   Ibid.

10   Dare, p. 12.

11   Even at the time of this writing, another Africa country, Ivory Coast, was fighting an economically induced conflict.   Soldiers facing the prospect of demobilization, a measure seemingly contemplated for economic reasons, undertook a coup d'etat.   The coup failed, but fighting was still ongoing in parts of the country at the time of writing.

12   John P. Renninger, *Multinational cooperation for development in West Africa*, New York: Pergamon Press, 1979, p. 2.

13   Ibid. p. 13.

14   Ibid. p. 12.

15   Bela Balassa, *The Theory of Economic Integration*, London: George Allen & Unwin LTD, 1965, p. 2.

16   John P. Renninger, The future of economic cooperation schemes in Africa, with special reference to ECOWAS,' in Timothy M. Shaw, ed., *Alternative futures for Africa*, Boulder, Colorado: Westview Press, 1982: 153-177.

17   Ibid. p. 159.

18   African Development Bank, 'Economic cooperation and regional integration policy,' African Development Bank (February 2000).

19   LaRay M. Barna, 'Stumbling blocks in intercultural communication,' in Larry A. Somovar and Richard E. Porter, eds., *Intercultural Communication, Sixth Edition*, Belmont, California: Wadsworth Publishing Company, 1991, pp. 345-353.

20   Ibid. p. 345.

21 Simon Otenberg and Phoebe Otenberg, *Cultures and societies in Africa*, New York: Random House, 1960.
22 Brian H. Spitzberg, 'Intercultural Communication Competence,' in Larry A. Somovar and Richard E. Porter, eds., *Intercultural Communication, Sixth Edition*, Belmont, California: Wadsworth Publishing Company, 1991, pp. 353-365.
23 Ibid. p. 364.
24 Dumisani O. Nkomo, 'Consultation needed in formulating economic policies,' *Africa News Service* (July 19, 2002).
25 Ibid.
26 L. Muthoni Wanyeki, 'Promoting socially responsible finance, trade and investment,' *Africa Economic Analysis* (2000).
27 Ibid.
28 Ibid.
29 Ibid.
30 Nelson Kariithi, 'Economics and business journalism in Africa,' *Nieman Reports* (Summer 2002).
31 Ibid.
32 Ibid.
33 Ibid.
34 Kevin Kelly, *New rules for the economy: 101 radical strategies for a connected world*, New York: Penguin Books, 1999.
35 Louise M. Bourgault, *Mass media in Sub-Saharan Africa*, Bloomington, Indiana: Indiana University Press, 1995.
36 R. L. Nwafo Nwanko and Teresa K. Mphahlele, 'Communication rule structure and the communication management of the South African crisis,' *Journal of Black Studies* 20, 3 (1990): 288.

Chapter 8

Communicating Through Political Development

Introduction

Much evidence supports David Abernethy's[1] contention that Africa has suffered more than its fair share of political crises in recent years. Since the 1960s, the territorial integrity of many African countries has been subjected to one or more forms of systemic instability. Countries such as Angola, Liberia, Nigeria, the Democratic Republic of Congo (Zaire), Sierra Leone and Sudan have endured protracted civil wars. Military coups have occurred frequently in Benin, Central African Republic, Ivory Coast, and Guinea. Ethnic violence has led to disruptions or decimations of political institutions in places like Burundi, Rwanda and Somalia. Religious intolerance has constantly threatened the governments in Algeria, Chad and a number of other countries.

Abernethy adds that an epidemic of governmental non-performance also has lingered across the continent, functioning both as a cause and effect of political instability. He notes that, theoretically, political institutions are established in order to alleviate—and, if possible, to eliminate—many of the problems people faced. But the African experience has been quite opposite. He says that in many African countries, the cost, policies, and priorities of government have been major constraints to efforts to emancipate the ordinary citizen from poverty and pestilence. As a result, not only have governmental institutions reduced African society's capacity for problem solving, but also they have effectively substituted selfishness and indiscipline for altruistic public service.

Abernethy says it is ironic that prior to attaining independence the majority of African nationalists believed the political system was the 'means through which the wants of the members of a society are converted into binding decisions.'[2] He explains that many thought central governments would provide the solution to their people's problems once power was wrested from the colonial authorities. In fact, the leading African nationalist at the time, Kwame Nkrumah, reasoned that once the political kingdoms were gained, all else would fall into place. To the contrary, the post-independence era has seen African political systems filled with widespread frustration and disillusionment. Governments seem unable or unwilling or both to deliver to the people what had been promised.[3] The institutionalization of a culture of mediocrity inclines public officials to pursue personal objectives rather than to search for excellence in public service to the nation. Why has this culture been allowed to entrench itself? Why has a continent once filled with economic and political promise become such a governance nightmare?

To answer these questions, scholars have generally pointed to the absence of political development. Robert Packenham highlighted the importance of political development as early as 1966, when he wrote:

> It is becoming increasingly evident, if it is not clear already, that one of the most critical problems in the modernization of developing countries is political development. In South Vietnam, in the Congo, in Brazil, in Indonesia—all over the underdeveloped world, the capacity of countries to deal with their own problems, and consequently the stance of the United States towards these nations, turns in varying degrees on the successes and failures of the political system.[4]

Packenham made this observation three decades ago, but the situation remains virtually unchanged in Africa. In almost every country, political failing still present the most formidable obstacles to the achievement of national integration, citizen empowerment and sustainable development. As a result, efforts have been continued across many fields of endeavor to find lasting solutions to the problems of political development on the continent. This chapter contributes to this effort through an exploration of the possible contributions communication can make to this enterprise. Specifically, the chapter discusses the possible effect that communication strategies might have on general and specific political development in Africa. The chapter first summarizes the definitions of political development and then establishes the intrinsic link between it and national integration.

Defining Political Development

Political development has been a rather elusive concept. Even recently, the literature had not offered a precise, conclusive or universally applicable definition of the concept. That is not to say, however, that research into the subject lacks a long and distinguished history. Packenham observes that scholars began paying serious attention to the concept in the 1960s, following the emergence of many new African and Asian nations from the shackles of colonialism. But the early studies were largely focused on understanding the conditions under which political development exists, as opposed to defining the phenomenon of political development.[5] Drawing from a wide variety of sources and writings, Packenham extrapolated the five conditions that were considered the primary correlates or determinants of political development. These were:

- The existence of a *legal-formal constitution*, which contains provisions for the rule of law, equal protection under the law, regular elections by secret ballot, federalism, and/or the separation of powers;

- The achievement of *a level of economic development* sufficient to serve the material needs of the members of the political system and to permit a reasonable harmony between economic aspirations and satisfactions;
- The existence of the *administrative capacity* to efficiently and effectively maintain law and order and to perform governmental output functions rationally and neutrally;
- A *social system* that facilitates popular participation in governmental and policy processes at all levels, and the bridging of regional religious, caste, linguistic, tribal, or other cleavages; and
- A *political culture* that orients the attitudes and personality of members of the social system to both accept the privileges and bear the responsibilities of a democratic political process.[6]

Proponents of these processes or conditions believed that political development could not occur in African social systems without them. African countries were judged to have a deficit in all but the existence of a legal formal constitution.

In contrast with Packenham's observation, Samuel Huntington[7] contends that many early attempts define the concept of political development. He reviews these definitions and notes that, with a few exceptions, the characteristics generally identified with political development are all related to processes of modernization. Four sets of categories routinely appeared in the various writings he reviews. The first set, derived from Parsonian pattern variables, emphasizes the movement from particularism to universalism, from diffuseness to specificity, from ascription to achievement, and from parochialism to affective neutrality. Huntington called this *rationalization*, defined in broad terms as the differentiation of political functions and establishment of achievement criteria. The second set is *nationalism* and *national integration*. Huntington observes that almost all of the writings he reviews recognized the crisis of national identity facing the newly created states and the necessity to delimit ethnic influences in the political community. He indicates that the writers considered nation-building an important aspect of political development. *Democratization* is the third set of characteristics. In general, writers who emphasized this characteristic thought that it should include pluralism, competitiveness, equalization and power, and other qualities in the politics of a nation-state. The fourth set of categories is *mobilization* or *participation*. The main belief expressed here is that:

> Increased literacy, urbanization, exposure to mass media, industrialization, and per capita income would expand the politically relevant strata of the population, multiply the demand for government services, and thus stimulate an increase in governmental capabilities, a broadening of the elite, increased political participation and a shift in attention from the local level to the national level.[8]

For Huntington, the concept 'modernization' means 'mass mobilization' defined as increased political participation. He adds that increased political participation is the key element in political development. He says participation was the main factor that distinguished modern politics from traditional politics.

Aside from reviewing the definitions, Huntington critiques them as well. First, he observes that the tendency of the various definitions to equate political development with modernization restricted the concept's applicability in both time and space. According to him, equating political development with modernization defines the concept in parochial and immediate terms, and limits its relevance to modern nation-states or the emergence of nation-states. As he put it, 'it becomes impossible to speak of a politically developed tribal authority, city-states, feudal monarchy, or bureaucratic empire.'[9]

In Africa, a number of politically developed entities existed prior to the colonial era. Much has been written, for instance, about the political systems of ancient Egypt, Mali and Songhai empires, Oyo city-states, Edo Kingdom and others. These were functioning political organizations before they were disrupted by colonialism. By restricting the definition of political development to the parochial and immediate, therefore, development planners seemed to miss the opportunity to learn from the success and failures of these systems, even though their cultural proximity made such learning imperative.

Secondly, Huntington explains that the definitions tended to sacrifice precision for comprehensiveness. The definitions seemed to suggest that political development should not be limited to characteristics of the modern nation-state, but should also be broadened to include almost all of the politically relevant aspects of the modernization process. The assumption was that political development is all a unit in which one good thing is related to another. Huntington observed that this assumption was misleading because it left the erroneous impression that political development was inescapable and easily attained. However, anyone familiar with Africa will have agreed with him. African countries have searched for political development since independence. Few, if any, have found it.

Thirdly, Huntington posits that many of the definitions failed 'to distinguish clearly the empirical relevance of the components going to the definition.'[10] He says the concepts of 'developed' and 'underdeveloped' are ideal types or states of the confusion about the concept of development as a process. He says they are also associated with the politics of the areas commonly called 'developing'. This association, he says, blurs the line between actuality and aspiration. Actual occurrences in the developing areas became hopelessly intertwined with what the theorists hoped should occur there. Huntington says the tendency here again was to assume that what was true for the broader processes of social modernization was also true of political changes. In reality, the vestiges of modernization (literacy, urbanization, industrialization, per capita income and gross national product) were showing perceptible growth. However, the measures of political development (development, stability, structural differentiation, achievement patterns and national integration) were far more elusive. Nevertheless, the theorists still believed that since modernization was taking place, political development was occurring as well.[11]

Although Huntington's critique of these definitions of political development was poignant and incisive, it came at time when the political situation in Africa ran counter to most theoretical formulations. During the 1960s, Africa had few competitive democracies and the dominant political trend was more towards autocracies and military dictatorships. There was great instability, with many coups and revolts. There were repeated ethnic conflicts and civil wars, and little unifying or nation building. Administrative failures and institutional breakdowns also were rife. With these prevailing conditions, Huntington's criticisms may have been both intuitively logical and basically unavoidable.

However, given the political changes that have taken place in Africa in recent years, it is debatable whether these criticisms still apply. Since the 1990s, Africa's political trends have become more positive. As Ransdell[12] notes, multiparty politics is now legal in 14 of the 47 sub-Saharan African countries. Many of the 14 countries have held elections in recent years. A majority of African leaders now seem to realize that Africa should participate in the political developments taking place around the world. Such alignment would mean that political development on the continent should be judged by its display of some, if not all, of the attributes that characterize most contemporary political systems. Of the possible attributes to choose from, those that Huntington extrapolated seem the most relevant to the particular needs of the continent. Thus, African countries would be better served to achieve rationalization, integration, democratization and mobilization in their political systems. Such qualities will give national systems legitimacy and allow African citizens to have a better political orientation.

Political Legitimacy in Africa

Political legitimacy in Africa is seen in terms of the degree to which a political system or government can claim popular support for its existence, policies and programs. As Tarifa Fatos[13] puts it, legitimacy implies that elites and a significant portion of the general population—particularly intellectuals, but even ordinary people, have confidence in the moral validity of their political system. Like the phenomenon of political development of which it is part, legitimacy is both a complex and multifaceted concept. Not only does it address the principles, means, and outcomes of the use of power, it also has objective and subjective connotations. Objectively, legitimacy may mean the existence of certain well-defined political processes or procedures that give rulers a systematic 'title to rule.'[14] Fatos notes that two important and relevant questions can be raised: first, what objective requirements might create a general propensity among citizens to obey the rulers and the rules? In other words, what would make power legitimate, or what would turn it from brutal force into civil authority? Second, who should accept formal authority, and how strong should this acceptance be?

Subjectively, a political system or government is considered legitimate when it has a high degree of acceptance by its citizens or is generally seen as having the right to govern.[15] This perception implies that legitimacy derives from two important sources: first is people's assurance that the government has a moral right to be obeyed; second is the approval or disapproval that they bestow on political norms.[16] According to Fatos, these definitions correspond with Weber's classical notion of legitimacy, which perceives that the concept involves the degree to which political institutions are valued for their qualities and considered right and proper.[17]

Based on these definitions, there is little question that African political systems and governments have long been beset by problems of legitimacy. The legitimacy of political institutions and decision-making organs, the right of certain individuals to rule, and the manner of their rule, have been repeatedly questioned and successfully challenged during the past quarter century of independence. The most visible signs of these legitimacy crises have been the frequent military coups instigated by junior officers in countries such as Nigeria, Benin (formerly Dahomey), Cote d'Ivoire and the Central African Republic (CAR). There is also the persisting civil unrest in Algeria, and the fact that military officers had served as executive heads of over 20 countries by 1986.[18] A more recent sign has been the upsurge in 'aggressive political behavior' in the early 1990s. Muller and Julian define aggressive political behavior as the 'collective action on the part of non-elites that is illegal and has a political focus in that it is intended to disrupt the normal functioning of the government.'[19] Since 1993, aggressive political behavior by disenfranchised peoples has unseated many formerly entrenched governments across Africa.

A main cause of the legitimacy crises is that the scarce resources available to most countries have been used almost exclusively to maintain the lifestyles, and to further the ambitions of the political, bureaucratic and business elites charged with overseeing or managing these resources. Through corrupt practices, public funds are diverted regularly and indiscriminately to meet private ends. As a result, public policies neglect or exploit the rural majority of the population, and undercut incentives for economic productivity and political stability. This exclusion of the populace has been the main source of contention between government and governmental policies and ordinary people throughout the continent.

Another cause is that ethnicity is put to various uses and misuses in different political contexts across Africa.[20] In Ghana, Nigeria, Liberia, Kenya and many other nations, ethnic sentiment, resistance and dissent are frequently activated for political gains. The tendency in these and other countries has been for governments and political leaders to derive their legitimacy from ethnicity rather than from altruism or nationalism. Yet, if African countries are to achieve their developmental objectives and be considered members of the elite group of politically advanced nations, the ethnic basis for political legitimacy must give way to more democratic national orientation. What specific role can communication play in this reorientation process? This question is addressed in the political communication section of this chapter. First, however, an assessment of the political orientation in Africa is presented.

Political Orientation in Africa

In order to determine the role of communication in political orientation in Africa, it is first necessary to review the definition of the concept. David Easton[21] distinguishes two types of political orientation: diffuse and specific. He describes *diffuse* orientations as deep-seated basic feelings people have towards their political system. According to Harrell Rodgers, 'It is generally conceded that diffuse support is critical to the stable functioning of a political system (especially a democratic system) since it provides a reservoir of positive effects which political authorities can draw upon during periods of stress.'[22] Measures of diffuse orientation include political efficacy, political trust and political partisanship. Political efficacy is the degree to which an individual feels that he or she can influence the political system.[23] An individual who possesses political efficacy feels 'it is worthwhile to perform one's political duties.'[24] Acock, Clarke and Stewart explain that efficacy has both internal and external dimensions:

> Internal efficacy is individuals' self-perceptions that they are capable of understanding politics and competent enough to participate in political acts such as voting. External efficacy is the belief that the public in general cannot influence political outcomes because government leaders and institutions are unresponsive.[25]

On the surface, it would seem that a high sense of internal and external political beliefs exist in Africa. This is suggested by the high percentage of registered voters who have actually voted in elections in recent years. As Afrobarometer[26] shows, 71 percent of people interviewed in a scientific survey conducted in 12 African countries in mid-2001 said they voted in the last election. When asked, these voters seemed to understand the main issues at stake during the elections. On the other hand, there appears to be a general belief that voters do not actually influence political outcome in Africa because of the prevalence of election tampering. It is thought that at the end of the day the incumbent government will have its way.[27]

Another measure of diffuse orientation is political trust, defined as an individual's perception that the political system works for him/her. Political trust is more or less an oxymoron in Africa. African electorates are aware that politicians are generally not trustworthy, and that politicians tend to abandon their promises and pledges as soon as they are voted into office. In some cases, this lack of trust has been taken to the extreme and combined with ethnicity to produce deadly conflict and social chaos. In Nigeria, for example, political supporters of one candidate or party have violently assaulted supporters of another candidate or party with deadly weapons, particularly if the opposing candidates differ in their ethnic background. The same has been true in Kenya and Zimbabwe.

The third and final measure of diffuse orientation is partisanship, defined as the emotional attachment or predisposition to vote consistently for one political party. Partisanship is extremely high in Africa. Political parties generally draw from a bountiful reservoir of loyal supporters. But there is much volatility as well,

as supporters tend to flow among parties based on the benefits promised or
delivered. Theoretically, schools and family are the most influential socializing
agents on diffuse orientations.[28]

According to Easton, *specific* political orientations are the immediate reactions
(cognitive, affective and behavioral) to the political environment. Specific
orientations focus not so much the political system, but on the people running the
system. Cognitive responses relate to what is known or perceived about the
environment. Political cognitions are almost entirely influenced by the media.
Affective responses relate to how people feel about what they know about the
political system. Like cognitions, political attitudes are also almost entirely
governed by media. Political behavior covers interest in politics and participation.
The most obvious form of participation is voting, but participation can also be
donations (money or time) to parties or campaigns.

Political Communication for Legitimacy and Orientation

Communication has an important role to play in the process of reorienting African
political systems for long-lasting legitimacy, as well as in citizen acquisition and
refinement of political orientation. As it is commonly known, political disposition
is not congenital. It is acquired through the socialization that environments
provide. Four main agents are generally discussed in the political socialization
literature: family, peers, schools and mass media. Individually and collectively,
the effectiveness of these agents ultimately determines how well political systems
work. But it is through communication that these agents exert their influence.
Therefore, communication should be pivotal to any attempt to restore the
confidence of most African citizens in their leaders, and in the way they are led.
But how specifically should communication be used?

Communication can be used to demystify the political process in Africa, under
which political leaders can detach themselves from the aspirations of their
constituencies. Throughout Africa, political leaders are revered and treated as very
important persons (VIPs), some even as demigods. This is largely because the
inherent and ubiquitous cultural orientation of deference to authority. In pre-
colonial times, authority figures were mainly those considered to be deserving of
leadership; they included heads of households, community elders, even monarchs.
From infancy, citizens were socialized to defer to these authority figures, even if
they thought their actions or decisions were questionable and debatable. Authority
figures were thought to possess infinite wisdom, which people believed that they
would use rightfully to guide their actions and decisions in the interest of the
population at large. Voters also believed anyone in a position of authority
understood clearly that their individual ambitions would have to be subjugated to
the broad aspirations of their communities.

This deference to authority was an important way of balancing oppositional
forces and maintaining social harmony. As Louise Bourgault points out, 'Social
values in the African systems of social organization strongly stressed group

orientation, continuity, harmony, and balance.'[29]   It was not surprising therefore that this culturally mandated deference for authority was also transferred to those who assumed power in the post colonial era.   Unlike their pre-colonial counterparts, politicians, government officials and elites who have taken the reins of power in the post-colonial period, have often been unscrupulous in the performance of their duties.   Their decisions and actions have not often reflected collective wisdom or respect for cultural norms.   Is it not senseless then for people to continue to trust and revere them?

If the best possible achievement is to be exacted from African governments and political systems, ordinary citizens must feel a sense of ownership of political power.   They must feel empowered to wrest political power from those they have elected to represent them, or from those who have imposed themselves without the benefit of elections, when such power has been misused or taken for granted. African citizens must remove the veil of invulnerability from their politicians and governments.   They must come to understand that it is their civic duty to hold leaders accountable for failed policies, unless their decisions are necessary or in their general interest.   But how can they fulfill this responsibility if they believe that politicians and government officials are inviolable and untouchable?

The effort to remove the veil of invulnerability from African politics and governments must begin with interpersonal communication at the family level. From childhood, African children are taught respect for elders who adhere to the tenets of their culture and appreciate the difference between what is right or wrong. Unfortunately, they are seldom taught that deference to authority must not be confused with obeisance to irresponsible political leaders.   When they become adults, children who have been reared in this manner often fail as adults to challenge officials who abuse their powers.   Fortunately, this indifference now seems to be waning.   Since the 1990s, more children have taken to the streets along with adults to protest against government stagnation and socio-economic decline. That is a positive stride forward for African political development.   When political sensitivity is as ubiquitous as corruption on the continent, people will be ready to hold their leaders accountable.

Communication among family and peers, at home and school, and through the media, exert disproportionate influences or changes to the political orientation of Africans.   However, the amount of influence each agent actually exerts varies across political contexts.   As in other areas of the world, African families tend to be more concerned with socialization than with the political values of honesty, morality and proper relations with others.   As a result, little political socialization generally takes place within African families.   Only in an educated African family would a parent sit down to talk politics with a child.

However, research done in the United States suggests that family communication patterns can have political implications; where there is an open line of communication between parents and children, partisanship may be transferred from parent to child.   This research has both a heuristic value towards a theory of family communications and for its impact on political orientation in Africa.   Given the diversity of cultures in Africa, it is logical to expect that different patterns of communication will exist within different family structures, in different countries. Studies are needed to examine the relationships between differing patterns of family communication and political orientations in Africa, and to compare and contrast the results of such studies with findings in the U.S.

Similarly, little research to determine the extent to which teachers and peers influence political orientations in Africa appears to have been done. Anecdotal evidence suggests that elementary and secondary school teachers and peers are probably not important influences on political orientation across Africa. Although social studies texts provide basic facts about the political systems of each country, teachers tend to shy away from politicizing the young at a very early age. The clear exception may be South Africa, where apartheid bred many political movements, and some of these co-opted the very young. Elementary and secondary schools students do receive some degree of political socialization through the glorification of past leaders in stories, pictures, and recitation of the pledge of allegiance.

In contrast to elementary and secondary schools, university campuses across Africa are a hotbed of political activity, and thus a vital agent of political socialization. Students attending universities often come in contact with radical or liberal faculty members and students. These associations help students to crystallize their own political cognitions and beliefs. University campuses are a regular staging ground for political revolts in many African countries. Although the revolts have led to the closure of many universities for extended periods of time, the closures have often not deterred political fermentation. That is heartening because some avenue must exist to keep pressure on governments to be transparent and efficient.

Mass media strongly influence specific political orientations. Through exposure to mass media, people acquire information that may lead to modifications in their political orientations. However, exposure alone does not guarantee influence. Media messages must contain politically relevant information and the person being influenced must be receptive to the socializing agent. Public affairs media (radio, television, newspapers, and magazines) have always been influential to the African political climate. As early as 1976, Fred Hayward[30] found that mass media were the most important source political information for Ghanaians. He says 48 percent indicated mass media as the major source of their political knowledge as opposed to 16 percent who indicated friends, eight percent who indicated chiefs or elders, and nine percent who chose political leaders. Today, political campaigns are regularly found in print media or on broadcast commercial messages at election time. These are in turn being supplemented with a tremendous amount of political news coverage. The impact of these messages has been greater in urban areas, where the majority of African media outlets operate. Because they are not easily accessible, the media do not influence power relations to a significant degree in the rural areas. As Paul Ansah explains:

> Whereas access to and availability of mass communication facilities are fairly even and widespread in the west, one notices glaring disparities in Africa. On the one hand,

there is a relative abundance of mass media facilities in the urban areas, where the elite minorities live and where the situation is close to what obtains in western societies; on the other hand, there is a media scarcity in rural areas, where the vast majority of the people live. This means in terms of penetration and possible effects, the situation is comparable to that of the west, and in the African situation it may be more accurate to examine issues at two different levels.[31]

Rural dwellers in Africa tend to favor traditional media. Thus, their political orientation is influenced more by face-to-face meetings with politicians or by dyadic relationships with other members of their social networks. That does not suggest that media influences are not felt beyond their urban area of dominant influence (ADI), but it is to say 'that such influence is likely to be a lot less than it could otherwise have been were the media infrastructure far more widespread.'[32]

In recent years, a number of sub-Saharan Africa countries have opened up their airwaves in response to the heightened concern about ordinary people's access to communication, and to particularly the electronic media. New laws were adopted to facilitate the breakup of state owned media monopolies and broadcast operations, but these laws gave little consideration to community media. Rather than decentralize broadcasting operations, they allowed 'independent, commercial broadcasters to establish their predominantly urban-based operations'.[33] Nevertheless, the new liberalized media environment has allowed community radio stations to surface in a few countries. The majority of these (82) are in South Africa. But there are also community radio stations in Benin, the Democratic Republic of Congo, Zambia, and Nigeria. For countries that have them, community radio stations have potential for a profound impact on citizens' political orientation. Whether they can live up to their mantra of 'voice of the people' will depend on how they are established, who controls them, how communities gain access to them and become involved in their program operation. In Benin, for example, community radio stations were represented in the negotiations that led to multiparty democracy.[34] Candidates for the parliamentary elections used this avenue to present themselves to their communities. Their supporters tended to be mobilized by 'stressing the socio-linguistic characteristics that united candidates and followers.'[35]

Conclusion

Political communication is crucial to political development. The objective of achieving rationalization, integration, democratization, and mobilization has a better chance of success in a permissive environment where political ideas are exchanged freely and openly. Where ideas are consistently stifled, the opportunities for civic engagement are limited or nonexistent. This allows a system to breed ineffectiveness and irresponsibility at many levels. Therefore, as more African countries lay a foundation for political development by building democratic governance, the main challenge will be developing institutions and processes responsive to the needs of ordinary citizens, particularly the poor. Meeting this challenge would mean confronting the issues of access, control, participation and freedom of expression. Each system must carefully examine itself to discover who really has a voice in the political system, has access to information, and truly controls intended meaning. Some international organizations, led by the United Nations Development Programme (UNDP), are helping countries strengthen their electoral and legislative systems, improve access to justice and public administration, and develop greater capacity to deliver basic services to those most in need.

But it should be noted that the effectiveness of any kind of communication usually depends on a number of factors, including the credibility of both sender and receiver, the quality (potency) of the message and the clarity of the channel. Political communication is no exception. Parties and their candidates rely on political broadcasts and spots advertising to explain their platforms to constituents. Given the ever-present diversity in African countries, parties and candidates for national offices suffer credibility problems, especially when their dress, speech, acts and actions tilt too heavily towards their ethnic or regional origin. The electorates interpret this as a betrayal of neutrality and sense of national devotion, and respond with apathy. Politicians in turn misinterpret the electorates' apathetic response as public compliance. The net result is a system fraught with patronage and clientelism.

Then there is the issue of what candidates and parties say to the electorate. All too often, politicians promise economic and political liberation, but deliver frustration and misery instead. This is counterproductive to political development, as it promotes civic disengagement. If African political systems are to achieve proper development, their politicians must learn better how to match their actions to their words. If politicians do not accept the opportunity to act more responsibly of their own free will, they may have to be compelled to do so by public advocacy groups, including the media (where they are free). Benin, the Democratic Republic of Congo and a host of other countries, where national conferences have led to political transformations, are clear examples of how public pressure can force political change.

In general, politicians need free publicity, gained from news coverage, current affairs discussion shows, and the like, to promote their image and get their message across. In countries, where media are heavily controlled, this often amounts to minimal access for opposition candidates. To remedy this situation, control of the media must be liberalized. Many countries have already taken steps towards this goal, but the total effort must include the development of community media. People at the grassroots need their own voices, controlled and operated by them. Without such avenues, the voices of those who matter most are often lost. Building community stations would require expenditures that many countries cannot soon afford. In the interim, African political systems can begin by ensuring that political messages disseminated through mass media are supplemented by traditional modes of communication. As George Ngwa writes, 'In strengthening grassroots democracy and development, there is virtually no substitute for face-to-face communication and people media.'[36]

Notes

1 David B. Abernethy, European colonialism and postcolonial crises in Africa,' in Harvey Glickman, ed., *The crises and challenge of African development*, New York: Greenwood Press, 1988, p. 4.

2 David Easton, 'The child's acquisition of regime norms: Political efficacy,' *The American Political Science Review* (1967): 25.

3 Abernethy, 'European Colonialism...', p. 4.

4 Robert A. Packenham, 'Political-development doctrines in the American Foreign aid programs,' *World Politics* 18, 2 (January 1966): 194-235.

5 Ibid., p196.

6 Ibid., pp196-197.

7 Samuel P. Huntington, 'Political development and political decay,' *World Politics* 17, 3 (April, 1965): 386-430.

8 Ibid., p.388.

9 Ibid., p. 389.

10 Ibid., p. 390.

11 Ibid., p. 391.

12 Eric Ransdell, 'Africa's trek to freedom,' *U.S. News & World Report* (August 10, 1992): 28-31.

13 Tarifa Fatos, ' The quest for political legitimacy,' *Social Forces* (December 1997): 437-473.

14 Seymour Martin Lipset, 'The social requisites of democracy revisited,' American Sociological Review 59 (1994): 1-22; See also Jurgen Habermas, *Legitimation crisis*. Translated by T. McCarthy, Beacon Press, 1975 and Max Weber, *The theory of social and economic organization*. Translated by A. M. Henderson and Talcott Parsons, New York: Free Press, 1947.

15 Anthony Giddens, *Sociology* (Polity Press, 1990); see also Seymour Martin Lipset, *The First New Nation, Expanded Edition* (Norton, 1979).

16 Fatos, 'The quest for political legitimacy,' p.434.

17 Ibid., p. 434.

18 Abernethy, 'European colonialism and postcolonial crises in Africa,' p. 4.

19 Edward N. Muller and Thomas D. Julian, 'On the meaning of political support,' *The American Political Science Review* (1977): 1561-1595.

20 Naomi Chazan, 'Ethnicity and politics in Ghana,' *Political Science Quarterly* 97, 3 (Autumn, 1982): 461-485.

21 David Easton, *A systems analysis of political life*, New York: John Wiley & Sons, 1965: 267-340.

22 Harrell R. Rodgers, 'Towards explanations of the political efficacy and political cynicism of black adolescents: An exploratory study,' *American Journal of Political Science* (1974): 257.

23 Ibid., p258.

24 Alan Acock, Harold D. Clarke and Marianne C. Stewart, 'A new model for old measures: A covariance structure analysis of political efficacy,' *The Journal of Politics* (1985): 1063.

25   Ibid., p1064.
26   Afrobarometer is a pioneering effort to systematically measure public opinion in 12 African countries (Botswana, Ghana, Lesotho, Malawi, Mali, Namibia, Nigeria, South Africa, Tanzania, Uganda, Zambia and Zimbabwe). It is produced collaboratively by social scientists from 15 African countries, and coordinated by the Institute of Democracy in South Africa (Idasa), the Center for Democratic Development (CDD-Ghana), and Michigan State University.
27   Ibid., p3.
28   Ibid., p3.
29   Louise M. Bourgault, *Mass media in sub-Saharan Africa*, Bloomington: Indiana University Press, 1995: 4.
30   Fred M. Hayward, 'A reassessment of conventional wisdom about the informed public: National political information in Ghana,' *The American Political Science Review* 70, 2 (June 1976): 433-451.
31   Paul A. V. Ansah, 'Communication research and development in Africa: An overview,' in C. J. Hemelink and O. Linne, eds., *Mass communication research on problems and policies: The art of asking the right questions*, Norwood, New Jersey, 1994.
32   Guy Berger, 'Media & democracy in Southern Africa,' *Review of African Political Economy* 78 (1998): 602.
33   Aida Opoku-Mensah, 'The future of community radio in Africa: The case of Southern Africa,' in Richard Fardon and Graham Furniss, eds., *African Broadcast Cultures: Radio in transition*, Westport, Connecticut: Praeger, 2000, p. 168.
34   Tilo Gratz, 'New local radio stations in African languages & the process of political transformation: The case of Radio Rurale Locale Tangueita in northern Benin,' in Richard Fardon and Graham Furniss, eds., *African Broadcast Cultures: Radio in transition*, Westport, Connecticut: Praeger, 2000, p. 123.
35   Ibid., p. 123.
36   George A. Ngwa, 'Communication and the empowerment of the people,' in Festus Eribo and Enoh Tanjong, eds., *Journalism and mass communication in Africa: Cameroon*, Lanham: Lexington Books, 2002, p. 30.

PART III
INTEGRATIVE COMMUNICATION
CONSIDERATIONS

Introduction

The preceding two parts of this book argued that communication is a vital component of strategies aimed at achieving the various dimensions of national integration. In accordance with this argument, it is necessary to address the practical considerations affecting integrative communication. Two primary considerations are research and planning. These considerations are the focus of the two chapters that comprise Part III. Chapter 9 addresses the research consideration. Research, as it used here, refers to the process of gathering information for structuring verbal, non-verbal and written integrative communications. There are many ways to gather information. Some are formal, others are informal. Some are scientific, others are nomothetic. This chapter addresses types of research and identifies which type is most suitable for integrative communication inquiry.

The chapter also examines the relationship between theory and planning. Windahl, Signitzer and Olson say 'all communication planners use theory to guide their work.'[1] In most cases, the theories used are the planners' original formulations, derived from personal experiences and from common professional practice. Windahl, et al explain, most planners are not aware that both formal academic and non-academic research have generated a 'continuously growing body of theories applicable to planned communication.'[2] They add that, in some respects, many of the academic theories gained their impetus from communication practice.

McQuail[3] created a typology to explain what theory means. He distinguished four main types: social scientific, normative, working and common sense. According to Windahl, Signitzer and Olson, *social scientific theory* is regarded as the most sophisticated type of theory for communication planning. This type of theory is the only one of the four derived from research using scientific rules and methods. It is formulated in the context of the scientific community and relies inherently on abstract concepts.[4]

Normative theory originates from societal values and ideological positions. It explains how communication is formulated and functions in specific social contexts. Normative theory differs from community to community. A planner working in Africa may find that different communities view and practice communication differently. For this reason, planners should understand operative normative theories in the social context in which they work.

Working theory prescribes how communication planning must be done to achieve desired goals. This prescription may derive from theories formulated by the planners themselves or those created by social scientists. Therefore, working theories are both practical and normative. A theory about communication patterns in tribal networks, which has its origin in observations of linguistic patterns, may help communication planners engage informal networks more efficiently. In the same vein, a social stratification theory of communal social order may alert planners to consider the role of opinion leaders in communication efficiency.

Common sense theory derives from individual experiences and guides individual conduct in everyday life. It is therefore unavoidable, even for the communication planner committed to social scientific theory. Lay people who criticize the work of communication planners often tend to rely on common sense theory. For this reason, Windahl, et al advises professional communication planners to understand that the knowledge base in communication does not command as much respect for the lay person, as it does say in engineering. They explain that everyone claims to be a communication expert; however, not everyone can claim to know how to build bridges. In spite of this, common sense theory is invaluable to the communication planner because it broadens discussion and participation. Additionally, it often leads to testing that can be used to validate social scientific theory.[5]

Although these theories have been treated discretely here, in practice they are highly interrelated. Social science theory and common sense theory complement each other in numerous ways. For example, common sense theory enriches social theory and social science theory suggests common sense theory. Similarly, the existence of normative communication theory in a country, community or organization may constrain the application of certain working theories. Or it may make testing of social scientific theory that runs counter to accepted theoretical principles impossible.[6]

The second chapter in Part III is Chapter 10. This chapter focuses on the practical aspects of communication planning. It is based primarily on the work of organization communication planners, Pat Innet and John Schewchuk.[7] Windahl, et. al note that the use of the term 'communication planning' is not as common as the ubiquitous human activity the term describes. They explain that this has to do with the pervasive reluctance to associate communication, usually thought of as a spontaneous activity, with planning, which implies strategy, management and control. They argue that that communication and planning must be combined to achieve good results.[8] Thus, this chapter examines the steps in communication planning within the context of what communication can and cannot do.

Notes

1   Sven Windahl and Benno Signitzer with Jean T. Olson, *Using communication theory: An introduction to planned communication* (London: Sage Publications, 1992).
2   Ibid, p. 1.
3   Dennis McQuail, *Mass Communication theory: An introduction*, 2nd edition, London: Sage, 1987.
4   Windahl and Signitzer with Olson, *Using communication theory*, p. 1.
5   Ibid, p. 2.
6   Ibid.
7   Pat Inett and John Shewchuk, "Communication planning for organizations," *Factsheet* (November 1997): 1.
8   Windahl and Signitzer with Olson, *Using communication theory*, p. 1.

Chapter 9

The Need for Research

Introduction

Knowledge is essential for decision-making, strategic planning and problem solving[1], and national integration is no exception. In order to better the odds of success, integrative policies and strategies must be formulated, implemented and evaluated on the basis of appropriate, accurate and timely information. Information must be obtained on three factors that bear on the success of national integration. First, the reasons why certain integrative strategies succeed in one country and fail in another must be clear. Second, knowledge must be gained of which structures, values, resources and outputs facilitate or hinder national integration.[2] Third, the most effective and prudent methods for evaluating integrative success or failure must be identified. To attempt national integration without this knowledge would be tantamount to navigating a dark labyrinth without a flicker of light.

There are three different ways one can acquire integrative knowledge. They are direct experience, reliance on authority (experts) or scientific inquiry. A person who resides or has resided in a volatile pluralistic country or has participated in the planning and execution of a successful or failed strategy should have reliable intelligence to add to an integrative strategic decision-making. Similarly, political scientists, sociologists, ethnographers or other such people, who generally know more about political or social problems than the ordinary person, should possess ideas salient to an integrative task. However, while knowledge gained from personal experience and from experts is ultimately indispensable, its immediate orientation may be too narrow or too broad. This means its utility must be further verified by scientific inquiry, with a focus on particular instances or undertaken in particular settings.

Science has many advantages over other modes of knowing. These include the following factors:[3]

- Scientific research relies on observation and measurement;
- Scientific research is testable;
- Science requires that researchers must explore all possible explanations in an effort to demonstrate that their propositions cannot be disproved;
- The results of scientific research are replicable, or repeatable;

- Scientific research is public;
- Scientific research recognizes the possibility of error and attempt to limit or control it;
- Scientific research requires the minimization of personal bias and distortion;
- Scientific research promotes the generalizability of results; and
- Scientific research is heuristic, in that it leads to further studies and future discoveries.

Paula Poindexter and Maxwell McCombs succinctly define scientific research as the structured inquiry that emphasizes systematic observation as opposed to casual observation, combines empiricism (direct observation) with logical thought, while constantly striving towards greater precision of observation.[4] As this definition suggests, scientific research can be seen as the most reliable way to explain, predict, understand and control a phenomenon.

However, this view is not shared by many African leaders, who seldom rely on scientific research for decision making. In the past four decades, African countries have formulated integrative policies largely from intuition, guesswork, hearsay or impromptu brainstorming. This is largely due to the fact that many African leaders have lacked opportunity for training in the scientific methodology. But, as Adidi Uyo notes, 'the next of kin to ignorance is guesswork, both of which involve high risks'.[5] James Madison, one of the principal framers of the American constitution writes that 'knowledge will forever govern ignorance'. It is vital, therefore, for African leaders to establish ongoing programs of scientific research inquiries to discern the individual and collective implications of the various dimensions of integration (social, cultural, political, and economic). Through scientific research, countries should be able to better understand the magnitude of the problem, and better able to discover strategies and tactics that would be most effective in dealing with it.

This chapter ponders the type of scientific research to be undertaken. It proposes who should conduct it, discusses how it should be planned, and considers the practical obstacles or limitations to overcome in order to achieve educationally significant and immutable results.

Types of Scientific Research

When deciding which type of scientific research to apply to integrative problems, there are two options to consider: *applied* or *basic*. The distinction between the two is not readily apparent, but applied (or pragmatic) research 'is generally thought of as problem-solving research'.[6] That is, applied researchers use scientific methodology to generate information to help solve an immediate, but recurrent, societal problem. Applied research spans many fields; academia, business, organizations, industry and government. In academia, this type of research is conducted across several disciplinary orientations, including business, communication, education, geography, political science, sociology, social work and psychology.

In contrast, basic (also called 'pure' or 'theoretical') research is conducted primarily in college and university settings. This academic context usually means that the research is theoretical or scholarly in approach; that is, the studies generally tend to originate from the need to create new knowledge or add to existing knowledge of fundamental human processes. Essentially then, the goals of basic research are to satisfy the natural curiosity of scholars and to explore questions relative to the understanding of various processes and effects occurring in the world. Control and absence of bias are vital requirements for basic research and this is normally achieved through laboratory experiments. This is not to imply, however, that applied researchers are willing to settle for something less than rigorous science. In actuality, applied and basic research is conducted in much the same way and with much the same amount of rigor.[7]

Still, there are other notable distinctions between applied and academic research. For instance, applied research is usually conducted with time constraints. The applied researcher often has to work within deadlines established by the research client. Such deadlines may be set by federal and state governments, governmental bureaucracies, legislatures, business corporations and organizations, service delivery organizations, professional and advocacy groups, foundations, among others. These clients usually have a specified period within which to make a decision and must have any necessary information within that time. Conversely, except when the research is funded by a grant, basic researchers seldom have specified deadlines for their research endeavors. The most common practice in academia is for researchers to 'conduct research at a pace that accommodates their teaching schedules'.[8]

Another difference between academic and applied research involves ownership. Academic research belongs to the public. Any researcher or organization interested in replicating or using academic research information can do so simply by asking the original researcher for the raw data. Most applied research, on the other hand, generates proprietary information that is considered the exclusive property of the sponsoring agency and is generally inaccessible to other researchers. There are times, however, when proprietary information is released into the public domain soon after it is collected, such as public opinion polls and projection of social and political trends. Sometimes, information may be released to the public after several years, but this practice is generally the exception rather than the rule.[9]

Still another difference between applied and academic research is how they are initiated. Typically, clients supply the applied research problems. Sometimes these problems are poorly conceptualized and somewhat incomprehensible. The clients are always in control, either 'through a contractual relationship or by virtue of holding higher position within the researcher's place of employment'.[10] Therefore, applied researchers must constantly negotiate with the client about the project scope, cost and deadlines. These negotiations often lead to compromises that require a researcher to make conscious trade-offs in selection of approach and depth of the research. In contrast, the academic researcher usually initiates his or her research, even when it is externally funded through a public or private grant. He or she is solely responsible for selecting the research idea, the approach to carrying it out, and setting the time frame for its completion. In reality, therefore, the basic researcher, in comparison with the applied researcher, operates in a more flexible environment, has less need to shape the research agenda by project cost, and has less time pressure to deliver results by deadline'.[11]

Also, academic research differs from applied research in terms of levels of analysis. In most cases, the applied researcher needs to examine a specific problem at multiple levels of analysis, including individuals, groups, organizations or even societies. For example, in evaluating integrative tendencies in a social system, a researcher must be concerned with individual or group attitudes and their implications for social integration. These additional levels of analysis may require 'that the researcher be conversant with concepts and research approaches found in a variety of disciplines, such as psychology, sociology, and political science. This may require the development of a multi-disciplinary research team capable of conducting the multilevel inquiry'.[12] It may also require the triangulation of research methods (that is using multiple research methods at the same time). When applied to difficult problems, this triangulation may strengthen confidence in the results.

Despite these differences, academic research and applied research are not entirely independent of one another. Academicians conduct research frequently for private sponsors. For example, academic researchers are often asked to conduct marketing studies and public opinion polls on behalf of private organizations. By the same token, private sector researchers also produce theoretical research. In Africa, for example, non-governmental organizations have been known to produce extensive research on social trends. It is ludicrous therefore, to believe as some people do, that one type of research is superior to the other.

The Need for Applied Integration Research in Africa

Academic research has constituted the bulk of the literature on national integration since interest in the topic was heightened when a large number of countries became independent in the 1950s and 1960s. The primary focus of this literature has been the nature and extent of individuals' identification with his or her country. Other areas of focus included the extent and cost of compliance with government directives, the relationship between individuals and the state, and the methods that determined the degrees of national integration.[13] The research goal has been to identify the factors that explain the persistence of political and social disintegration in the developing world. By producing theories that explain the nature and processes of national integration, scholars hoped to isolate which factors are integral or peripheral to the integrative strategic decision.

To a great extent, academic researchers have been successful. Today, there is a vast repository of academic materials (integration models, ideal types, and paradigms) to draw from in the study of national integration. This material has specified the possibilities applicable when attempting to isolate the specific variables that affect integration. Those variables may include goals, homogeneity, mobilization, degree of political participation, proximity, exchange relationship (transactions), governmental effectiveness, pluralism, autonomy, common experiences, size of units, styles, degree of institutionalization, ideological dispositions, and so on.[14] However, as Fred Hayward observes, when taken as a whole studies on national integration to date have been far too 'subjective to substantiate authoritative judgments about which are 'key' variables or what additional variables might be more useful'.[15] This absence of authoritative information creates a need for applied research on national integration in Africa.

Specifically, applied researchers can be employed to test the efficacy of existing integration models, ideal types and paradigms, under certain conditions and in specific countries. This would greatly enhance the ability of individual countries to formulate and execute new integrative strategies, and to evaluate existing policies. The evidence suggests that theoretical assumptions about the processes leading to integration have failed to hold, especially in African countries. For instance, it was generally assumed that centralized political structures would break down parochial loyalties and lead to political integration. However, in countries where dictatorships or one-party rule have persisted in Africa, there have been non-integrative consequences. John Young gives the example of Ethiopia. He writes:

> For centuries Ethiopia's rulers have attempted to overcome local bases of power and establish a strong central government. To the extent that this was achieved, it produced many largely ethnically based rebellions, which plagued the country until the Ethiopian People's Revolutionary Democratic Front's victory in 1991.[16]

However, Ethiopia is not an isolated case. Similar situations existed in Malawi during the reign of Kamuzu Banda, Zaire under Mobutu Sese Seko and in Guinea and the Sudan. It currently exists also in the Central African Republic, Guinea Bissau and a host of other countries.

Applied research can also be used to understand integrative perceptions, attitudes and behavior in Africa. As Hayward[17] notes, one of the fundamental areas of concern in national integration is the attitude of the people towards the nation and the government. Do people perceive themselves as members of the state? Do they identify with the aspirations and policies of the government? However, the concern is not with the population as a whole but with sections of the populace. Groups invariably differ in almost all countries, thus the issue is the intensity of difference. If particular groups have negative feelings towards the government or major government policies, the consequences of this negative orientation may drastically affect the level of integration. In Cote d'Ivoire, for example, disagreements between certain ethnic groups and the national government led to armed rebellion in 2002 that effectively divided the country into two parts for some time. In Nigeria, tensions between the Ibos and the federal government led to a civil war, which lasted for almost five years (1966-1970).[18] It is vital, therefore, for policy makers and strategists to monitor the prevailing loyalties in a country at periodic intervals. Formulating integrative policies and strategies based on analysis of actual conditions will be the most assured way of enhancing their effectiveness and overall success. Accomplishing this task require concentrated efforts.

Topical Areas for Integration Research in Africa

National integration is not entirely a communication problem. Therefore, it would be presumptuous to argue that researching communication topics exclusively can provide solutions to all of integration's problems. However, there is ample evidence in the literature to suggest that communication can mediate the direction (positive or negative) of the integrative tendencies displayed at the social, economic and political levels of society. Based on the works of Karl Deutsch, John Coleman, Myron Weiner, Adelumola Ogunade and Christine Drake, the exploration of communication research topics must be considered a vital necessity in the quest for integration solutions.

The communication issues that arise from national integration are not essentially different from those that occur in routine interactions. Fundamental questions revolve around source motivation and credibility, message clarity and comprehension, channel effects, receiver inclination and interest. Throughout the world, these communication factors are routinely taken for granted. Africa is no exception. But the African case is more distressing because the study of communication is superficial or practically nonexistent. Speech communication courses are seldom offered at academic institutions in Africa. And the communication arts and media courses offered are usually too theoretical to have practical value. It is no surprise then that influential African leaders seldom consider the essential factors before engaging in a communicative situation. For example, most heads of state or government officials who deliver a lengthy speech urging unity and tolerance after a civil or religious disturbance, usually do not know how the audience will react to their address. They do not know or care how many people heard the address. Or how many people understood the message or shared their meaning. Or how many people believed them. Neither are their speech-writers, who seem oblivious of the 'receivers, the message, the information reaching the audience via radio or television, and their likely effects'.[19]

Sadly, the situation is no different among media professionals or practitioners. Uyo writes that few editors in Angola, Benin, Eritrea, Ghana, Kenya, Senegal or Uganda can claim to know their audience. Few can claim direct knowledge of their audience size and composition. Few understand the reading, listening or viewing habits of their readers, listeners or viewers. Few care how much news the audience actually read in a newspaper, listen to on radio or watch on television. He compares the communicative conduct of African leaders to that of a surgeon who performs surgery without knowledge of human anatomy. He says,

'Government officials and media practitioners in many developed countries conduct their communication like a surgeon who goes straight to opening up the chest of a patient without knowing where the heart is, its constituent parts or its functions'.[20]

As this analogy demonstrates, research is essential to the planning and execution of an important event. And communication (the sharing of ideas and meaning) is an important event. In a complex communication environment as exists in Africa, research must address a number of general and specific questions. Uyo suggests some of the specific questions, including how does communication function in the rural areas? Is communication in rural settings different from communication in urban areas? What are the perceptions of people in particular communities? How can communication be used to change attitudes dysfunctional to society? How can communication be used to inculcate or reinforce those values that lead to the development of individuals and society?[21]

The general questions are suggested by existing social science theories. To date, a large number of theories have been formalized in interpersonal and mass communications. Prominent among these are selective-exposure, group dynamics, agenda setting, knowledge gap, spiral of silence, cultivation, media framing, media hegemony and normative values. Although the global utility of these theories has not yet been fully established, common sense suggests they can help to further knowledge about integration-related issues. The following pages discuss the relevance of these theories to integration-issues, as well as the possible questions they may raise for integration.

Selective Exposure

Selective perception is one of the widely accepted principles in sociology and social psychology used to explain why communication campaigns rarely have persuasive impact.[22] Selective exposure theory states, 'people prefer exposure to communications that agree with their pre-existing opinions'.[23] This suggests that people purposely seek out messages that support their opinions and purposely avoid materials that challenge them. For example, the US has spent more than 600 million dollars since September 11 on campaigns aimed persuading Muslim countries that the 'War on Terrorism' is not a 'War on Islam,' and that the US is not an enemy of the Islamic world. However, studies show that the campaign has been ineffective. The majority of people in Islamic countries have been turning away from the main messages in the campaigns. The reason given is that people in the Islamic countries feel that the US media blitz has shied away from the real issue, the overt tendency of US policies to lean heavily towards Israel.[24] As Stanley Baran and Dennis Davis explain, people employ selective exposure to preserve existing attitudes by avoiding messages that challenge them.[25]

Three other psychological processes are associated with selective exposure. These are *selective perception*, *selective retention* and *selective attention*. Baran and Davis define selective perception as the mental process of interpreting a message to make its meaning fit a person's belief and attitudes. An illustration of this is the violent reaction to a newspaper article, published during the truncated Miss World contest in Nigeria 2002. In the article, journalist Isioma Daniel wrote that the prophet Mohammed would not have complained about the Miss World competition, and may even have chosen a wife from among the contestants. Islamic religious fanatics, who had opposed the contest from the outset on the basis that their religion prohibited the exhibition of scantily clad women, interpreted the remarks as blasphemy. They staged riots that led to the death of more than 250 people and the destruction of property. The riots led to the relocation of the contest to London. The journalist who wrote the article complained that she meant to treat a serious topic with humor. This intention however was lost on the rioters.

Selective retention is the tendency to 'remember best and longest information that is consistent with pre-existing attitudes and interest'.[26] Selective attention suggests that we concentrate more on those things that agree with our dispositions, to the possible obscurity of materials with which we might disagree. Dominic Lasorsa[27] summed up all three processes when he wrote that people tend to expose themselves to messages they 'are likely to agree with, to attend to such messages more carefully, and to retain such messages'. He adds that each process is not discrete because one cannot retain information to which one has not been exposed. Neither can one interpret a message that has not been retained.

To what extent do these psychological processes exist generally in Africa? How are they applied specifically to integrative communications? How can they be overcome? In short, what methods can be used to ensure that integrative communications agree with people's existing attitudes and are clearly understood? How long do people retain integrative messages and act on them? These are some of the questions that must be answered before appropriate and effective integrative strategies can be found. Answers to these questions are paramount for three reasons. First, individuals in a diverse society must share experiences before they can communicate efficiently. As Wilbur Schramm explained, 'the extent to which two persons share overlapping fields of experience affects how easy it is for them to communicate'.[28]   He noted that communication is more than just the transmission of messages from senders to receivers. Such transmission models imply that a communicator's task is merely to 'get messages out'. However, human communication is more about sharing meaning. And it is quite difficult to share meaning with someone you do not know well or who comes from a different background. Thus, the impact of the integrative message may be subject to whether different groups in the society feel they share a common 'field of experience'.

Second, the ability to share common experiences is mediated by attitudes and cultural expectations. Attitudes and cultural expectations affect selective processes in powerful ways. A good demonstration of this is the HIV/AIDS issue in South Africa. There are people who believe that having sex with a virgin can insulate them from contracting the virus or can cure them of it (if they already have it). They rape young girls on the basis of this belief. To other people, this is unfathomable and reprehensible behavior. To these people, the practice is quite reasonable. Attitude is therefore is powerful predictor of behavior. On the basis of a person's prevailing attitude, one may be able to predict the person's future course of action. Therefore, it is necessary to understand people's attitude toward their other ethnic groups, as well as the general idea of integration.

Group Dynamics

In collective societies (such as are found in Asia, African, Latin America and the Middle East), groups have more power over their members than in Western societies (such as the United States or Britain).[29] In Africa, for example, where an individual is generally subordinated to his or her group, 'a high degree of conformity is expected'.[30] Ethnographic studies have shown that African groups assume a central role in shaping their member's norms, personal judgments and how each member uses interpersonal communication to mediate media effects.[31] This co-orientation of values is said to be a vital means for determining individual self-concept, individual status within the group,[32] and for maintaining group identity.[33]

Accordingly, 'group identification' and 'group consciousness' are said to be the important factors associated with harmony or discord among groups.[34] Pamela Conover defines group identification 'as having two related components: a self-awareness of one's objective membership in the group, and a psychological sense of attachment to the group'.[35] Arthur Miller, Pamela Gurin and Gerald Gurin define group consciousness as 'a politicized awareness, or ideology, regarding the group's relative positions in society, and a commitment to collective action to realize the group's interests'.[36] These definitions suggest that ethnic attachment and ethnic politicization are relevant to the national integration discourse.

In recent years, interethnic and inter-religious conflicts have increased in a number of African countries. These conflicts suggest that African countries are far from being a 'melting pot'. As a result, it is necessary for African leaders to understand fully the nature of the 'interface between attachment to the nation as a whole and attachment to one's ethnic group'.[37] Empirical studies have been carried out in Israel, Mexico and the United States, but none have so far been conducted in Africa. In attempting to understand the psychologies of patriotism and nationalism in Africa, a number of relevant questions must be asked. For example, what is the influence of ethnic group identification on national group identification? How does ethnic group attachment affect the national group's integrative agenda? In other words, how do group dynamics influence specific dimensions of national integration, including value and normative congruence, integrative behavior and political awareness? What motivates a group to protest collectively? How does this collective protest enhance or hinder national integration? Answers to these questions may point to the particular integrative appeals that apply to certain groups.

Agenda Setting

McCombs and Shaw's[38] agenda-setting theory holds that the issues the media focus on the most often and the longest become the issues that the general public will think about and talk about. That is to say, as media emphasize some news and neglect others, they highlight the issues that the public would consider salient. An important principle to note here is the relationship between media coverage and public cognition. Vincent Price[39] explains that because public opinion is a social and communicative process, individual opinions depend in many ways, for both form and content, on the larger context of the public debate. He says social cues received through communication give suggestions on how individuals should proceed in forming their opinion. In this manner, individual views become public cognitions.

Price explains that in the course of deciding their stand on an issue, individuals are not so much determining their own opinion, or 'where they stand' on the matter. Instead, they are 'interpreting the issues through their relationships to broader social movements and emerging opinion groups'.[40] In other words, they are choosing 'with whom they stand'. Because this choice is based on what one knows, the public opinion process transcends the process in which each person independently considers a problem and decides on a reasoned course of action. It becomes 'a process of social "structuration" in which the public gradually organizes into some number of opinion groups via interpersonal discussion and widespread mass communication, and in which the public comes to define and express their opinion primarily through support for or opposition to groups'.[41]

In describing the elements most consequential to the context of the public opinion processes, Price notes the potential of media coverage to influence people's perceptions on developments in public affairs. He says the media determine the social terms in which public issues are framed. Price says, the media highlight the personalities or groups that emerge eventually to represent various stands on an issue. He says that by weaving discrete events into a continuing story, media reporters and commentators help the public make sense out of complicated social issues, as they present all sides of an issue. Through this contextualization of social issues, the media exert their influence both on the issue agenda and public opinion.

In Western countries, research on the agenda setting function of the mass media is advanced and ongoing. The same is not true for Africa, where research on the topic is relatively scant. However, agenda-setting research can help to verify the social status and influence of African media systems. It can also help to understand the relationship between media coverage and issue salience among African populations. Increasingly, the media are fast becoming the main source of news and information for most Africans. Radio in particular continues to be a main avenue for forming and manipulating African public opinion. Therefore, agenda-setting studies should be helpful in determining not only the issues that are most important to Africans, but also how ethnic and individual variances affect the public agenda. As an intrinsic part of such inquiries, a number of integrative questions should be explored. These may include, but should not be restricted to:

- What is the public's conception of the important issues in integration?
- What is the media's conception of the important issues?
- To what extent do the media influence the integrative agenda of the public?
- In general, where does the integration issue rate on the public's agenda?
- And how do the media form their agenda?

Knowledge Gap

The knowledge gap theory proposes that socioeconomic status affects acquisition of mass media information in a social system to the extent that a gap in knowledge will exist between those in the high and low social strata. In a formal statement of the theory, Tichenor, Donohue and Olien wrote:

> As the infusion of mass media information into a social systems increases, segments of the population with higher socioeconomic status tend to acquire this information at faster rate than the lower status segments, so that a gap in knowledge between these segments tend to increase rather than decrease.[42]

As part of the theory, Tichenor, Donohue and Olien predicted a relationship between an increase in knowledge and receptivity to social change. They wrote that an increase in knowledge leads to 'increased rate of acceptance of a particular behavior, a belief, a value, or an element of technology in a social system'.[43]

This could mean that increased knowledge will lead African populations to demonstrate a willingness to engage in integrative behavior. To prove such a hypothesis, the sort of knowledge that is required (general or specific) must be identified. In addition, planners must also define what is meant by integrative knowledge, and how much of it is to be presented via mass media? Other questions need answers as well. For example, is there ethnic and religious variance to the information gap? Can increased national knowledge lead to greater ethnic consciousness and parochialism? In other words, what are the positive and negative effects of bridging the knowledge and information gap between the fortunate and the less fortunate, between various ethnic and religious groups, and between socially stratified classes, on the national integration process in African countries?

Spiral of Silence

Noelle-Neumann's spiral of silence theory holds that people who perceive their views to be in the minority opinion will forego public expression of those views for fear of being isolated. As Price explains, people who sense from media reports that trends of opinion are running against their views will refrain from expressing their opinions, 'except to those who share them, for fear of social isolation'.[44] Price adds that even if these people constitute a numerical majority, the failure to express their views leads invariably to a strengthening of the opposition. An important principle is the linkage between media coverage and social conformity. By telling us 'what ideas are popular, are in the majority, and are gaining in strength,'[45] the mass media may be subtly and indirectly influencing system-level opinion towards convergent outcomes. Price explains the ways by which mass media contextualizes these public opinion outcomes. He says the media represents an issue socially, and depicts 'how various groups of people within the public are crystallizing into opinion factions'.[46]

Based on these definitions, the spiral of silence theory implications for integration research in Africa. First, is there is a spiral of silence surrounding the national integration issue in African countries? Is the public opinion favoring value and normative congruence in the minority or majority? This determination is a crucial necessity and greatly aids efficient and effective integrative strategizing.

Secondly, if it is found that a silent majority favors integration, Lasorsa notes that it is possible to 'fight the spiral of silence under certain conditions'.[47] He says that vocal minority voices are required to stimulate group pressure. Ideas that are unpopular today may become universal maxims tomorrow. Take the case of Louis Pasteur who was banished from the French Academy for suggesting the invisible organisms (microbes) were making people ill. Or Rosa Parks who was arrested for daring to believe that she should have an equal right to sit in the front of a public bus. Lasorsa notes that at one time, both Pasteur and Parks were a minority of one. However, in time, their ideas caught on.[48] Must national integration in Africa await individual voices to manifest? What are the main obstacles to nation building?

Cultivation

Cultivation theory postulates 'entertainment media do play a role in shaping viewers' conceptions of reality.'[49] The theory claims that prolonged exposure to dominant television themes will skew viewers' perception of the world towards messages implicit in these themes. George Gerbner and his colleagues[50] stated the cultivation hypothesis when a series of their studies showed a link between heavy viewing of violent television content and the development of a scarier view of the world. However, as Baran and Davis argue, cultivation's point is more complex than simply stating that heavy television viewers give answers more similar to 'TV answers' than real world answers. They say the 'central argument is that television 'cultivates' or creates a world view that, although possibly inaccurate, becomes the reality simply because we, as a people, believe it to be the reality and base our judgments about our own, everyday world on that reality'.[51]

Based on this argument, cultivation's implication for integrative studies may seem self-evident. A modified version of cultivation theory could predict that if people see only positive information about social interactions, governmental affairs, economic growth and economic distribution, their view of the national integration process would be more positive in tone. It should be noted that 'television's cultivation process does not exert a one-way influence. Rather, it is a dynamic, ongoing process of interaction between the medium and the environmental context and attributes of the viewer'.[52] The nature of the changes that this interaction brings must be constantly understood through research.

Cultivation questions in Africa may include: What are the dominant themes on African television programs? What are the effects of these themes on the integrative agenda? How feasible is cultivation as an integrative theory?

Media framing

Thomas Nelson, Rosalee Clawson and Zoe Oxley define framing as 'the process by which a communication source, such as a news organization, defines and constructs a political issue or public controversy'.[53] They say *frames* focus attention on the possible effects of media content rather than the mere coverage of issues as agenda-setting does. As Robert Entman explains, 'Frames call attention to some aspects of reality while obscuring other elements, which might lead audiences to have different reactions'.[54]

Throughout Africa it is commonly understood that the lens through which people receive media messages and images is not neutral. What people generally see or hear is more often than not a particular point of view, a particular kind of explanation, or a particular type of description, largely determined and managed by the person bearing the news or information. Africa is not the only continent where media and other information sources use *frames* to describe events. However, it appears to be one of the few environment where ethnicity provides additional color to these frames. This is because the frame of reference for most Africans is largely the ethnic group. For example, in coverage of conflicts on the continent, the most common frame used to explain cause is ethnicity, rather than politics or economics. For this reason, it is necessary to explore how media frame national integration? Possible questions may include: how does framing affect African society's acceptance or rejection of the national integration phenomenon and its attendant goals? And is there a difference in the way private and public media frame societal conflicts?

Media Hegemony Theory

Media hegemony theory holds that ideas of the societal elites, particularly the ruling social class, are the dominant or governing ideas. The theory further states these ruling class ideas 'control the mass media, which then exert this control over this rest of this society'.[55] As Karl Marx[56] observed, those who control the means of industrial production also control the means of information generation and dissemination. Thus, journalists are socialized to cater to the dominant social class,[57] whose 'routine and taken-for-granted structures of everyday thinking contribute to a structure of dominance'.[58]

This is true of Africa, where most media institutions are still controlled by governments, and those employed by media are members of the dominant elites. Throughout the continent, newspapers, radio and television content caters to the urban elite. Though the media landscape has become liberalized in recent years, little has been done to reorient media focus towards the disenfranchised in society. Not even the presence of community media in a few countries has balked this trend. Necessarily, therefore, research must be done to determine the effect of this conscious bias on media credibility. Similarly, it is important to determine the relationship between media credibility and integrative effectiveness.

Values Theory

James Spates defines values as the 'moral beliefs to which people appeal for the ultimate rationales of action'.[59] Values theory posits that the basic moral beliefs of all people are the same, but that people differ in how they rank these beliefs—that is, the importance they assign to different beliefs. According to Lasorsa, 'the theory maintains that by showing people inconsistencies in their value structures (that is in how they prioritize their values), it is possible to get them to change'.[60] Based on this theory, one could discover how many Africans value ethnic unity, but not national integration. One could discern the real differences between the values of various ethnic groups, and how these differences impact the national integration agenda. Such findings would be critical to designing effective integrative strategies.

Obstacles to Scientific Research in Africa

Conducting scientific research in Africa is not easy. The most daunting problems are shortage of funds, inadequate research infrastructure, and lack of a social science research culture. Little domestic money is available for scientific research and development in Africa. African governments seldom allocate huge sums to research endeavors, and African private organizations rarely support or initiate research. For example, spending on health research is less that 0.5 percent of the gross domestic product (GDP) in Africa.[61]

There are two primary reasons for this lack of support. First, since independence, African economies have been overwhelmed by 'increased debt, export market share decline, redirected foreign investment and increased reliance on aid'.[62] In this environment of capital paucity, research funding has had to take a back seat.

Second, most African governments see the restriction of funding as a way of exerting political control over the production and dissemination of knowledge. In his article, 'The Politics of Historical and Social Science Research in Africa,' Paul Zeleza[63] explains how this pecuniary control over universities and research institutions evolved through the years. He writes that relations between state officials and academicians were cooperative at the outset, as academics were allowed to shape many of the goals and aspirations of the nationalist ideology:

> In the heady years immediately after independence academics were as intoxicated as the nationalist leaders were by the totalizing dreams of nation building and development, and contributed, deliberately or not, to the construction of an authoritarian ideological edifice that would later consume them.[64]

But the academics desired more than practical application of knowledge. A majority of them also believed basic research was an important means of writing Africa into the empirical and theoretical corpus of their disciplines, and of promoting scientific and technological development'.[65] By contrast, government officials perceived academic research as 'irrelevant' mostly because it was not applied research, but also because 'African academics were adversarial, ... or blindly followed western research themes that did not address local conditions'.[66] To those who pulled the purse strings, this academic tilt in research meant African universities had lost their mission.

Today, foreign donors are the main source of funding for research in Africa, not alumni or industry, as is common in the United States. For example, Zeleza reports that the Ford Foundation alone awarded 259 grants, totaling $52.7 million between 1990 and 1999 to universities and NGOs in 15 African countries. Much of this research was in the social sciences and was policy oriented. Conversely, African bourgeoisie remained still mired in 'primitive accumulation' and were yet to develop the habit of public institutional charity. This lack of domestic participation in research leaves African social scientists caught in a bind of addressing African realities by 'conversing with each other through publications and media owned by foreign academic communities'.[67]

In addition to scant funding, research facilities in Africa are grossly inadequate. Africa lacks internal capacities for research. The manpower is certainly there, as the number of Africans holding doctoral degrees has grown tremendously in the past four decades. However, the amenities to conceptualize, execute and analyze scientific studies are clearly lacking. Only a few universities have computer hardware and software to undertake data analysis. In many countries, there are no indigenously-generated theories on which to base research, and few offices to house research institutes. These deficits are complicated further by the problem of erratic power supply. The prevalence of power interruptions in most countries limits the ability to maintain the integrity of studies dealing with perishable materials. At the institutional level, libraries are poorly equipped. Books and journals are few and most of what is stocked is outdated. For example, when this writer visited the University of Nairobi in the summer of 2002, he found few current journals in mass communication. What were termed communication journals dealt with computing and computer communications. The most current of these were published in the 1980s.

There also is the issue of the lack of a social science research culture in Africa. Zeleza alluded to this lack when he says that African universities do not have a long and established history of scholarly production. He writes that the majority of African universities have been in existence only since the 1960s. In this period, the universities have been plagued by frequent government intrusions and absence of academic freedom. These problems have left the universities largely devoid of a research culture. In an effort to overcome this deficit, African academics resorted to 'imported scientific consumerism,'[68] or what Paulin Houtondji calls 'theoretical extroversion'.[69]   This engendered a prevailing culture dominated by the 'importation of paradigms, problematics and perspectives, and the search for legitimation and respectability from the intellectual institutions of the north'.[70]

This culture is more evident in the field of communications.   As Enoh Tanjong[71] corroborates, the early scholars of mass communication in Africa were mostly Americans and Europeans who had research interest in African media systems. These were the people who established the journalism and media schools found on the continent today. Meanwhile, African scholars have contributed little to African media studies as an area of scholarly endeavor.

To illustrate this, Tanjong notes that the few journalism and mass communication schools in existence tended to follow American and European models of media effects. However, the Africans who administered them tended to lack any rigorous tradition of mass communication research. The majorities had backgrounds in the humanities, such as linguistics, history, or political science. Thus, historical discourse and content analysis dominated the early studies of mass communication in Africa. There were no surveys or experiments. As Tanjong notes, the application of the survey methodology required the availability of qualified and competent survey researchers, who were scarce or not available in Africa.

Conclusion

This chapter has argued that scientific research is central to knowledge acquisition and application, and that knowledge in turn is instrumental to decision-making. Specifically, the chapter has argued that applied research is vital for formulating effective integrative strategies in Africa. To support this argument, the chapter reviewed several prominent mass communication theories. These theories were then used to suggest possible research topics on national integration. Accordingly, the chapter called on African leaders to establish infrastructures for scientific research in Africa. It noted that until this was done, much of what we know about the process, effects, and systems of communication in Africa would be derived from 'sources of knowledge other than the scientific method, which is the pivot of the research process'.[72]

Notes

1   Paula M. Poindexter and Maxwell E. McCombs, *Research in mass communication: A practical guide*, Boston: Bedford, 2000: 5.
2   Fred M. Hayward, 'Continuities and discontinuities between studies of national and international political integration: Some implications for future research efforts,'

International Organization, 24, 4, Regional Integration: Theory and Research (Autumn 1970), p. 923.

3   Joann Keyton, *Communication Research: Asking questions, finding answers*, Mountain View, California: Mayfield Publishing Company, 2001, pp. 9-10.

4   Poindexter and McCombs, *Research in mass communication*, p. 5.

5   Adidi Uyo, 'Communication research: An African discourse,' in Festus Eribo and Enoh Tanjong, eds., *Journalism and mass communication in Africa: Cameroon*, Lanham, New Jersey: Lexington Books, 2002: 82.

6   Michael Singletary, *Mass Communication Research: Contemporary methods and applications*, New York: Longman, 1994, p. 48.

7   Leonard Bickman and Debra J. Rog, 'Introduction: Why a handbook of applied social research methods?,' in Leonard Bickman and Debra Rog, eds., *Handbook of applied social research methods*, Thousand Oaks, California: Sage Publications, 1998, p. x.

8   Roger D. Wimmer and Joseph R. Dominick, *Mass media research: An introduction*, Belmont, California: Wadsworth Publishing Company, 1991: 11.

9   Ibid. p. 11.

10   Bickman and Rog, *Handbook of applied social research methods*, p. xii.

11   Ibid. p. xiii.

12   Ibid. p. xiv.

13   Hayward, 'Continuities and discontinuities between studies of national and international political integration,' p. 922.

14   Ibid. p. 934.

15   Ibid.

16   John Young, 'Regionalism and democracy in Ethiopia,' *Third World Quarterly* 19, 2 (06-01-1998).

17   Hayward, 'Continuities and discontinuities between studies of national and international political integration,' p. 934.

18   Ibid.

19   Uyo, 'Communication research: An African discourse,' p. 86.

20   Ibid. p. 86.

21   Ibid. pp. 86-87.

22   David O. Sears and Jonathan L Freedman, 'Selective exposure to information: A critical review,' *Public Opinion Quarterly* 31, 2 (Summer 1967): 194-213.

23   Ibid. p. 197.

24   Dan Murphy, 'US ads miss mark, Muslims say,' *The Christian Science Monitor* (January 7, 2003): p. 6.

25   Stanley J. Baran and Dennis K. Davis, *Mass Communication Theory: Foundations Ferment and Future*, Belmont, California: Wadsworth Publishing Company, 1995: 40.

26   Ibid. p. 141.

27   Dominic L. Lasorsa, 'Diversity in mass communication theory classes,' *Journalism & Mass Communication Educator* 57, 3 (Autumn 2002): 246.

28   Wilbur Schramm, The processes and effect of mass communication (New York: Free Press, 1956).

29   Richard E. Porter and Larry A Samovar, 'Basic principles of intercultural communication,' in Larry Samovar and Richard Porter, eds., *Intercultural Communication: A reader*, Belmont, California: Wadsworth Publishing Company, 1991: 39.

30   Ibid., p. 39.

31   Lasorsa, 'Diversity in mass communication theory classes,' p. 250.
32   Cecilia L. Ridgeway and James W. Balkwell, 'Group processes and the diffusion of status beliefs,' *Social Psychology Quarterly* 60, 1 (March 1997): 14-31.
33   Richard R. Lau, 'Individual and contextual influences on group identification,' *Social Psychology Quarterly* 53, 3 (1989): 220-231.
34   Peter Grant and Rupert Brown, 'From ethnocentrism to collective protests: Responses to relative deprivation and threats to social identity,' *Social Psychology Today* 58, 3 (September 1995): 195.
35   Pamela Conover, 'The influence of group identifications on political perceptions and evaluation,' *The Journal of Politics* 46, 3 (August 1984): 760-785.
36   Arthur H, Miller, Patricia Gurin and Gerald Gurin, 'Electoral implications of group identification and consciousness: The reintroduction of a concept,' Presented at the Annual Meeting of the American Political Science Association (New York, 1978): 18.
37   Jim Sidanius, Seymour Fesbach, Shana Levin and Felicia Pratto, 'The interface between ethnic and national attachment: Ethnic pluralism or ethnic dominance?' *Public Opinion Quarterly* 61, 1, Special issue on race (Spring 1997): 102-133.
38   Maxwell E. McCombs and Donald L. Shaw, 'The agenda-setting function of mass media,' *Public Opinion Quarterly* 36 (1972): 176-187.
39   Vincent Price, 'Social identification and public opinion: Effects of communicating group conflict,' *Public Opinion Quarterly* 53, 2 (Summer 1989): 197-224.
40   Ibid. p. 198.
41   Ibid.
42   P. J. Tichenor, G. A Donohue and C. N. Olien, 'Mass media and the differential growth in knowledge,' *Public Opinion Quarterly* 34 (1970): 159-170.
43   Ibid. p. 159.
44   Price, 'Social identification and public opinion,' p. 199.
45   Lasorsa, 'Diversity in mass communication theory classes,' p. 252.
46   Price, 'Social identification and public opinion,' p. 199.
47   Lasorsa, 'Diversity in mass communication theory classes,' p. 252.
48   Ibid. p. 199.
49   Mollyann Brodie, Ursula Foehr, Vicky Rideout, Neal Bael, et al., 'Communicating health information through the entertainment media', *Health Affairs* 20, 1 (January 2001): 192.
50   George Gerbner, Lynne Gross, M. Morgan, and Nancy Signorielli, 'Living with television: The dynamics of the cultivation process', in Jennings Bryant and Doff Zillmann, eds., *Perspectives on media effects*, Hillsdale, NJ: Lawrence Erlbaum, 1986: 17-41.
51   Baran and Davis, *Mass Communication Theory: Foundations Ferment and Future*, p. 303.
52   Jeremiah Strouse, Nancy Buerkel-Rothfuss, and Edgar C. J. Long, 'Gender and family as moderators of the relationship between music video exposure and adolescent sexual permissiveness,' *Adolescence* 30 (September 1, 1995): 505-522.
53   Thomas E. Nelson, Rosalee A. Clawson and Zoe M. Oxley, 'Media framing of a civil liberties conflict and its effect on tolerance,' *American Political Science Review* 91, 3 (September 1993): 567-583.
54   Robert M. Entman, 'Framing: Toward clarification of a fractured paradigm,' *Journal of Communication* 43 (1993), p. 55.
55   Lasorsa, 'Diversity in mass communication theory classes,' p. 254.

56   Karl Marx, A communist manifesto (1954).
57   Lasorsa, 'Diversity in mass communication theory classes,' p. 254.
58   W. A. Gramson, D. Croteau, W. Hoynes and T. Sasson, 'Media images and the social construction of reality,' *Annual Review of Sociology* 18 (1992): 373-393.
59   James L. Spates, 'The sociology of values,' *Annual Review of Sociology* 9 (1983): 27-49.
60   Lasorsa, 'Diversity in mass communication theory classes,' p. 252.
61   Author not available, 'Forum established to promote research on health in Africa,' *APWorldstream* (December 14, 2002).
62   M. B. Gleave and W. B. Morgan, 'Economic development in tropical Africa from a geographical perspective: A comparative study of African economies,' *The Geographical Journal* (June 2001): 139-145.
63   Paul Tiyambe Zeleza, 'The politics of historical and social science research in Africa,' *Journal of Southern African Studies* 28, 1 (2002): 9-23.
64   Ibid. p. 11.
65   Ibid.
66   Ibid.
67   Ibid. p. 9.
68   Ibid. p. 21.
69   P. Houtondji, 'Introduction: Recentering Africa,' in P. Houtondji (ed), *Endogenous Knowledge: Research Trails*, Dakar: Codseria Book Series, 1997: 1-39.
70   Zeleza, 'The politics of historical and social science research in Africa,' p. 21.
71   Enoh Tanjong, 'Using survey methods in communication research,' in Festus Eribo and Enoh Tanjong, eds., *Journalism and mass communication in Africa: Cameroon*, Lanham, New Jersey: Lexington Books, 2002: 105-119.
72   Uyo, 'Communication research: An African discourse,' p. 87.

Chapter 10

Planning
Integrative Communications

Introduction

Integrative communication is undertaken for a variety of reasons—to inform, persuade, develop relationships, prevent misunderstandings, promote ideology, advocate a point of view or break down barriers. Therefore, it must not be conducted haphazardly. Careful thought must be given to how to deliver messages 'in a way that enables recipients to understand, react to, and act upon the information received'.[1] The intended audience must receive, understand and act upon the message. This requires a straightforward, step-by-step process called 'communication planning'. This process clearly and logically summarizes what to say, how to say it and how to evaluate its success or failure.[2]

Windahl, Signitzer and Olson[3] write that communication planning is broader in scope than communication campaigns. According to them, campaigns usually have a specific and fixed objective—'to influence some or all groups in society with a specific message or set of messages'.[4] On the other hand, communication planning, although it contains campaigns as an important component, encompasses comprehensive goals, objectives, structure and functions. Inett and Shewchuk explain[5] describe these goals, objectives, structures and functions. They see communication planning as a foundation on which to base decision and generate ideas. It is a means of focusing where you want to be and what needs to be done to get there. It is a tool for discovering opportunities, optimizing challenges and initiating change. Also, it is a means of monitoring communications efforts.

According to Windahl, et al, work associated with communication planning is done from a short or long-term perspective, with emphasis on long-term planning. The characteristics of this work are:

- Communication efforts planned from the bottom up instead of from the top down;
- Communication with more general and widespread goals, as opposed to the specific and fixed goals of campaigns;

- Communication viewed from the receiver's perspective instead of from the sender's.[6]

These characteristics show communication planning requires a 'deeper understanding of what communication is and what different forms of communication can achieve'.[7]

Since the mid 1980s, communication planning has been an intrinsic component of development support communication (DSC) efforts in the developing countries. Before that time, development messages were structured and conveyed by technocrats who appeared more concerned with the content of messages than with the process and effects of the delivery. Initially, DSC experts focused primary attention on health and agricultural communication. In recent years, attention has been extended to political communication. But, much of this effort has focused on the promotion of good governance and civil society participation. Efforts toward specific integrative communication planning either have been superficial or non-existent. However, the success of communication depends upon preparation, strategy and feedback. Therefore, it is necessary to treat communication planning as a vital part of a purposeful integration strategy. This chapter discusses communication-planning steps within the context of their specific application to integration. Before discussing the steps, the chapter reviews the general limitations and strengths of communication to provide an appropriate context for their application.

What Communication Can't Do

Windahl, et. al say the most frequently cited reason why planned communication fails is: 'something that is not a communication problem is treated as though it were'.[8] For example, an African leader explains public dissatisfaction with government officials and policies by saying, 'The media have not adequately presented our programs to the people,' or, 'People just don't understand what we are trying to do,' implying that his or her policies are flawless. A more honest explanation would require statements such as, 'Official policies do not address people's needs,' or, 'There is overt favoritism and nepotism in the distribution of national resources'. Such utterances are unlikely from an African statesman. Similarly, a mediator seeking resolution of internal conflicts in Africa might call for more dialogue between combatants, implying that dialogue alone would solve the problems. But if the political, cultural and economic basis of conflict is addressed prudently and adequately, dialogue may not be even necessary.

In the foregoing examples, inadequate communication is wrongly described as the problem. Windahl, et. al note that blaming communication when some other factor should be blamed is a common mistake many communication professionals make. Before something can be called a communication problem, two conditions must be met. First, the problem must result from a lack of, or the wrong type of, communication, implying the problem should be caused directly by communication, or the lack of it. Secondly, the problem must be susceptible to a communication solution. For example, the conflict mediator's thinking above is that conflict will stop when combatants start talking.[9] However, the African situation has proven this not to be the case. In virtually every conflict that has occurred on the African continent, combatants have continued to fight during cease-fire negotiations or conflict mediation.

Thus, it is incumbent for every communication planner to ask questions such as, 'What specifically can solve the problem at hand?' Is it communication alone, communication in conjunction with other measures, or other measures alone? The answer to these questions determines the specific options that the planner must consider. Windahl, et. al note that only issues resulting from proper communication can truly be labeled a communication problem. Only this type of issue calls specifically for the first option described above.[10]

Another shortcoming of communication solutions is that they are superficial at times. Although they are not always inadequate, they are often insufficient and should be supplemented by other measures. An example is the 'war against indiscipline' waged in Nigeria in 1984 and 1985. The war was meant to eradicate 'indiscipline' in the areas of environmental sanitation, public decorum, corruption, smuggling, and disloyalty to national symbols such as the flag and the anthem. For 18 months, the Buhari/Idiagbon regime sought to promote acceptable forms of public behavior through carefully prepared radio, television, radio, newspaper, and billboard advertisements. While the campaign was symbolic, both critics and the public judged it to have been largely ineffective. This is because in general it failed to institute the necessary social changes.

Some attributed this failure to the campaign's short duration. But Alufa Yemsi[11] presents the more truthful explanation. He explains that there was far too much 'word' than sincere action. For contrary to the government's belief, the lack of discipline in Nigeria did not originate from the lack of communication, but rather from the socio-psychological predispositions cultivated as a result of antipathy to colonialism. Robert Stock writes, 'the roots of the contemporary sanitation crisis are found in the colonial attitude toward Nigerians and their living environments'.[12] Critics said the campaign needed the addition of both an educational and infrastructure component to be effective. Education could have instilled the macro and micro benefits of orderly behavior. Also the provision of infrastructures, such as buses, affordable market stalls and housing units could have alleviated the need for cues at banks, post office and the like. Yet, the government did little else to change the factors or circumstances that bred the widespread lack of discipline.

Lastly, receivers must be activated before communication solutions can have the desired effect. Many communication planners have stories about a campaign that failed to galvanize the audience to action. Simply putting out information does not guarantee audience involvement or behavioral change. Extra measures must be taken to generate receiver interest, participation and behavior. Locketz[13] cites the case of a national health campaign against schistosomiasis in Surinam. This campaign used an art contest that presented the disease as its theme. This made the health message more interesting for participating school children. Therefore, it is important for integrative communication planners to think of added resources and organization that will ensure campaign resonance with the target audience and generate the needed action.

In thinking about the limitations of communication solutions, planners should consider Suchman[14] and Hornik's[15] distinction between 'theory failures and program failures'. Theory failures result from mistakenly choosing and applying a communication solution to a problem. An example is the African leader who puts policy inadequacies to communication failure. Program failures occur because communication-based solutions have been poorly designed and implemented. Such failures include overestimating the potential reach of a medium or using technical language to convey information to uneducated people.

Hornik discovered a third type of failure based on his evaluation of development communication projects in developing countries. He calls it 'political failure'. The problem of political failure is not so much caused by the political system per se. It arises when planners fail to appraise properly and account for all constraints (opportunities exercised by those holding political power.[16] To be successful, a communication plan must fit the general political climate, and be useful to politicians responsible for the issues it addresses. Politicians shape policies when they are conceived. Invariably, they are the ones controlling the necessary financial and organizational resources to execute the plans. Thus, no matter how frustrating it may be, it is not sufficient for the planner to simply avoid theory and program failure. Planners must anticipate and address emergent political failures.[17]

What Communication Can Do

Despite its inherent limitations, there are many roles communication and communication technology can play in integrative communication planning. Hornik[18] extrapolates these roles from his analysis of agriculture and nutrition programs in developing countries. One role is that of a 'low-cost loudspeaker'. Mass communication media are used to extend the reach of individual communications in development projects. They reach 'large numbers of receivers at a higher level of quality than would be possible were communication to occur in individual communication acts'.[19] As a result, they are an inexpensive and effective way to define, refine or conceptualize an integration problem and to present applicable solutions and strategies for public debate. Until such issues are in the media, most people are not aware of the extent of ethnic or religious discord in communities outside their own. Nor do they actively consider the implications of such discord on national cohesion. It is often through media frames that social and political problems are defined, refined, analyzed or solved.

Another role is that of an 'institutional catalyst'. By its existence, a mass communication campaign can mobilize particular sectors of society. To illustrate this, consider the common practice among African leaders to pay lip service to or to deny the existence of issues or problems of which the public is not yet aware. Once media coverage has broadened awareness of a problem, the potential for public backlash tends to force government officials to react. An example of this is the environmental degradation problem in Nigeria. Environmental destruction caused by oil pollution in the Niger delta went unnoticed for many years until mass media began to cover the activities of the late Ken Saro Wiwa and others opposed to the destruction. This coverage brought mass and international attention to the issues. This attention exerted pressure on the Nigerian government and Shell Oil Company and forced them to compromise. Such experiences indicate that if media are persistent in drawing attention to the origin, causes and solutions to an integration problem, sooner or later people will react.

The cynical corollary of this is the role of 'political lightning rod'. In the same way that media campaigns are used to galvanize action, they are also used to feign action. For example, the power structure can use communication campaigns as a ruse, 'an elaborate scheme to pretend to do something about a problem while really doing nothing substantive in terms of resources and conflict'.[20] This commonly occurs in Africa. Following religious or tribal conflicts, governments usually set up a committee to find the causes of and solutions to the crisis. The establishment of a committee usually gives people the impression that the government is genuinely concerned and taking action. But in reality, the committee's findings are never made public and further action is seldom ever taken.

Another role for media is that of 'maintainer'. Planners often work on the assumption that media campaigns can change behavior, at least sometimes and in certain areas. For this reason, they also give serious thought to how to sustain and reinforce these changes. Communication plays an important role through repeated messages over a period of time. However, the long-term duration must be planned and budgeted for at the beginning.

Finally, there is the role of 'feedback accelerator'. Successful campaigns are those that enable receivers to interact quickly with the sender. This interaction provides an early evaluation of the success or failure of the campaign. In a campaign against ethnic violence, for example, the success of the campaign will depend on witnesses committing to call the police immediately. The campaign may advocate, 'If you see or know anyone committing acts of violence against another person, call 01-254-378 immediately. Don't hesitate'. Such information included in the campaign allows witnesses an immediate opportunity to do what was suggested. Other devices are also used to facilitate interaction between senders and receivers. These include hotlines, suggestion and complaint boxes, prepaid surveys, telephone polls, computer bulletin boards, to mention a few.

Steps in Communication Planning

It is knowledge of the strengths and weaknesses that the communication planner applies specific steps. Inett and Shewchuk[21] describe the series of steps communication planners should follow:

- Research and analysis (Taking stock of the current situation)
- Goals and objectives
- Identify target audience
- Identify key messages
- Communication strategy, and
- Evaluation.

Step 1 – Research and Analysis (Taking stock of the current situation)

Communications planning begins with research. The topic of research has been dealt with comprehensively in Chapter 9. Therefore, only aspects relative to communication planning are presented here. Planning research can be as extensive as conducting a nationwide public opinion poll or as simple as conducting a focus group among 10 to 12 members of specific communities. Regardless of its scope, research should reveal the state of integration in a country and the various conditions that affect it. It should present a clear picture of the integration goals that help to determine a good course of action for using communications. Research should be driven by the following questions:

- What resources are already available? Information, people, money, time and public support are all valuable assets. Determining which assets are already available and which ones are needed will help in the decision regarding the scope of the communication program.
- Is the any previous research on this issue to help the current effort? And is there any need for research now?
- Has this type of communication activity taken place before? If so, what were the results?
- What are the major communication opportunities for the intended research? What is the likelihood that media in certain parts of the country will strongly favor the integrative cause and will willingly promote it? Or is there an upcoming meeting of traditional or local leaders where the integrative message can be presented?
- What are the communication obstacles? Is there sufficient funding to sustain a campaign? Or are there communities where persuasion cannot break their resistance?

Once all of the relevant data are gathered, they need to be analyzed to determine what will be helpful in framing the communication plan. This analysis enables the planner to:

- Define the communication challenge;
- Identify support or opposition and their underlying motivations;
- Help to analyze audiences, order their importance for the research goal, and determine how each audience perceives the nation; and
- Suggest what messages should be directed to different communities.

Step 2 – Goals and Objectives

Following data gathering, it is necessary to specify goals and objectives for the integrative communication plan. Is the goal to provide information about the benefits of integration? Or is it to promote a specific type of integrative behavior, for example, intermarriage among distrusting ethnic groups? Or is it to activate support for a particular government strategy? Or is it some combination of these objectives? The goals and objectives must be clearly and specifically defined. Defining the goals and objectives or what is to be achieved will help to focus on the 'who,' 'why,' 'when' and 'how' of the communication plan. Goals are the overall changes to be made. Objectives are the short-term measurable steps to research that goal. For example, if your goal is to increase community support for nation-building initiatives, your objectives might be:

- To promote intermarriage;
- To promote concern for other ethnic nationalities in the country;
- To promote respect for the nation and its symbols;
- To promote emotional attachment to the nation;
- To inform people of the dangers of tribal conflicts;
- To reinforce the virtues of the country; and
- To promote accountability in government, such as sufficient funding.

When deciding goals and objectives, it is important to answer the following questions:

- Are you trying to provide new information?
- Are you calling for action?, or
- Are you seeking to change behavior?

Whatever the objective, it should be expressed as a clear statement of what the planner hopes to achieve. It should be specific, realistic and prioritized in order of importance. It should also be measurable and under the control of the planner. All these qualities are important because objectives are the baseline against which the results of communication plans are measured. Windahl, et. al present a schema to help determine who ultimately defines the problem, goals and solutions in communication planning and where (see Figure 10.1 below). The schema indicates that problems, goals and solutions are defined within or outside a community or social system. Subsequently, the communication planners' role will change according to the strategy chosen.

Figure 10.1 Four Communication Strategies

Communication Solution Defined

	Traditional communication information campaign	External impetus requiring internal follow-through
Outside the System		*External Initiative*
	1	2
PROBLEM AND GOALS DEFINITION	Internal impetus requiring external follow-through	Grassroots Initiative
Inside the System	*Communication Support*	
	3	4

Reprinted by permission of Sage Publications Ltd from Sven Windahl, Benno Signitzer with Jean T. Olson, Using Communication Theory, P. 40, Copyright, (Owner, 1991)

The first cell in the Figure presents the traditional communication/information campaign approaches, where the problem, goals and objectives and solutions are conceptualized by people outside the target community or social system. Critics have labeled this strategy, which typifies the model promoted under modernization theory, by adherents of the now discredited dominant paradigm, as undemocratic and authoritarian. The main problem with this strategy is that people are not easily motivated by communication coming from the outside with goals set by others. Communication planners may prefer this approach, however, because it gives them total control over message content.

Cell 2 illustrates situations where the government of a country suggests that ethnic and religious communities at odds get along, but are doing nothing more to facilitate or encourage more cordial relationships. In this strategy, the government believes that the communities will take upon themselves to evolve strategies that can achieve the government's goals. The main task for the communication planner in this approach is to promote the goals and objectives and to motivate the target group of the social system to find its own solutions. This is sometimes called 'dumping the problems on your doorstep'. Like the traditional strategy, it may fail to motivate people to generate the desired solutions.

In Cell 3, the community or communities involved determine the problem, goals and objectives, but the solution is left to people outside the community. For example, the need to get along, as well as the goal of getting along, is determined by the communities involved in an ethnic or religious conflict. For whatever reason, they may be unable to come up with solutions. So they approach federal and state governments or outside groups or organizations for the solution. In this strategy, the planner provides the communication resources to achieve community goals. An obvious advantage of this strategy is that people can be motivated because they themselves defined the problem and the end goals. However, there is the problem of outsiders not knowing the kind of communication support that will best serve the group in question.

Cell 4 is appropriately called the grassroots initiative because the target group or social system determines the problem, goals and solutions. This allows a problem to be solved without cost to those outside the group. The planner in this strategy merely acts as a facilitator, helping with logistics for communication initiatives designed by the group. This has been the strategy adopted in many development support communications in Africa in recent years. Nevertheless, the extent to which the approach is deemed suitable for integrative communication will depend on the degree to which warring communities accept national unity as a priority. Assuming that is possible, this strategy would be the better accepted in communication planning.

Step 3 – Identify Target Audiences

Not everyone in a diverse country will go against integration. As Lau[22] notes, there are individual and contextual influences on group identification. Thus, integration is more likely to be opposed by specific communities that feel some sense of disconnection or fear domination by the national community. Messages aimed at promoting integration should therefore be directed at specific audiences.

Determining the specific target audience is the next logical step in communication planning. As the planner thinks about the people and communities that need to be influenced, he or she may consider stratifying them by demographics and psychographics. Each group must be listed and analyzed. That is, they should be sorted by age, gender, education, income, and location of residence, and also by likes and dislikes, motivations and lifestyle. The more clearly the audience is described, the easier it is to choose the message and communication vehicles. When analyzing the individuals or communities, it is important to consider the following:

- What do they already know about the state of integration in the country?
- How likely are they to respond to messages calling for integrative behavior and why are they responding as they do?
- What factors are influencing the audiences receiving the message—for example, what effect may poverty, literacy, or cultural sensitivity be having on their responses?
- Are there any difficulties in communicating with each group and what are the root causes of these difficulties?

Possible target audiences could include mass communication representatives, government officials, business people, professional people, educators and ordinary people. Knowing the particular characteristics of each group will help in determining what to say and how to say it.

Step 4 – Identify Key Messages

Once the objectives of the campaign and target audiences are known, the basic idea or set of ideas that the planner wishes to communicate should be formulated. This begins with audience appraisal. What does the audience already know about the issue? What do they need to know? And what does that planner want to tell them or involve them? Following this, the planner develops the message or messages that he or she wants the target audience to hear and believe. Each message should be written as a simple, specific statement. To motivate people, the message must indicate how audience needs will be met. A clear statement of benefits to the audiences will help ensure that the message is received, processed, understood, and acted upon.

Step 5 – Choose communication vehicle

Next, the planner can choose the communication vehicle or vehicles to deliver the structured message. Figure 10.2 lists the possible media channels to reach the target group. According to the Figure, there are two broad types of channels to consider: mass media and group media. Mass media make the better choice when the goal is to reach a diverse group of people separated by space and distance simultaneously. Group media are more efficient in interpersonal and small group situations. In other to make the best choice, the planner must undertake analysis of the communication channel. Among the questions to be answered are what are the strengths and limitations of each medium and does the medium fit the message?
    Once the analysis is completed, the planner will be able to narrow the choices of communication vehicles. The vehicle chosen should be one that:

- Is the most effective in reaching the specified target audience and influence them with the message(s);
- Fits the resources available; and
- Delivers the best desired goals and outcomes.

Timing is an important consideration when choosing the communication vehicle. The planner may not want messages to compete with other significant events. The planner must also decide the campaign's duration. If it is short, the frequencies of messages may be increased to achieve the desired effect. If the campaign is to be sustained, messages may be repeated at longer intervals. The campaign's duration depends, of course, on budget. Although budget might pose a severe limitation, there are many effective inexpensive communication vehicles.

Figure 10.2 Possible Media Channels to Reach Target Audiences

Mass Media	Group Media
Banners	Audiotape
Billboards	Blackboards
Booklets	Drama
Calendars	Extension Kits
Cinema Spots	Films
Exhibits	Flannel Boards
Newspapers	Flip Charts
Pamphlets	Games
Posters	Models
Stamps	Slides
Stickers	Transparencies
Television	Wall Charts
Radio	Videotape

Source: Planning Communication Support for Rural Development Campaigns; Assifi and French; UNDP Asia; 1986.

In recent years, entertainment-education has been seen as a highly effective way to communicate development messages. Singhal and Rogers[23] define entertainment-education as 'the process of purposefully designing and implementing a media message to both entertain and educate, in order to increase audience knowledge about an educational issue, create favorable attitudes, and change overt behaviors'. Similar to social marketing and health promotion, entertainment-education is designed to produce social change at both the macro and micro levels. To do so, it focuses on using entertainment media such as soap operas, songs, cartoons, comics and theater to present information that can result in pro-social behavior. Entertainment-education is not an entirely new concept. Entertainment has been used for social purposes for centuries. What is new is the systematic research and implementation of educational, pro-social messages in entertainment media throughout the world.

Step 6 – Evaluation

Finally, the planner must formulate an evaluation scheme to assess the campaign, either at the front-end, back-end or both. Generally, public communication campaigns use four basic methods of evaluation.[24] Table 10.2 presents each method, along with its definition and examples of questions it may address. Coffman[25] writes that the first method—formative evaluation is usually done at the front end of a project; the last three methods—process, outcome, and impact— usually occur at the back end. She says information collected during formative evaluation helps to shape the campaign. This evaluation is done during the creative design stage. Valente[26] lists the primary functions of formative evaluations:

- They help to define the scope of the problem;
- Identify possible campaign strategies;
- Provide information about the target audience;
- Sense what messages work best and how they should be framed;
- Determine the most credible messengers, and
- Identify the factors that can help or hinder the campaign.

Coffman adds that this usually involves testing issue awareness and saliency through public opinion polls or extended interviews conducted within the target population or focus groups.

Process evaluation assesses the overall implementation of a campaign on how well it was delivered. This involves tracking the distribution of campaign materials or the amount of media time bought or received. It also estimates how many people the campaign reached; however, reliable results are more difficult. Coffman says that while process evaluations are important, they do not capture campaign effects and are not meaningful in terms of providing effect or causal explanations.

Table 10.1 Four Evaluation Types

Evaluation Type	Definition/Purpose	Example Questions
1. Formative	Assesses the strengths and weaknesses of campaign materials and strategies before or during the campaign's implementation.	• How does the campaign's target audience think about the issue? • What messages work with what audiences? • Who are the best messengers?
2. Process	*Measures effort* and the direct outputs of campaigns-what and how much was accomplished. Examines the campaign's implementation and how the activities involved are working.	• How many materials have been put out? • What has been the campaign's reach? • How many people have been reached?
3. Outcome	*Measures effect* and changes that result from the campaign. Assesses outcomes in the target populations or communities that come about as a result of grantee strategies and activities. Also measures policy changes.	• Has there been any affective change (beliefs, attitudes, social norms)? • Has there been any behavior change? • Have any policies changed?
4. Impact	*Measures community-level change* or longer-term results that are achieved as a result of the campaign's aggregate effects on individuals' behavior and the behavior's sustainability. Attempts to determine whether the campaign caused the effects.	• Has the behavior resulted in its intended outcomes (e.g., higher incidence identification, integrative, and political awareness) • Has there been any systems-level change?

Published with permission from Harvard Family Research Project from Coffman, J. (2002). Public Communication campaign evaluation: An environmental scan of challenges, criticism, pracfice, and opportunities. (p. 13). Cambrigde, MA: Harvard Family Research Project

Outcome evaluation measures the overall effect of the campaign in terms of changes in attitudes, behavior or policy. Has the audience received the intended message or has it gotten a totally different message? Has it acted according to the planner's intentions or in the opposite direction? These are critical questions that must be answered after the campaign has run its course. By undertaking this summative evaluation of the campaign, the planner can learn how well the plans or procedures have worked with various target audiences. The planner can also learn which activities have had the most effect and which parts have failed. Various formal measurement techniques may be used for comparing results to objectives. They include readership surveys, attitude audits, focus group sessions, content analysis and experiments. An informal evaluation can be done by assessing media coverage on the issue and by reactions received in talking to people. The evaluation should constitute the foundation for the next communication plan. According to Coffman, impact evaluation is the most resource-intensive in terms of design and implementation. Its objective is to produce with near certainty the most definitive answers about whether the campaign has delivered its intended results. This requires an experimental design that may be expensive and resource-intensive. Usually, considerable cost is involved in 'getting a large enough sample to observe effects, being able to support data collection with a treatment and control or comparison group, and being able to support multiple waves of data collection'.[27]

Conclusion

This chapter has argued that communication planning is essential for the formulation of successful integrative communication strategies. In making this argument, the chapter reviewed the strengths and weaknesses of communication and discussed the seven steps associated with communication planning. In this discussion, an attempt was made to demonstrate how each step applied to the context of integrative communication. As much as possible, integrative issues involving the recipient community were used to illustrate the various steps in communication planning.

The necessity for the presented argument is illustrated by the *Edo*[28] proverb, which states: 'The stone that a person sees thrown at him/her will not blind him or her'. This proverb suggests that vigilance produces better anticipation of outcomes and effects. Effective communication planning is the attempt to maintain vigilance over every aspect of communication, including the establishment of goals and objectives, the structure of messages and choice of channels, and response to audience feedback.

Notes

1   Ibad Rashdi, 'Communication and rural development,' *Pakissan.com* (February 19, 2003).
2   Pat Inett and John Shewchuk, 'Communication planning for organizations,' *Factsheet* (April 2003): 1.
3   Sven Windahl and Benno Signitzer with Jean T. Olson, *Using Communication Theory: An introduction to planned communication*, London: Sage Publications, 1992:19.
4   Ibid. p. 19.
5   Inett and Shewchuk, 'Communication planning for organizations,' p. 1.
6   Ibid. p. 19.
7   Ibid.
8   Ibid. p. 30.
9   Ibid. p. 31.
10   Ibid. p. 31.
11   Alufa Yemsi, 'War against indiscipline and corruption,' *U.S. African Eye* 9, 12 (June 15, 2001): 39.
12   Robert Stock, 'Environmental sanitation in Nigeria: Colonial and contemporary,' *Review of African Political Economy* 42, 15 (Summer 1988): 19-31.
13   L. Locketz, 'Health education in rural Surinam: Use of videotape in a national campaign against schistosomiasis,' *Bulletin of the Panamerican Health Organization* 10 (1976): 219-226.
14   E. Suchman, *Evaluative Research* (New York: Russell Sage Foundation, 1967).
15   R. C. Hornik, *Development communication: Information, agriculture and nutrition in the Third World* (New York: Longman, 1988).
16   Windahl and Signitzer with Olson, *Using Communication Theory*, p. 38.
17   Ibid. p. 38.
18   Hornik, *Development communication*.
19   Windahl and Signitzer with Olson, *Using Communication Theory*, p. 36.
20   Ibid. p. 37.
21   Inett and Shewchuk, 'Communication planning for organizations,' pp. 1-7.
22   Richard R. Lau, 'Individual and contextual influences on group identification,' *Social Psychology Quarterly* 53, 3 (1989): 220-231.
23   Arvind Singhal and Everett Rogers, 'Entertainment Education'.
24   National Cancer Institute, *Making health communication campaigns work: A planner's guide* [Electronic Version], Washington, DC: Author, 1992.
25   Julia Coffman, *Public communication campaign evaluation: An environmental scan of challenges, criticisms, practice, and opportunities*, Cambridge, Massachusetts: Harvard Family Research Project, 2003.
26   T. Valente, 'Evaluating communication campaigns,' In R. E. Rice and C. K. Atkin, eds., *Public communication campaigns*, Thousand Oaks, CA: Sage, 2001: 105-124.
27   Ibid. p. 3.
28   Edo is a language spoken by an ethnic group, residing in the Midwestern region of Nigeria.

Chapter 11

A Model of
Integrative Communications

African countries, especially those in the sub-Saharan region, are paying a high price for social heterogeneity. This price includes the inability to achieve social mobilization for development. Throughout sub-Saharan Africa, a mentality of 'every man or woman for himself or herself' seems to permeate group and individual attitudes and behavior. This mentality is generally reinforced by persistent inefficient and subjective economic management, improper functioning of national institutions and persistent political instability.[1] As recent studies show, ethnic diversity may make a society more susceptible to 'corruption, political instability and slow economic growth, due to political conflict and lack of cooperation among ethnic groups'.[2] For example, Edward Miguel found that a 'higher level of local ethnic diversity is associated with sharply lower primary school funding and worse facilities in Western Kenya'. He found that distinct and deeply-rooted types of ethno-linguistic and religious differentiations severely limited social pressures for contributions to schools. He notes that ethnically diverse communities in western Kenya were less able than ethnically homogenous communities to pressure parents to make school payments.

Another price is the misplacement of economic policies and priorities. Easterly and Levine note:

> Although ethnic diversity is not significantly correlated with every economic indicator, the evidence is consistent with the hypothesis that ethnic diversity adversely affects many public policies associated with economic growth.[3]

They say ethnically diverse economies have made it more difficult to agree on public good and policies. To illustrate this point, Asante observes that the very structure of the African economy is one of dependency rather than self-reliance. He says this dependency obliges Africa to keep producing commodities such as coffee it does not need and its people do not consume. Production is geared toward export to the detriment of domestic consumption. People consume few of the commodities they produce while depending on others to produce what they need. This dependency is further complicated by the existence of a large informal sector of economic activity supported by weak institutional capabilities.[4]

A third price is the mentality of divide-and-conquer or exploit-the-fundamental-ignorance-of-the-masses for personal gain that seems to permeate political cognition, attitude and behavior in most of Africa. Asante says this mentality is partly responsible for the prolonged absence of basic human rights, individual freedoms and democratic participation in many countries. Even though democratization or political liberalization has occurred in a few countries in recent years, the general mental state of people across much of the continent is one where 'people feel alienated and unable to devote their energies to development and productivity'.[5] Asante explains why this political condition is not conducive for national development:

> Indeed, in places where injustices are the norm rather than the exceptions, it is almost impossible to expect a momentum of progress. What you find often is disillusion, lethargy, repression, civil disorder and an environment where fear and man's inhumanity against man prevail. Given such circumstances, people do not work hard or produce optimally, and naturally if people do not work hard, the pace of development, if any, is at snail's speed.[6]

When the pace of development is slow, accrued gains are small and difficult to distribute equitably across diverse groups in a social system. Even in a healthy economy, the spatial impact of development is almost always uneven. This disparity in the distribution of economic gains produces unhealthy competition among differing ethnic and religious groups. Drake[7] notes that this competition exacerbates regional differences and tension. Easterly and Levine[8] add that it sets the stage for political instability. Invariably, all of this leads to social disintegration. As the main thesis of this book states, without social integration, development is difficult to attain or sustain.

It is fair to say that the consequences of social heterogeneity keep Africa's development in a state of permanent crisis. It is a crisis in which government and people are trapped in poverty and debt and in danger of being left behind as other nations become richer and stronger. The depth of the crisis is such that merely building physical infrastructure has not helped to overcome its concomitant social and political malaise. As Ouma-Onyango explains, 'Emphasis on physical infrastructure has failed to cement a heterogeneous society'.[9] This is because the soft and intangible infrastructure has not been given adequate attention. The infrastructure never developed to the degree required to enable it to deliver the necessary basis of commonness and unity in diversity that hold socially diverse nation states together.

Given these circumstances, national integration must remain a cardinal objective of national development in many parts of Africa. The continuing challenge is how to ensure that disparate peoples in Africa are motivated to a greater degree by national sentiments rather than by primordial attachments of ethnicity, kinship and religion. Many countries have segments of their population who are yet to cultivate an appropriate appreciation for the supremacy of nationhood. Nor do they yet understand the place of the goodwill of each citizen in the subsistence of nationhood. Geoffrey Oswald[10] was accurate when he opined that for as long as tribal words and adjectives fill the air and the sense of nationness continues to evaporate without trace, African countries may find their stability threatened for years to come. It is ironic that, to date, there have been hardly any specific communication theories or strategies devoted to national integration. Scholars and planners have tended to subsume integrative strategies within general development theories and policies.

Modernization Theory

Prior to the 1980s, 'modernization theory' was the principal framework that governed integrative communication thinking and planning. This theory is a linear theoretical model of development in which communications is seen as the intervening variable between socio-economic factors and modernization. As Sonaike[11] explains, theorists of the period (Daniel Lerner, Wilbur Schramm, Karl Deutsch, Lucien Pye and others) accorded mass communications 'a place of honor' in development planning. They believed mass media would catalyze a country's effort to keep pace with the demanding requirements of the modern state, as well as rupture those ties that bind a population to an existence of collective poverty and ignorance.[12] However, Coleman[13] pondered if emphasis on modernization could reduce racial and tribal attachments and cleavages. He observed that elites tend to use their ethnic or racial group as a base or springboard for seeking political power.

Nevertheless, in keeping with the postulation of modernization theory, most African countries established mass media facilities. In fact, as Sydney Head[14] put it, they saw the establishment of a national media system as a rite of passage into true nationhood. But it soon became abundantly clear the mere existence of media services was not sufficient, in and of itself, to bring about national integration. In some countries, the media were politicized and this tended to exacerbate divisive tendencies. In Nigeria, for example, media politicization entrenched deep rivalries between the federal and state governments, 'between the states, and between ethnic groups within the states'.[15]

Oduko[16] cites the case of Lagos State Television (LTV) to illustrate how this politicization gave rise to a competitive structure of federal and state broadcasting. He notes that prior to LTV's inception, the federal government adopted a policy permitting state television stations only on the UHF band. However, the various states in Nigeria saw this policy as a directive to prevent them from operating independent stations. At the time, television sets available in Nigeria could only receive VHF signals. The states countered that the federal government desired to maintain political advantage over the states by monopolizing telecasting. In defiance of this directive, LTV began broadcasting on the VHF band without a license. No formal order was issued to ban LTV telecasts. However, the federal government's Nigerian Television Authority (NTA) began to jam LTV broadcasts. LTV audiences were infuriated. The Lagos state government asked other states to pressure the federal government to permit states to broadcast on VHF. Several did.

Today, there is a parallel system of national and state broadcasting systems in Nigeria, supplemented by a small private system. Similar politicizations have been found in Benin, Ivory Coast,[17] Kenya, South Africa and a number of other African countries.

In sum, modernization theory did not help the integrative cause of African countries. Instead, it intensified existing ethnic fragmentation and attachments. In many countries, the sentimental attachment to ethnic identity posed a severe threat to participation in a national system, thereby hindering the development of national identity.[18] However, it should be noted that Collier[19] has presented empirical data showing that the mere existence of ethnic fragmentation is not by itself dysfunctional. According to Collier, the negative effects of ethnic fragmentation usually derive from the action of elite groups who manipulate and subvert ethnic loyalties for personal gain.

Humane Development

Based on the lessons learned from the failures of modernization theory in the 1980s, development communication scholars proposed the alternative principle of 'humane development'. This principle marked a departure from emphasis on growth in economic indicators and modernization. It stressed achievement of national development through 'community involvement, interactive two-way communication and small media'.[20] Stating its basic premise, Moemeka wrote:

> True and effective community development requires the participation of every segment of the nation—rural, urban, city, suburban; and every sector—government and private and public business. These groups and sectors must establish new social relations with one another before they can collectively be effective. It is the task of development communication to facilitate the growth and development of such human relationships.[21]

Accordingly, proponents argued that communication in humane development should be more than merely a way of exchanging problem-solving messages. They said it should generate empathy or psychological mobility and raise aspirations, cultivate a willingness to work hard to meet those aspirations, teach new skills and stimulate local involvement in development activities.

Indeed, if African countries are to experience complete and long-lasting national development, individual and group goals or aspirations must be consistent with those of the nation at large. This convergence of micro and macro outlooks is a prerequisite for national involvement, and national involvement is a cohesive mechanism. But under what conditions can society have sufficient participation to enable development in Africa without introducing forces of cleavage that will undermine national cohesion? This is a question begging an urgent answer in light of the ethnic violence that continues to plague emergent and existing democracies in Africa. As Makonnen notes, African democracies 'may have relatively free and fair elections from time to time, but they are democracies only in name and not in deed'.[22] The majority of them are ethnically based regimes with pretentions of liberty and freedom.

Take for example, Nigeria, Africa's largest democracy. In mid April 2003, legislative elections were held, but these were marred by ethnic and religious violence. A week later, presidential elections were also held. While this was considered largely peaceful, ethnic violence was recorded in some states, including Bayelsa, Delta and Rivers.[23] Similarly, the election in Ivory Coast was subsequently followed by a civil war prompted by the disillusion of certain ethnic groups. This is in sharp contrast to Collier's finding that incidence of ethnic violence is fewer in democracies than in dictatorships.[24]

Overall, it is evident that the philosophical change from the 'top-down' approach of modernization theory to a 'bottom-up' approach of humane development has done little to strengthen interethnic relations in many parts of Africa. The main reason for this appears to be the politicization of development theories and practice. The selection, planning and allocation of resources to development projects have been subject to political machinations at both domestic and international levels. This politicization has impeded efforts to erode differences in social structures and values between ethnic groups. It has also allowed the traditional ways of life to sustain a variety of negative influences on the development of national consciousness.

According to Nelson, several factors impede interethnic relations among most people in Africa's rural areas. These include:

- Enmities arising from ancient warfare;
- Language barriers;
- Religious convictions; and
- Jealousies over access to educational and economic opportunities.[25]

An example is Cameroon. There, interethnic tensions are clearly visible in attitudes toward the Fulani, who have dominated the north—initially through conquest and subjugation. These tensions have achieved political prominence in the modern state. Nelson adds that many other groups also dislike the aggressive attitudes and superior economic position of the Bamileke. He notes that even though a certain unity exists among peoples of the western highlands and those of the forested region in the south, a degree of cleavage created by Roman Catholic and Protestant religious competition still exists in southern Cameroon.[26]

Simmons and Montagne[27] present another example in Nigeria. As in Cameroon, the Hausa/Fulani group in the north has dominated political power and the military in Nigeria since independence in 1960. This has apparently led the Hausa/Fulani to believe that this situation is part of the divine order of things. However, Mogekwu[28] notes that the Hausa/Fulani feeling of superiority has incensed some of the other ethnic groups who also want to assert their own rights as a people. These other groups have violently resisted the Hausa/Fulani domination from time to time. For example, in the early 1990s, the Katafs of southern Zaria in Kaduna state began to show signs of resentment in their relations with the Hausas living in their region. Such feelings of resentment came to a head in 1992, setting in motion a catastrophe that resulted in hundreds of deaths on both sides. In Kogi state, ethnic distrust among the three major tribes that make up the state[29] was a frequent source of worry during the parliamentary and presidential elections of April 2003.

In a similar vein, Mogekwu[30] found that the past decade of fighting in Liberia is related to the mutual distrust between two ethnic groups represented by Charles Taylor and Alhaji Koroma. In Kenya, long-standing mutual suspicion and distrust among different ethnic groups have created an environment for the frequent outbursts of violence that have occurred over the years. Throughout the continent, some ethnic groups like the Temnes of Sierra Leone and the Urhobos of Nigeria are stigmatized as 'aggressive'. Unfortunately, rather than dispel this image, members of these groups validate it by deliberately trying to live up to it. Thus, they project an aggressive image as a way of intimidating other groups. Mogekwu says it is not unusual for a Temne to threaten a member of another ethnic group with violent acts just to prove that he or she is indeed a Temne. They usually threaten, 'I will show you I am a Temne'.[31]

These examples suggest that implementation of development theories have not significantly altered the basis of 'outgroup' members' evaluation in Africa. As Mogekwu aptly notes, throughout Africa ethno-linguistic identities remain the basis for prejudgment, intolerance, bigotry, xenophobia, ethnocentrism and the like. He says Africans have the tendency to place premature cognitive fixes on others prior to consideration of the relevant evidence. He says members of one group may reject outright members of another group simply on the basis of ethnic/linguistic differences. This is what breeds the readiness to act violently.[32]

Mogkwu notes another lingering effect of the persistence of ethno-linguistic identities. This is the propensity among dominant tribal groups (whose dominance may not necessarily accrue from numbers) to try to impose their language on others. He writes that some dominant groups in African hold their language superior out of sheer ethnocentrism. For example, he notes that, in Algeria, the dominant group has tried to impose Arabic as the language for all official transactions. Speakers of the Berber language have vehemently opposed this. In most cases, the dominant group seeking imposition of its language on others are those occupying positions of political and economic power, and others have to look up to them for patronage. In some cases, whether one receives patronage depends on a demonstrated willingness and effort to be integrated into the dominant group. A typical demonstration of this integration is learning the language of the dominant group and overtly showing off one's proficiency in it. This is still the case even if the language in question is not the official language or lingua franca. The supplicant usually believes that he or she needs the language to 'get along'.[33]

These examples testify to the need to reverse certain social trends before African countries can evolve into true nationhood. This reversal must involve building long-lasting and mutually rewarding exchange-relationships among the diverse groups that make up the majority of African countries. Such exchange-relationships must act to subjugate ethno-linguistic pressures to nationalistic counter-pressures. In building these relationships, communication must be seen as an important enabler and nurturer. As Rogers notes, 'Communication is the process in which participants create and share information with one another in order to reach mutual understanding'.[34] But how is this communication to be conducted or studied? To answer this question, it is necessary to present a conceptual model.

The EDNA-4 Model of Integrative Communications

Any conceptual approach for communicating social integration should be anchored in a dialogic process that grants participants sensitivity to cultural, historical, economic and political realities. The proposed model is called 'The EDNA-4 model of integrative communications. EDNA is the acronym comprising the first letter of each of the four categories of the model: enablers, domain, nurturers, and application. Although EDNA is labeled a model, the intent is not to prescribe a schema that is applied in a mechanistic fashion. Rather it is to offer a space for recognizing and dealing with:

- Differences in meaning as disparate individual and groups discuss the development, execution and evaluation of socio-political and economic programs;
- Differences in perceptions, interpretations and judgments, feelings and intentions relative to individuals and group acts, actions and activities (especially in positions of power); and
- The ramifications of these influences on social cohesion.

The EDNA-4 model encourages attention to both the rhetorical and relational functions of communication; it advises that the process should be engaged each time there is need to converge outlooks among disparate groups and interests. It is important for integrative communication planners to employ a dialogic process that affirms the pervasiveness of cultural exigencies in the life of pluralistic social systems. Moreover this approach challenges social, economic and political communications to address cohesion issues at the macro (policy, government, societal, and international) level as well as the traditional micro level of development policy implementation. The efficacy of this approach therefore relates to its potential to aid accomplishment of the altruistic goals stated by Ali Mazrui.[35] He advocates nationalization of what is sectional or ethnic, indigenization of what is alien, idealization of what is indigenous and emphasis on what is African. In this context, the model incorporates existing theories and frameworks in communication and cohesion studies.[36]

The EDNA-4 model is diagrammed in Figure 11-1. As the figure illustrates, each of the model's four dimensions is dynamically interrelated and interdependent.   So are each of the four categories contained within each dimension. The first dimension of the model is *environment*, the four categories of which are social differentiation, history, economic conditions and political situation. This dimension provides the impetus for social interaction.[37]

Figure 11.1   EDNA-4 Model of Integrative Communication

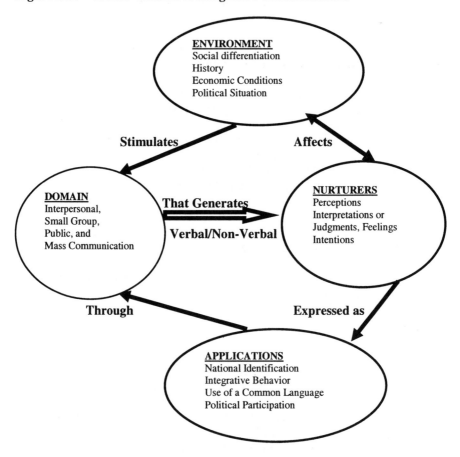

Social differentiation

The basic context for discussing any integration problem in Africa is social differentiation. One simply cannot talk of conflict in an African country without considering the role played by ethnic, linguistic, and/or religious diversity. To this end, integration policies and strategies must be geared toward creating a new supranational community that supersedes or overshadows ethnic identities. This requires information, education and communication.

History

The important role which history plays in forming national identity has been discussed fully in Chapter 5. To recapitulate, all nations are a product of history. History is the main mechanism through which nations establish and differentiate their identities. History provides the perennial structural context in which the meaning of national events is generated and realized. History thus provides the elements that are subsequently extrapolated into national traits or characteristics, including culture, language, religion, and politics. Therefore, it would be a veritable act of omission to believe that one has assessed Africa's integration problems sufficiently without taking stock of the historical context. It is clear, as noted in Chapter 5, that the dissemination of common history should be seen as a quintessential part of the national integration process.[38]

Economic conditions

During times of plenty, the problem of national integration is often latent in a pluralistic country, especially if economic policies have not been subject to ethnic and religious manipulation. The reverse is true in austere times. When the economy is bad and resources are scarce, ethnic diversity tends to translate from a cultural phenomenon into an economic one. Different groups begin to compete unwittingly for the scarce resources. When this competition exists in an atmosphere of corruption and mismanagement (as is often found in Africa), ethnic and religious interests tend to be elevated above all others. In countries like the Democratic Republic of Congo, Ivory Coast, Liberia and Sierra Leone, this combination has resulted in violent ethnic conflict. Therefore, the state of the economy is an integrative consideration that African countries must address with appropriate policies and strategies. It is important to ensure that the country's economy is sufficiently healthy to minimize divisive tendencies.

Political situation

Africa's political situation can be summarized into two main trends. The first is the preponderance of authoritarian regimes. Although a number of countries have moved towards political liberalization in recent years, it is fair to say that autocratic or one-party states still dominate the continent. Many of these have justified their existence by claiming to be the only force of stability in a volatile political environment. But more often than not, this dominance becomes a basis for political conflict that inevitably upsets system stability.

The second trend is the manipulation of ethnicity by unscrupulous political elites. It should be noted, however, that in most cases ethnicity is not mobilized among the lower classes to a great extent because there is usually no political structure to mobilize it.[39] Most of the time, ethnicity is principally a cultural phenomenon.[40] Every now and then, an African politician comes along who considers it astute to exploit ethnic diversity for political expediency. Like the late Samuel Doe of Liberia[41] or Daniel Arap Moi of Kenya, these leaders reserve key government positions for members of their ethnic group. They discriminate against other ethnic groups, whom they consider dangerous. By doing so, they introduce the ethnic element as the most significant variable in their countries' politics. In these countries, as in others, this nepotism creates a basis for volatility in governance. As a result, when programs are designed to address the root causes of national disintegration in Africa, recognition is often given to the need to discuss the volatility of the political situation.

The second dimension of EDNA-4 is the communication *domain* in which the social, historical, political and economic issues affecting national integration are normally discussed. The main domains are interpersonal, small group, public and mass communication. Interactions in these domains serve many functions. But the most relevant of these to integrative communication are those identified by Thunberg, Novak, Rosengren and Sigurd:[42]

- *The expressive function.* Individuals and groups express themselves effectively so as to create an identity for themselves and their group.
- *The social function.* Through interaction, people develop a sense of community and reach consensus on various issues.
- *The information function.* Through communication, individuals and their groups share and receive information and increase their knowledge.
- *The control activation function.* Communication leads to joint action, modifying the environment and improving the situation of individuals and their groups.

Windahl, Signitzer and Olson[43] note that these functions are related to one another. They note that when communication is used to satisfy one function, other functions are fulfilled as well. As a result, mastering these functions may enhance the ability of individuals and groups to accomplish certain objectives, such as social integration and empowerment.

Interpersonal Communication

This is the communication that occurs when we interact on a one-to-one basis, usually in an informal, unstructured and comfortable setting. This domain of communication mostly involves two people, though it may include more than two.[44] It is the main avenue through which dissatisfaction with conditions in a country are initially expressed. For example, persons may express their frustration about joblessness to a family member or friend. This dyadic interaction may trigger involvement in increased discussion, which may produce concerted action. It is important, therefore, that integrative communication strategies are discussed at the lowest possible level of interaction. As Hybels and Weaver note, interpersonal communication offers the greatest opportunity for feedback.[45]

Small-Group Communication

This refers to a small number of people who gather to discuss and to find solutions to a problem. The group must be small enough so that each member has a chance to interact with all other members. Integrative issues may be discussed in small groups. For example, opinion leaders of an ethnic group may meet to discuss the impact of a poor national economy on their community. The occurrence of such meetings in different communities simultaneously may become the wellspring for broader social mobilization. Such meetings have been the genesis for military coups that have destabilized many countries in Africa.

Public Communication

In this communication domain, a speaker or group of speakers delivers a speech to a congregated audience. An example of this is a political rally where a candidate addresses the issues in his or her campaign to a large audience. When applied to social, political and economic issues, public communication can become an effective avenue through which individuals or groups may express their support for, or condemnation of, government policies and strategies. Thus, it can be a vital avenue for stimulating social integration or systemic instability.

Mass Communication

Print and electronic media are generally used to address various issues facing a country. Mass communication contains all of the previously discussed types of communication: interpersonal, small group and public. For example, a television station may air an interview program where two people or a small group of people discuss social, political and economic issues. News reports may cover public demonstrations over a contested policy of strategies. When employed, mass communication targets a large and differentiated mass simultaneously. For this reason, it is the avenue preferred for the mobilization of public opinion. It is no surprise therefore that Africans generally consider mass communication a vital integrative medium.

The third and most critical dimension of the EDNA-4 model is the *nurturers*. Integrative communication and behavior *nurturers* include perceptions, interpretations and judgments, feelings and intentions by individuals. These are pivotal to the existence of integrative environments because they determine the type of social transaction that occurs in a social system. When there are positive nurturers, social transactions are positive and foster an atmosphere for harmonious coexistence. On the other hand, when negative nurturers predominate, the result may be contentious social environments that breed conflicts inimical to integration.

Perceptions

In its simplest sense, perceptions are the unique social realities we construct by attributing meaning to the social objects and events we encounter in our environment. Perceptions are developed through an internal process by which we select, evaluate, and organize objects and events in our external environment. In this process, we translate the physical energies of elements in our external environment into meaningful experiences.[46]

Three major socio-cultural attributes directly influence our perceptions and the meanings we derive from them. According to Samovar and Porter, these attributes are beliefs/attitudes/values, worldview and social organization.[47] Samovar and Porter note that these attributes are intrinsically linked with our cultural background that directly influences our subjective interpretations of events. They explain that people from different cultures may witness the same event and agree on it in objective terms, but they might disagree completely on its meaning. For example, Gore and Pratten observe that northern, western and eastern tribal groups in Nigeria have divergent imaginings of the country as a nation.[48] According to them, the Hausa-Fulani in the north envision Nigeria as a predominantly Muslim state, where Islamic Sharia law is the dominant legal system. The Yoruba in the west desire a Nigerian confederation where states or regions are operated autonomously along tribal lines. And the Ibos and Ibibios in the east envision a Nigeria where resources are controlled by each state that generates it.

Another example is the different interpretation of patriotic songs by government and rebel forces in Ivory Coast. Take for instance the song 'Free My Country' by the singer Waizey, which has been quite popular in both government and rebel-held areas. Both sides in the war see the song as justifying their respective positions. Both sides believe they are fighting for the liberation of Ivory Coast. The government believes Ivorians must be liberated from the divisive ambitions of rebels. The rebels, on the other hand, believe the Ivory Coast must be liberated from the mal-administration of the government. It should be noted that both sides comprise different ethnic nationalities.

In these examples, cultural background is the main influence that differentiates the perceptions of the different groups. Thus, it is important during planning and implementation of strategies, to carefully consider the influence culturally engineered perceptual differences may have on integrative communication and behavior. This is because socially differentiated people may not always understand integrative messages the way they were intended. These misunderstandings that ensue from this varied perception not only hinder the ability to find common ground among disparate groups, but also can lead to violent conflict.

Interpretations or Judgments

These are the basic premises people establish from the meanings derived from what they see, hear, remember or imagine. These premises act as precursors to the feelings individuals will develop and as a signal to the course of action each person or a group of people will likely take. Take, for instance, the conclusion reached by members of the Movement for the Actualization of the Sovereign State of Biafra (MASSOB) that there is a double standard of policing in Nigeria. MASSOB 'is a collection of quixotic individuals who have existed more on the pages of the newspapers, threatening to actualise the ill-fated Biafran dream, if the situation of the Igbo people is not turned around for the better by the Nigerian state'.[49] MASSOB members believe that Nigerian law enforcement agencies are treating their organization with double standards. They point to the constant arrests, harassments and detentions of their members, while at the same time members of another ethnic-based organization Oodua's Peoples Congress (OPC) are allowed to go free. This has happened despite the fact that the OPC was proscribed by both the Nigerian government and the United States. They state that this double standard of treatment is meted out to them because 'the Igbos are without godfathers in the current dispensation, while OPC can continue to murder because the presidency and the police now speak Yoruba'.[50]

Feelings

Depending on the perceptions formed and the meanings attached to them, individuals or groups may develop emotional reactions to past, present or future sets of circumstances. They may feel happy, sad, intimate, distant, united, disunited, angry or afraid. Feelings form the basis for actions. Therefore, integrative communication planners must anticipate the feelings that may develop from historical, social, political, and economic activities. They must ensure that positive, rather than negative, feelings are developed about the country and its symbols.

Intentions

These are the actions people take on the basis of their perceptions, interpretations and judgments, and feelings. These actions are positive, negative or neutral. If it is true that much of the time we act to vindicate our own set of perceptual and attitudinal orientations, efforts must be made to ensure that are our perceptual and attitudinal sets are consistent with the aims and objectives of national harmony.

The fourth and final dimension of EDNA-4 is the *application*. This comprises four categories: national identification, integrative behavior, use of a common language and political participation. These categories are the intended objectives of positive developments in each of the other three dimensions of the model.

National Identification

As indicated in the introduction to Part I of this book, national identification occurs when individuals or groups perceive and describe themselves as members of a national community.[51] In this manner, they differentiate themselves from members or other nationalities.   There are three broad aspects of national identification. Verbal identification is the oral acknowledgement that one is a member of a national entity. For example, an Englishman would say, 'I am British,' or 'Britain is my country'. A Kenyan would say, 'I am Kenyan,' etc.   Identification with salient national symbols refers to the acknowledgement of the icons symbolizing national existence. Examples of this include the celebration of independence days or wrapping oneself with the national flag at sporting events.   Affective identification is the emotional attachment to the nation and its symbols. For example, people will generally feel a sense of accomplishment when their national teams excel at sporting events. By the same token, people will feel disillusioned if anything happens to bring their nation to disrepute. National identification is generally considered a positive development and is encouraged.

Integrative Behavior

As stated previously in the introduction to Part II, Abernethy[52] defines integrative behavior as the readiness of individuals or groups to work in an organized fashion for common purposes and to behave in a manner conducive to the achievement of these common purposes. Deutsch[53] says it is the mental state in which groups or individuals interlock their communication habits, share meaning, learn to predicts each other's behavior and coordinate each other's action. It is one thing for diverse groups to acknowledge that they are members of a nation, it is quite another for them to behave as one community. For example, members of the Ibo and Hausa groups in Nigeria or Luo and Kalenjin groups in Kenya may readily admit that they are Nigerians or Kenyans, but they may frown on intermarriage between the groups. Thus, cultivating integrative behavior is perhaps the most difficult aspect of the national integration process. History suggests that it takes an inordinate amount of time and requires extraordinary patience on the part of everyone to accomplish.

Use of a Common Language

The importance of language in national integration has been discussed in Chapter 6. Suffice it to say here that language is essential because the process can be considered as a communication problem. This problem existed in colonial times, since the European administrators had to find ways to communicate with the indigenous populations. But the colonial governments established only, or chiefly, what Pierre Alexandre[54] termed 'vertical channels of communication'. They were not interested 'in trying to build up a nationwide network of crosswise, intergroup links; in some cases it actually tried to prevent the formation of such a network'.[55]

But it is basically this type of crosswise, horizontal channels that post-independence African governments must build if their countries are to develop a national feeling of common purposes and interests.

Many African countries do not yet have an explicit language policy. In formulating one, countries should note that to choose any local language as the official language is to risk 'generating political problems even more serious than those resulting from the lack of homogeneity'.[56] The few exceptions have been Rwanda and Burundi (where an overwhelming majority of the population already speak the new language), and Kenya, Tanzania and Central African Republic (where the new national language is a widespread, non-tribal language—Swahili and Sango). All other countries where a local language has been chosen—be it that of a small majority or that of a strong minority—have had troubles on a pattern quite familiar in other parts of the world. On the other hand, the use of either English or French or both (as in Cameroon) as national language will be seriously resisted on nationalistic grounds. For this reason, the language issue will require thorough research to establish a language policy that will satisfy a majority of the population.

Political Participation

The political process in present day Africa is devoid of popular participation in the sense of active involvement of ordinary persons. Political parties are elite organizations that marginalize the political stakeholders. The public tends to equate voting with participation. Yet, most people who vote cannot explain the context for their actions. They cannot articulate the issues in the various campaigns, nor can they explain why they have chosen particular candidates, nor what they hope to benefit from casting a vote. Voting is done perfunctorily, more as a social behavior than an expression of rights. As a result, critics believe that equating political participation to voting is a limited interpretation of the construct.

Indeed, if political participation is to be truly meaningful in Africa, people must know what they are voting for and be ready to mobilize against under-performing public servants. NGOs, such as Norway's World Voices, and local interest groups, such as Women in Nigeria, have begun to take steps towards educating youths and women for greater participation in political affairs. This trend must permeate all segments of the societies before meaningful political participation can be institutionalized.

Notes

1   S. K. B. Asante, *African development: Adebayo Adedeji's alternative strategies*, London: Zell Publishers, 1991.
2   Edward A. Miguel, *Ethnic diversity and school funding in Kenya*, Paper C01-119, Berkeley, California: University of California Institute of Business and Economic Research, Center for International and Development Economics Research, 2001: 1-50.

see also William Easterly and Ross Levine, ' Africa's growth tragedy: Policies and ethnic division,' *Quarterly Journal of Economics* 112, 4 (1997):1203-1250 and Paolo Mauro, Corruption and growth,' *Quarterly Journal of Economics* 110, 3 (1995):681-712.

3   William Easterly and Ross Levine, 'Africa's growth tragedy: Policy and ethnic divisions,' *The Quarterly Journal of Economics* 112, 4 (November 1997):1203-1250.

4   Ibid.

5   Asante, *African development*.

6   Ibid.

7   Christina Drake, *National integration in Indonesia*, Honolulu: University of Hawaii Press, 1989.

8   Easterly and Levine, 'Africa's growth tragedy,' pp. 1203-1250.

9   Richard Ouma-Onyango, *Information resources and technology transfer management in developing countries*, London: Routledge, 1997: 198.

10   Godfrey Oswald, 'The North vs the South' *Internet newsgroups: soc.culture.nigeria* (January 22, 1996).

11   Adefemi Sonaike, 'Communication and Third World development: A dead end?' *Gazette* 41, 2 (1987): 83-103.

12   Gladstone Yearwood, 'Mass media in Nigeria'. The Nigerian Media Journal (1985):8.

13   James S. Coleman, Political integration in emergent Africa, *Western Political Quarterly* 8 (March 1955):45-57.

14   Sydney Head, *World broadcasting systems* (Belmont, California: Wadsworth, 1985).

15   Brian Smith, Federal-state relations in Nigeria. *African Affairs* 80 (July, 1981): 377.

16   Segun Oduko, 'New technologies upset the political communication balance in the Third World,' (Paper presented at the International Television Studies Conference, London, 1986, July).

17   See W. Joseph Campbell, The emergent independent press in Benin Cote d'Ivoire: From voices of the state to advocates of democracy, Westport, Connecticut: Praeger, 1998.

18   Eddie C. Y. Kuo, 'Language, nationhood and communication planning: The case of a multilingual society,' in Syed A. Rahim and John Middleton, eds. *Perspectives in communication policy and planning*, Honolulu, Hawaii: East-West Communication Institute, 1977.

19   Paul Collier, 'Implications of ethnic diversity,' *Policy Research Working Paper #* 13840, Washington, DD: The World Bank, 2000.

20   Arvind Singhal and William Brown, 'Entertainment-education: Looking backwards and forward,' *CommDev News* 6, 2 (1995):1-5.

21   Andrew Moemeka, 'Development communication: A historical and conceptual overview,' in Andrew Moemeka, ed. *Communicating for Development: A New Pan-Disciplinary Perspective*, New York: State University of New York Press, 1994: 13.

22   Raphael Makonnen, 'Democracy or Autocracy?: Opinion' *Addis Ababa Tribune* (April 18, 2003).

23   Abdullahi Tasiu Abubakar, 'Violoence, intimidation and electoral fraud in Rivers, Bayelsa,' *Weekly Trust* (April 19, 2003).

24   Collier, 'Implications of ethnic diversity'.

25   Harold D. Neslon, Cameroon: Chapter 1. General characteristics of the society (01-01-1991).

26 Ibid.
27 Anne Simmons and Renee Montagne, Nigeria's Political Transition, *NPR Morning Edition* (July 21, 1998).
28 Matt Mogekwu, 'Overcoming violence in language in Africa,' *Peace Review* 10, 4 (December 1, 1998): 593.
29 Mamman Akpena, 'We'll provide responsive government in Kogi State: PDP gubernatorial candidate,' *Africa News Service* (April 15, 2003).
30 Ibid.
31 Ibid.
32 Ibid.
33 Ibid.
34 Everett M. Rogers, *Communication Technology: The new media in society*, New York: The Free Press, 1986, p. 199.
35 Ali A Mazrui, *Cultural Engineering and Nation-building in East Africa*, Evanston, Illinois: Northwestern University Press, 1972: 278.
36 See for example 'The transactional model of communication' by Saundra Hybels and Richard L. Weaver, II, *Communicating effectively*, New York: Random House, 1986; and 'The convergence model' by Rogers, *Communication Technology*, p. 199.
37 E. Lisbeth Donaldson and Suzanne M. Kurtz, 'Applications of an interpersonal communication model to educational environments,' *Canadian Journal of Communication* 22, 1 (1997).
38 Christina Drake, *National integration in Indonesia*, Honolulu: University of Hawaii Press, 1989.
39 Luca Renda, 'Ending civil wars: The case of Liberia,' *The Fletcher Forum of World Affairs* 23, 2 (Fall 1999): 64.
40 Eghosa E. Osaghae, *Ethnicity, class and the struggle for state power in Liberia* (Dakar: CODESRIA, 1996). 19.
41 Renda, 'Ending civil wars: The case of Liberia,' 64.
42 A. Thunberg, K. Nowak, K Rosengren and B. Sigurd, *Communication and Equality: A Swedish perspective*, Stockholm: Almquist & Wicksell, 1982.
43 Sven Windahl, Benno Signitzer and Jena T. Olson, *Using communication Theory: An introduction to planned communication*, London: Sage Publications, 1992, p. 79.
44 Hybels and Weaver, II, *Communicating effectively*, pp. 19-20.
45 Ibid.
46 Richard E. Porter and Larry A. Samovar, 'Basic principles of intercultural communication,' in Larry A. Samovar and Richard E. Porter, eds., *Intercultural communication: A reader*, Belmont, California: Wadsworth Publishing Company, 1991: 5-22.
47 Ibid.
48 Charles Gore and David Pratten, 'The politics of plunder: The rhetoric of order and disorder in southern Nigeria,' *African Affairs* 102 (2003): 211-240.
49 Africa News Service, 'Between OPC and MASSOB: A double standard of policing?' (May 23, 2003).
50 Ibid.
51 Amos Sawyer, 'Social Stratification and National Orientations: Students and Non-students in Liberia,' in *Values, Identities and National Integration*, ed. John Paden, Evanston, Illinois: Northwestern University Press, 1980, 285-303.

52   David Abernethy, *The Political Dilemma of Popular Education: An African Case*, Stanford, California: Stanford University Press, 1969.
53   Karl Deutsch, *Nationalism and Its Alternatives*, New York: Alfred A. Knopf, Inc., 1969.
54   Pierre Alexandre, 'Some linguistic problems of nation-building in Negro Africa,' in *Language problems of developing nations*, eds. Joshua A Fishman, Charles, A Ferguson, and Jyotirindra das Gupta, New York: John Wiley & Sons, Inc: 119-127.
55   Ibid. p. 123.
56   Ibid.

Chapter 12

Summary and Conclusions

Political scientists and sociologists have undertaken most of the research and writing on national integration. Their efforts have successfully established the complexity, dimensions, problems and prospects of the construct. Also, they have been indispensable in outlining the difficulties associated with the quest for national unity and cohesion in African countries. However, they have generally not included the conceptualization of Africa's national integration difficulties as a communication problem. This is the void this book attempts to fill. Its central argument is that communication research and planning can no longer be ignored in national integration strategic thinking in Africa. This argument is presented through an interpolation of a review of existing integration theories and strategies, with a discussion of how communication is applicable to each dimension of the construct.

To briefly summarize the content of this book, national integration is essential for the social, economic and political development of African countries. Christina Drake[1] says without national integration a country will spend most of the human and material resources needed for development on coping with the forces of rebellion. As I note in chapter 1, national integration is a complex construct, with social, historical, economic and political dimensions. These dimensions must be addressed individually with communication strategies, without losing sight of their interrelatedness. The social dimension comprises national identification and integrative behavior. National identification is expressed verbally, affectively and through representative symbols. The communication issues that relate to these dimensions are discussed in Chapters 2, 3 and 4. Integrative behavior is exhibited through historical commonness, social interaction and social mobilization. As I point out in Chapters 5 and 6, the communication issues related to integrative behavior is not only structures, but also organization and control. Economic performance and distribution are the main focus of the economic dimension and they are discussed in Chapter 7. Chapter 8 examines the political dimension, and discusses specifically the issues of trust, efficacy and legitimacy within the context of their difficulties as communication endeavors. Chapters 9 and 10 address the research and planning aspects of communicating national integration.

As I note in these chapters, communicating national integration will require African leaders to replace rhetoric, insensitivity and self-aggrandizement with observable solutions to the values, identities, linkages and structures issues that hinder cohesive existence. An important aspect of this communication is abandoning the politics of division, nepotism and favoritism. As I have previously stated, many African politicians establish their political legitimacy within their ethnic group. This happens so much so that the fact that certain groups dominate the government becomes far more important than the ideological orientation or overall performance of the government. In Ethiopia for instance, Roe and Aadland[2] note, 'Today people are far more preoccupied with the fact that the present government has its power base related to ethnicity, than that it calls itself democratic.' This is true of other African countries, including Liberia, Democratic Republic of Congo (formerly Zaire), Kenya, Nigeria, Uganda, Sudan and numerous others.

Not surprisingly, politicization of ethnicity remains a major polarizing force in Africa. Political politicization fuels distrust and allegations. As Roe and Aadland note, African people have developed an uncanny ability 'to interpret anything that emerges from government quarters: The basic assumption is that what they hear is not true'.[3] Roe and Aadland say this widespread mutual distrust between government and the public leads to entrenchment of political positions. They say these entrenched political positions breed defensiveness that makes it difficult to establish constructive dialogue between different actors or interests. Accordingly, each actor or interest perceives the other as adversary, always suspecting it of hidden motives. Each believes it has the best solution to the nation's problems. Each actor or interest provides total and unyielding criticism of the other that creates a sense of exclusiveness, and does not allow for anything other than disruption and destruction to be expected from the other groups. As a result, political positions become self-assertive and absolute, and every new revelation about the adversary, every new suspicion instantly adds credibility to one's own position. Roe and Aadland conclude that in this environment political arguments have little value.[4]

Based on these assertions, it is logical to say hypothesize that if national populations are to regard national integrity inviolable, African political systems must be purified. This purification would require establishing cooperative, broad-based, participatory democracy, and creating constructive dialogue between different interests in the society. As Elliot Skinner predicts:

> African countries will continue to be racked by conflicts unless leaders agree about how to govern their multi-faceted nation-states and how to distribute their economic resources equitably. Without a compromise that would ensure 'ethnic justice', neither so-called 'liberal democracy', nor any other species of government will succeed in Africa.[5]

Skinner says African 'liberal democracies' will have evolutionary advantages, if they adapt to local realities, and shape their contours by indigenous African socio-cultural traditions. The way African economic and political systems adopt and manage local realities or traditions will determine whether disagreement between groups continue to result in enmity and polarization.

It is imperative for African leaders to begin to see establishment of liberal democracy as an effective way to communicate national integration. Liberal democracy is the best way to promote and institutionalize good governance. Hoekman says good governance is the essential foundation for achieving sustainable economic development, social cohesion and a healthy environment.[6] He defines governance as:

> the exercise of the economic, political and administrative authority to manage a community's affairs at all levels. It comprises the mechanisms, processes and institution through which community members articulate their interests, exercise their legal rights, meet their obligations and mediate their differences.[7]

Hoekman says good governance must involve popular participation, government transparency and public accountability. It must be based on administrative effectiveness, resource allocation equitability, application of the rule of law, and the derivation of social, political and economic priorities by broad consensus in society.

Contrary to these suggestions, many African governments still operate in secrecy and with little regard for the rule of law. Many discount the ethics of public service by using the authority and responsibility associated with their offices to subvert the political and economic system for personal gain, or to elevate the social status of their ethnic groups.[8] However, leaders such as Ronald Reagan, Winston Churchill, Valerie Giscard D'Estang and Nelson Mandela have shown that espousing democracy and upholding the highest standards of public service is the best platform from which national leaders can advocate national unity.

Good governance rejects corruption for the good of the society. Hoekman says corruption is a universal concept and one of the most enduring dilemmas facing society throughout history. Heywood[9] notes, in the last decade, no state, not even the most mature democracy, has been immune from the phenomenon. Therefore, corruption is not peculiar to Africa, as it most often seems. However, corrupt practices in Africa appear to be more blatant and unscrupulous, and the consequences seem more far-reaching than in other areas. In general, corruption:

- Undermines social and economic development;
- Hampers poverty reduction efforts;
- Steals resources for education and health; and
- Deprives ordinary people from responsive and even-handed public administration.

Research estimates suggest 'corruption is costing Africa more than 148 billion dollars a year, increasing the cost of goods by as much as 20 percent, deterring investment and holding back development'.[10] Because of its prevalence, it is assumed that no business can be done without money or a present changing hand. Corruption is so ingrained into the African psyche that efforts to clean it up have so far proved futile.[11] Regardless of the difficulty, governments must continue to fight corruption by enacting and enforcing codes, rules and laws against it. Other actions that are necessary in this regard are:

- The creation of general public awareness;
- The establishment of high expectations of good conduct;
- The establishment of clear standards of performance; and
- Transparency in procedures.[12]

Good governance also promotes civic-mindedness. A study in Germany showed that of the different ways to hold society together, the most effective is to have people 'with community-oriented skills, who trust one another and who take an interest both in one another and in the welfare of the community'.[13] The research concludes, 'Mutual interest and trust, together with shared goals and a variety of resources, result in commitment and involvement'.[14] It notes people must believe that something they have in common is at stake and be involved in social life in order to be integrated into society and help society cohere. It restates the widely shared view that the key to integration is participation.

According to the study, the civic-minded person is characterized by a sense of belonging to a community, an orientation to the common good, and a willingness to work for the community. The sense of belonging to a community is the emotional dimension of civic-mindedness. This is because civic-mindedness develops only if an individual feels he or she belongs to and can identify with the community. An individual must feel valued and recognized by the other members of the community. This feeling helps to build a community's belief that it belongs together. As previously noted in Chapter 2, an individual's sense of identity is tied to this concept of belonging to a community. People tend to define themselves in relation to their communities—such as the immediate or extended family, friends, religion, culture, ethnic group, or nation.

However, the conditions under which the social connections and ties needed for social identity are developed are far different today than in the past. Today, personal decisions play the most important role. With the increased potential for social mobility and spatial dislocation, individuals have more flexibility in developing their own network of relationships. The need to establish these relationships actively and build their social identity means the individual must possess appropriate relationship-building resources. These are tied partly to material resources.

In establishing social identity, individuals may choose multiple communities or just a few. In extreme cases, they could choose to identify with just a single community. Viewing this single community as absolute might lead them to devalue other communities. Thus, to reduce conflicts between groups with competing social identities, members of different groups must get to know one another personally, or form a social identity that embraces both groups. However, in complex societies, individuals never belong exclusively to just one community. They belong to several communities at the same time (for example, a religious community, a workplace community and also the community they live in). This decreases the potential for developing an exclusive social identity.[15]

According to the German researchers, orientation to the common good is a normative aspect of civic-mindedness. Orientation to the good of the community requires that individuals know their own needs, goals and interests, and weigh them against those of other members of the community. This means being able to 'see things from the other's point of view, to modify their own viewpoint, and to acknowledge that everyone has an equal right to develop freely'.[16] Exactly what constitutes the common good of a community should be decided by a negotiation-process in which all members can participate. This is what sets free, democratic, pluralistic communities and societies apart from authoritarian and totalitarian ones. In the latter, the common good is structured by ideology, determined at the top and sent downward. However, the democratically negotiated common good does not just emerge from formal procedures, nor is it just the sum of all individually coordinated interests. It is a normative idea that should be tied to values like justice and human dignity. It should be premised on the preservation of fundamental human rights. Thus, it should take into equal account the interests of all.[17]

The civic-minded person is ready to 'accept responsibility within a community and to work for the good of that community'.[18] The German researchers call this the practical or behavioral aspect of civic-mindedness. This aspect requires individuals to know how to get involved and to realize what opportunities exist for participation. Individual willingness to be involved cannot be fulfilled unless opportunities exist to help shape the community and to make a productive contribution.

Because the individual's communal participation reinforces social cohesion, the focus in promoting civic-mindedness must be on enabling participation. Individuals need to perceive the community as 'an enriching space for experience, negotiation and life-structuring'.[19] An environment must exist where individuals can experience civic-mindedness as a means of self-determination. An important way to accomplish this is to encourage them to act independently and on their own responsibility. They must possess the freedom to determine when they can contribute according to their own abilities, interests and solutions to problems. Family, peer groups and school can be exceedingly helpful in cultivating civic skills, especially in the young. Thus, the individual person is the starting point for cultivating civic-mindedness. As the German researchers note:

> When individuals are given the opportunity to experience themselves as belonging to a community and when they receive positive recognition as community members, they can develop a sense of belonging and build a positive social identity.[20]

However, community orientation does not just emerge from abstract references to the value of community for the individual, or by bemoaning the supposed decline of civic skills. Rather, the values are 'taught and learned, conveyed and instilled, mainly through experience'.[21] The community's values become credible when it contextualizes an individual's previous positive social interactions, or facilitates new experiences. Thus, the learning processes must be structured in such a way that they allow people to share experiences and feel emotionally connected.

An orientation to the common good presupposes sound ethical judgment. Accordingly, 'perhaps the most important aspect of ethical judgment is the ability to see one's own viewpoint in relative terms, to compare it with other viewpoints, and to incorporate it into the social context'.[22]   Ethical reflection enables individuals to exercise rational insight and conscience. It encourages civic courage, which individuals need to distance themselves from group prejudices and pressures. Africans, especially the leaders, need this civic courage to do what is ethically (or morally) proper to move their countries in positive political and economic directions that will make them unified entities. Such positive shifts in the behavior of African leaders will help to reduce the communicative distance that polarizes various segments of society. People will be able to relate to their leaders and the leaders will possess the sensitivity to empathize and respond to the problems and needs of the masses, at all times. This responsiveness is the emotional impetus needed to mobilize African populations towards embracing the spirit of national participation. It is required for people to develop the sense of putting their nation first in thoughts, words and deeds.

Whether it is intended or not, the social, economic and political speeches, mannerisms, acts, actions and behaviors of governments, community leaders and others in society are communicative. Individually and collectively, they constitute rhetorical and relational communication[23] with consequences for national integration. As previously discussed, they determine the type of relationships individuals will have with their own group members and members of other groups in the society.

Relational communication is about creating and maintaining lasting human relationships. The way Africans cultivate this relationship will determine whether people are receptive to national persuasions or not (rhetorical communication). As McCroskey explains, relational communication helps to move public opinion toward consensus, or what he terms 'a shared perspective satisfactory to all'.[24] This perspective is necessary to appreciate the role and importance of national landmarks, national holidays and national heroes in maintaining national identification and cohesion. It is vital in extrapolating ritual ceremonies and celebrations that help to crystallize the nation's identity. It is essential for agglomerating the diversity of each country's history into a common narrative that can be reified through oral tradition and the electronic media. Throughout Africa, individuals are aware that overt and covert actions or activities can produce polarizing effects and non-integrative behavior. It is important, therefore, that all public and private speeches, writings, acts, actions, activities and adopted policies are seen by the general public to be devoid of sectional leanings.

Africa's Road to National Development

To synthesize the foregoing recommendations, the critical criteria for achieving positive African development must contain a number of concrete actions that African people must use to achieve national cohesion. These actions include:

The desire to overcome past and present failures

The rate at which Africans, in both the public and private sectors, repeat mistakes across all facets of life is despairing. The recurrence of mistakes seems to suggest that Africans, particularly the leaders, lack the determination or ideas to overcome past and present failures. Despite the fact that African and foreign writers present many new and interesting ideas on the way forward for Africa, ineffectual policies are adopted and implemented repeatedly.

However, Alexander Pope writes, 'a man [or woman] should never be ashamed to own up that he has been wrong, which is but saying in other words that he is wiser today than he was yesterday'. If Africa is to truly develop in the coming years, leaders must understand that 'the person interested in success has to learn to view failure as a healthy, inevitable part of the process of getting to the top'. Therefore, they must be willing to reverse course when failure is imminent or has occurred. As the legendary racecar driver, Mario Andretti, notes aptly, 'desire is the key to motivation, but it's the determination and commitment to an unrelenting pursuit of your goal—a commitment to excellence—that will enable you to attain the success you seek'.

The will to accept policies of liberal democracy

An important tenet of effective management is the *authority level principle*. It states that the authority to make decisions should be utilized at the lowest possible level, and everyone with authority must account for how they have used it to accomplish their duties. This principle aids the diffusion of power. It brings accountability to the exercise of power, checking excesses where necessary.

In many African countries, political and economic power tends to be concentrated in a single individual or small group of individuals. This concentration allows politicians to disregard necessary checks and balances. It leads political leaders, even the well-meaning ones, to entrench themselves as they loose track of their public responsibilities. If Africa is to truly develop, the *authority level principle* must be seen as the most effective way to meet the need of national populations. Leaders must be willing to share political and economic power through unflinching acceptance of liberal democratic policies. For it is only through commitment to shared-governance and effective representation that Africa can transcend political tribalism, the bane of progress across the continent.

Building a civic-minded community

No country or community can achieve national development if citizens actively distance themselves from its goals and aspirations. Studies have shown that the productive capacity of a community or country depends upon the participation and involvement of its citizens.

Civic-mindedness is the 'social capital' a community can use to make people's lives more productive. In his book, *Bowling Alone: The Collapse and Revival of American Community*, Robert Putnam shows a relationship between 'social capital' and positive outcomes for individuals, neighborhoods, and communities in several areas. These include:

- Education and children's welfare;
- Safe and productive neighborhoods;
- Health and happiness; and
- Democracy and civil society.

He says the 'connections among individuals and social networks and the norms of reciprocity and trustworthiness that arise from them' are the essential ingredients in achieving economic growth and political stability in a community.

The development of social capital is essential for Africa's progress. This agrees with the current thinking that development must occur from the bottom-up. But much to the dismay of many people, Africans leaders have generally not empowered citizens to undertake projects that will benefit their communities and the nation as a whole. They have always believed that government alone had the responsibility for development. If Africa is to fulfill its full developmental potential, individuals and communities must be empowered to become more civic-minded. Measures such as voting, membership in civic organizations, religious participation, informal social connections, volunteerism and philanthropy must lead to community growth. As each community grows, so will the nation as a whole.

Adherence to ethical behavior in all aspects of national affairs

As previously noted, unethical behavior is pervasive, but not unique to Africa. People in other parts of the world, including Asia, Europe and North America, are not exempt from the unethical behavior of bribery and corruption. However, it is fair to say that Africa's situation is bleaker because there are no effective measures in place to curb unethical practices.

Yet, Africa cannot hope to develop without taking positive steps in this direction. Chan Sup Chang, Nahn Joo Chang and Barbara Freese define *ethics* as the 'code or principles that enable one to tell what is right from what is wrong'.[25] An inherent component of African culture is the socialization that ethical behavior is the right thing to do. But Africans must practice ethical behavior not just because it is right, but also because it can improve the economic and political bottom line.

Communication that expresses national identification and cohesion

As I note in the preface, African leaders frequently promote national unity in speeches and writings. At the same time, their personal acts, actions, activities, policies and programs tend to remain decidedly sectional. This unwittingly sends mixed integrative messages to the receiving audience who, more often than not, pay closer attention to the polarizing politics than to the integrative speech.

If national integration is to take hold in African countries, the verbal and non-verbal aspects of disseminated integrative message must be mutually reinforcing. In other words, people must back up their articulated sense of nationhood by what they do, wear or infer.

In sum, integrative communication must be viewed as an all-encompassing task that transcends official speeches and polemics. It must include decisions that eliminate policies that promote spatial dislocation and cultural polarization. It must include the overt avoidance of any individual and collective action or activity capable of derailing the integrative intentions. It must include the provision of physical infrastructure for creating linkages among people. Above all, it must include the overt display of fairness and logic in the management and distribution of national resources.

Notes

1   Christina Drake, *National integration in Indonesia*, Urbana, University of Illinois Press, 1982.
2   See for example Knut Roe and Oyvind Aadland, *Assessment Study on media educational involvement in Ethiopia: Media involvement in building democracy and civic institutions in Ethiopia*, Gimlekollen School of Journalism and Communication: Extension and Consultancy Department, Holland: November, 1999.
3   Ibid.
4   Ibid.
5   Elliot P. Skinner, 'African political cultures and the problem of government,' *African Studies Quarterly: The Online Journal for African Studies* 7, 1 (Spring 2003).
6   Ibid.
7   Arie Hoekman, 'e-Governance and the promotion of transparency in governance,' presented at the Regional Workshop on Building e-Governance Capacity in Africa.
8   John Mukum Mbaku, 'Bureaucratic corruption in Africa: The futility of cleanups,' *The Cato Journal* 16, 1 (Spring/Summer 1996).
9   Paul Heywood (ed.), *Political corruption*, Oxford: Blackwell for the Political Science Association, 1997: 250.
10   Elizabeth Blunt, 'Corruption cost Africa billions,' *BBC News World Edition* (September 18, 2002).
11   Mbaku.
12   Hoekman.

13   Bertelsmann Foundation, Bertelsmann Policy Research Group (eds.), Civic-Mindedness: Participation in modern society (Germany: 2003).
14   Ibid.
15   Ibid.
16   Ibid.
17   Ibid.
18   Ibid.
19   Ibid.
20   Ibid.
21   Ibid.
22   Ibid.
23   James C. McCroskey, 'Human Communication Theory and Research: Traditions and Models,' in *An Integrated Approach to Communication Theory and Research*, ed. Michael B. Salem and Don W. Stacks, Mahwah, New Jersey: Lawrence Erlbaum Associates, Publishers, 1996.
24   Ibid.
25   Chan Sup Chang, Nahn Joo Chang and Barbara T. Fresse, 'Offering gifts or offering bribes? Code of ethics in South Korea' *Journal of Third World Studies* 18 (April 2001): 145.

Bibliography

Abernethy, David, *The Political Dilemma of Popular Education: An African Case*, Stanford, California: Stanford University Press, 1969.

Abernethy, David B., 'European colonialism and postcolonial crises in Africa', in Harvey Glickman, ed., *The crises and challenge of African development*, New York: Greenwood Press, 1988: 4.

Abubakar, Abdullahi Tasiu, 'Violoence, intimidation and electoral fraud in Rivers, Bayelsa', *Weekly Trust* (April 19, 2003):

Achebe, Chinua, *The Trouble with Nigeria*, Enugu: Fourth Dimension Press, 1980.

Acock, Alan, Clarke, Harold D. and Stewart, Marianne C., 'A new model for old measures: A covariance structure analysis of political efficacy', *The Journal of Politics* (1985): 1063.

Adedeji, Adebayo, 'Introduction-Marginalisation and Marginality: Contexts, Issues, and Viewpoints', in *Africa Within the World: Beyond Dispossession and Dependence*, ed. Adedeji, Adebayo, London: Zed Books, 1993: 3.

Africa News Service, 'Between OPC and MASSOB: A double standard of policing?' (May 23, 2003).

African Development Bank, 'Economic cooperation and regional integration policy', African Development Bank (February 2000).

Ahlburg, Dennis A. and Brown, Richard P. C., 'Migrants' intentions to return home and capital transfers: A study of Tongans and Samoans in Australia', *The Journal of Development Studies* 35, 2 (December 1998)pp. 125-151

Ajayi, J. F. Ade, 'The Place of African History and Culture in the Process of nation-Building in African South of the Sahara', *Journal of Negro Education* 30, 3 (Summer, 1961), PP. 206-213.

Ajayi, Rotimi, Omonobi, Kingsley and Ehigiator, Kenneth, 'Obasanjo apologizes, cancels US trip', Vanguard (January 31, 2002)

Akpena, Mamman, 'We'll provide responsive government in Kogi State: PDP gubernatorial candidate', *Africa News Service* (April 15, 2003).

Akukwe, Chinua, 'Integration will improve Africa's competitiveness', *African News Service* (May 21, 2002).

Alexandre, Pierre, 'Some linguistic problems of nation-building in Negro Africa', in *Language problems of developing nations*, eds. Fishman, Joshua A., Ferguson, Charles, A., and Jyotirindra das Gupta, New York: John Wiley & Sons, Inc.: 119-127.

Allison, Lincoln, *The Politics of Sports*, Manchester, England: Manchester University Press, 1986: 13.

Amienyi, Osabuohien P., 'Obstacles to Broadcasting For National Integration in Nigeria', *Gazette* 43 (1989): 1-15;

Amienyi, Osabuohien P., *The relationship between mass media and national integration in Nigeria*, Unpublished Ph.D. dissertation, Bowling Green State University, Bowling Green, Ohio, 1989.

Amienyi, Osabuohien P., with Igyor, Gerard 'Sub-Saharan Africa', in *World broadcasting: A Comparative view*, ed. Allan Wells, Norwood, New Jersey: Ablex Publishing Corporation, 1996.

Amienyi, Osabuohien P., 'Adult Perception of the Integrative Contribution of Mass Media in Nigeria', *Southwestern Mass Communication Journal* 6 (1990): 53-63;

Amienyi, Osabuohien P., 'The Association Between Mass Media Exposure and National Identification in Nigeria', *International Third World Studies Journal & Review* 2 (1991):337-346.

Amienyi, Osabuohien P., 'Communication and development quintessentials: The focus of development agencies and theorists', *The Journal of Development Communication* 9 (June, 1998): 1-16.

Amienyi, Osabuohien P., Technology Transfer and Media Development in Nigeria, *Southwestern Mass Communication Journal*, 9 (1993): 44-53.

Amienyi Osabuohien P., and Abraham, Gilbert T. 'An Experimental Investigation of the Influence of Photographs on College Student Perceptions of Africans', *Southwestern Mass Communication Journal* 11 (1995): 67-80.

Anderson, Benedict *Imagined Communities: Reflections on the Origin and Spread of Nationalism*, London: Verso, 1991: 224.

Andrade-Watkins, Claire, 'Portuguese African Cinema: historical and contemporary perspectives – 1969 to 1993', *Research in African Literatures* 26 (1995), pp. 134 (17).

Ankromah, Baffour, 'African Media Are Stuck in Time Warp', *African News Service* (June 19, 2002).

Anon, 'The National Anthem', *Compton's Encyclopedia Online* (1999). Http://www.optonline.com/comptons/ceo/03358_A.html April 13, 2000.

Anon, 'South Africa has to build new roads in rural areas', *Xinhua News Agency* (May 21, 2002).

Anon., 'A New Strategy to Empower People in Africa', *World Health* 6 (November-December, 1997): 4.

Anon, 'Brain Drain: An Endless Stress in Africa', *African News Service* (April 17, 2000).

Anon, 'Football violence Takes its Toll', Inter Press Service (November 5, 1993).

Anon, 'A new Strategy to Empower people in Africa', *World Health* 6 (November-December, 1997): 4.

Anon, 'Finance and economics: A look on the brighter side: Africa's economies', *The Economist* (July 20, 2002), p. 69.

Anon, 'Corrupt political elites and businessmen kill economic development: Transparency International Says', *www.Arabicnews.com* (September 23, 2002).

Anon, 'Murtala Mohammed: The Untold Story', *Africa One Stop Service* (December 17, 1998).

Anon., 'Steve Biko: Martyr of the Anti-apartheid Movement', *BBC News Online*: Background (December 8, 1997).

Anon, 'Forum established to promote research on health in Africa', *APWorldstream* (December 14, 2002).

Anon., 'Newsmakers: Nelson Rolihlahla Mandela', *ABCnews.com*

Anon., 'Troubled skies: airlines in Africa', *The Economist* 334 (March 4, 1995), pp. 69 (1).

Anon, 'Kwame Nkrumah, His Rise and Fall, 7 march 1957 - 24 February 1966: Part III', *Great Epic Newsletter* 2, 1 (January, 1998).

Ansah, Paul A. V., 'Problems of localizing radio in Ghana', *Gazette* 25 (1985)1: 1-16.

Ansah, Paul A. V., 'Communication research and development in Africa: An overview', in Hemelink, C. J. and Linne, O., eds., *Mass communication research on problems and policies: The art of asking the right questions*, Norwood, New Jersey, 1994.

Asante, S. K. B., *African development: Adebayo Adedeji's alternative strategies*, London: Zell Publishers, 1991.

Ashurst, Mark, 'Africa's ringing revolution', *Newsweek International* (August 27, 2001): 16.

Awolowo, Obafemi, *Path to Nigerian Freedom* (London: Oxford Univeristy Press, 1947), pp. 47-48.

Azikiwe, Nnamdi, 'Essentials for Nigerian survival', *Foreign Affairs* 43 (1965): 457.

Balassa, Bela, *The Theory of Economic Integration* (London: George Allen & Unwin LTD, 1965), p. 2.

Baran, Stanley J. and Davis, Dennis K., *Mass Communication Theory: Foundations Ferment and Future*, Belmont, California: Wadsworth Publishing Company, 1995: 140.

Baran and Davis, *Mass Communication Theory: Foundations Ferment and Future*, p. 303.

Barna, LaRay M., 'Stumbling blocks in intercultural communication', in Somovar, Larry A. and Porter, Richard E., eds., *Intercultural Communication, Sixth Edition*, Belmont, California: Wadsworth Publishing Company, 1991: 345-353.

Bass, Abraham, 'Promoting nationhood in Africa', *Journal of Broadcasting* 13 (1969) 2: 165-169.

Battersby, John, 'Nelson Madela's Moral Legacy', *The Christian Science Monitor* (May 10, 1999), p. 9.

Berger, Guy, 'Media & democracy in Southern Africa', *Review of African Political Economy* 78 (1998): 602.

Bertelsmann Foundation, Bertelsmann Policy Research Group (eds.), Civic-Mindedness: Participation in modern society (Germany: 2003)

Bickman, Leonard and Rog, Debra J., 'Introduction: Why a handbook of applied social research methods?', in Leonard Bickman and Debra Rog, eds., *Handbook of applied social research methods*, Thousand Oaks, California: Sage Publications, 1998, p. x.

Bienen, Henry, 'The State and Ethnicity: Integrative Formulas in Africa', in *State versus Ethnic Claims: African Policy Dilemmas*, ed. Donald Rothschild and Victor Olorunsola, Boulder, Colorado: Westview Press, 1983: 100-126.

Blunt, Elizabeth, 'Corruption cost Africa billions', *BBC News World Edition* (September 18, 2002).

Bornman, Elirea and Applegryn, Ans E. M., Ethno-linguistic vitality under a new political dispensation in South Africa', *The Journal of Social Psychology* 137 (1997): 690-707.

Bourgault, Louise M., *Broadcasting in Sub-Saharan Africa*, Ames: Iowa University Press, 1995.

Bourgault, Louise M., *Mass Media in Sub-Saharan Africa*, Bloomington, Indiana: Indiana University Press, 1995.

Bourghis, R. Y., Giles, H. and Rosenthal, D., 'Notes on the construction of a 'Subjective Vitality Questionnaire' for Ethnic Groups', *Journal of Multilingual and Multicultural Development* 2 (1981): 145-155.

Brodie, Mollyann, Foehr, Ursula, Rideout, Vicky, Bael, Neal, et al., 'Communicating health information through the entertainment media', *Health Affairs* 20, 1 (January 2001): 192.

Brody, Paula Rae, 'Zambian Reflections', *Great Epics Newsletter* 3, 3 (March, 1999).

Browne, Stephen, 'Governance and Human Poverty', *Choices Magazine* 10, 3 (September 2001): 8.

Buddick, Emily Miller, Fiction and Historical Consciousness: The American Romantic Tradition, New Haven: Yale University Press, 1989: 1-240.

Cabral, Anna Maria, 'Amilcar Cabral.' Fundacion Amilcar Cabral (Praia, Cabo Verde).

Chang, Chan Sup, Chang, Nahn Joo and Fresse, Barbara T., 'Offering gifts or offering bribes? Code of ethics in South Korea' *Journal of Third World Studies* 18 (April 2001): 145.

Calamistsis, Evangelos A., 'Adjustment and growth in Sub-Saharan Africa: The unfinished agenda', *Finance & Development* (March, 1999), p. 6.

Campbell, W. Joseph, The emergent independent press in Benin Cote d'Ivoire: From voices of the state to advocates of democracy, Westport, Connecticut: Praeger, 1998.

Carey, Kathleen, 'A theory of group stability', *American Sociological Review* 56, 3 (1991): 331-332.

Cecilia, L. Ridgeway and James W. Balkwell, 'Group processes and the diffusion of status beliefs', *Social Psychology Quarterly* 60, 1 (March 1997): 14-31.

Chazan, Naomi, 'Ethnicity and politics in Ghana', *Political Science Quarterly* 97, 3 (Autumn, 1982): 461-485.

Chisiza, D. K., 'The Outlook for Contemporary Africa', *The Journal of Modern African Studies* 1 (1963): 25-38.

Clignet, Remi and Stark, Maureen, 'Modernization and Football in Cameroun', *Journal of Modern African Studies* 12, 3 (1974): 409-421.

Coffman, Julia, *Public communication campaign evaluation: An environmental scan of challenges, criticisms, practice, and opportunities*, Cambridge, Massachusetts: Harvard Family Research Project, 2003.

Coleman, James S., Political integration in emergent Africa, *Western Political Quarterly* 8 (March 1955):45-57.

Collier, Paul, 'Implications of ethnic diversity', *Policy Research Working Paper* # 13840, Washington, DC: The World Bank, 2000.

Conover, Pamela, 'The influence of group identifications on political perceptions and evaluation', *The Journal of Politics* 46, 3 (August 1984): 760-785.

Cornell, Stephen and Hartmann, Douglass, *Ethnicity and Race: Making Identities in a Changing World*, Thousand Oaks, California: Pine Forge Press, 1998.

Coulibaly, Abdou L., 'Media growth poses training challenges', *InteRadio, 9 (1998)*:2-5.

Cowan, Gray, *The dilemmas of African independence* (New York: Walker and Company, 1965).

Cuba, Vuli, 'Developing Visionary Leaders - An African Imperative', Vuli Cuba Safika Investment Holdings Ltd, 1997: 3.

Dare, Sunday, 'A continent in crisis', *Dollars & Sense* (July 1, 2001), pp. 12.

Dawkins, Kristin, 'Food Self Reliance and the Concept of Subsidiarity: Alternative Approaches to Trade and International Democracy', paper presented at the Tenth Annual Pan-African Studies Conference, Indiana State University, Terre Haute, Indiana, April 15-16, 1993.

Deng, Francis M., 'Ethnicity: African Predicament', *The Brookings Review* 15, 3 (Summer 1997), pp. 28-31.

Deutsch, Karl, *Nationalism and its Alternatives*, New York: Alfred A. Knopf, Inc, 1969.

Domatob, Jerry, 'Sub-Saharan African Broadcasters: Social Influence and Status', *The Third Channel: IBS Journal of International Communication* 5 (1987): 660-675.

Domatob, Jerry, The Status and Influence of Nigerian Media', *The Third Channel: IBS Journal of International Communication* 5 (1987): 632-643.

Donaldson, E. Lisbeth and Kurtz, Suzanne M., 'Applications of an interpersonal communication model to educational environments', *Canadian Journal of Communication* 22, 1 (1997).

Dossier, 'Mozambique: Making a Song and Dance About Peace', *The Courier* 168 (March-April, 1998), p. 27.

Drake, Christina. *National integration in Indonesia*, Honolulu: University of Hawaii Press, 1989.

Dunbar, Clark D. and Moore, Ann, eds., *Africa Yesterday and Today*, New York: Prager Publishers, 1969: 27.

Dyer, Gwynne, 'Africa takes a step in the right direction', *The Toronto Star* (July 10, 2002).

Easterly, William and Levine, Ross, 'Africa's growth tragedy: Policies and ethnic division', *Quarterly Journal of Economics* 112, 4 (1997):1203-1250.

Easton, David, *A systems analysis of political life*, New York: John Wiley & Sons, 1965: 267-340.

Easton, David, 'The child's acquisition of regime norms: Political efficacy', *The American Political Science Review* (1967): 25.

Entman, Robert M., 'Framing: Toward clarification of a fractured paradigm', *Journal of Communication* 43 (1993), p. 55.

Etieyibo, Edwin E., 'Opinion: Nigerian at 40: 4 decades of wasted years?', *African News Service* (October 10, 2000).

Etzioni, Amitai, Political Unification: A Comparative Study of Leaders and Forces. New York.

Eyre, Banning, 'The Griot is the elder, the Keeper of Tales, the Tribes Memory', The Kennedy Center (April, 1998).

Fair, Laura, 'Kickin' it: Leisure, Politics and Football in colonial Zanzibar, 1900s-1950s', *Africa* 67, 2 (1997): 224-251.

Faris, Stephan, 'Hollywood, Who Really Needs It? Nigeria's homegrown film business is booming, but is this a case of too much of a good thing?', *Time International* (May 20, 2002), p. 39.

Fatos, Tarifa, 'The quest for political legitimacy', *Social Forces* (December 1997): 437-473.

Fernandez, Maria Elena, 'Grand Old Flags: Symbols of Our Unity, Our Purpose, Ourselves', *Los Angeles Times* (Sunday, June 11, 2000): 1.

Foster, Robert J., 'Making National Cultures in the Global Ecumene', *Annual Review of Anthropology* 20 (1991), pp. 235-260.

Geertz, Clifford, *The Interpretation of Cultures*, New York: Basic Books, 1973: 234-243.

Geertz, Clifford, 'The Integrative Revolution, Primordial Sentiments and Civil Politics in the New States', in *Old Societies and New States*, ed. Clifford Geertz, New York: Basic Books, 1973.

Gerbner, George, Gross, Lynne, Morgan, M., and Signorielli, Nancy, 'Living with television: The dynamics of the cultivation process', in Bryant, Jennings and Zillmann, Doff, eds. *Perspectives on media effects*, Hillsdale, NJ: Lawrence Erlbaum, 1986: 17-41.

Giddens, Anthony, *Sociology*, Polity Press, 1990.

Giles, H. and Johnson, P., 'The Role of Language on Ethnic Group Relations', in *Intergroup Behavior*, ed. J. C., Turner and Giles, H., Oxford: Basil, 1981: 199-243.

Glasberg, David, 'History and the Public Legacies of the Progressive Era', *The Journal of American History* (1987), pp. 957-980.

Gleave, M. B. and Morgan, W. B., 'Economic development in tropical Africa from a geographical perspective: A comparative study of African economies', *The Geographical Journal* (June 2001): 139-145.

Goldman, Robert and Jeyaratnam, Wilson, eds., *From Independence to Statehood: Managing Ethnic Conflict in Five African and Asian States* (New York: St. Martins Press, 1984).

Gore, Charles and Pratten, David, 'The politics of plunder: The rhetoric of order and disorder in southern Nigeria', *African Affairs* 102 (2003): 211-240.

Gramson, W. A., Croteau, D., Hoynes, W., and Sasson, T., 'Media images and the social construction of reality', *Annual Review of Sociology* 18 (1992): 373-393.

Grant, Peter and Brown, Rupert, 'From ethnocentrism to collective protests: Responses to relative deprivation and threats to social identity', *Social Psychology Today* 58, 3 (September 1995): 195.

Grant, P. R., 'Ethnocentrism in Response to a Threat to Social Identity', *Journal of Social Behavior and Personality* 8 (1993): 143-154.

Grant, P. R., 'Ethnocentrism Between Groups of Unequal Power in Response to Perceived Threat to Social Identity and Valued Resources', *Canadian Journal of Behavioral Science* 24 (1992): 348-370.

Gratz, Tilo, 'New local radio stations in African languages & the process of political transformation: The case of Radio Rurale Locale Tangueita in northern Benin', in Richard, Fardon, and Furniss, Graham, eds., *African Broadcast Cultures: Radio in transition*, Westport, Connecticut: Praeger, 2000: 123.

Gray, Weller, 'Letter of Opinion', *The Saturday Evening Post* (January 1943).

Gumisai, Mutume, 'South Africa-Sports: More Than Just a Soccer Victory', *Inter Press Service English News Wire* (February 6, 1996).

Guyonvarc'h, Christian, 'The Basis of Prejudice', *The Courier* 140 (July-August, 1993), p. 53.

Habermas, Jurgen, *Legitimation crisis*. Translated by T. McCarthy, Beacon Press, 1975.

Hachten, William A., *The Growth of Media in the Third World: African Failures, Asian Successes*, Ames: Iowa State University Press, 1993: 14-15.

Harman, Danna, 'Nigeria Nips at Hollywood's Heels', *Christian Science Monitor* (June 26, 2002), pp. 01.

Harris, Michael D., 'African-American Baseline Essays: An Excerpt', *Editorial Research Reports* (November 30, 1990): 690-694.

Haynes, Jonathan and Okome, Onookome, 'Evolving Popular Media: Nigerian Video Films', *Research in African Literature* 29 (1998), pp. 106 (23).

Hayward, Fred M., 'Continuities and discontinuities between studies of national and international political integration: Some implications for future research efforts', *International Organization*, 24, 4, Regional Integration: Theory and Research (Autumn 1970), p. 923.

Hayward, Fred M., 'A reassessment of conventional wisdom about the informed public: National political information in Ghana', *The American Political Science Review* 70, 2 (June 1976): 433-451.

Head, Sydney, *World Broadcasting System*, California: Wadsworth Publishing Systems, 1985.

Heywood, Paul (ed.), *Political corruption*, Oxford: Blackwell for the Political Science Association, 1997: 250.

Hoberman, John, The Olympic Crisis: Sports, Politics and the Moral Order, New Rochelle, New York: Aristide D. Caratas, Publisher, 1986.

Hoekman, Arie, 'e-Governance and the promotion of transparency in governance', presented at the Regional Workshop on Building e-Governance Capacity in Africa.

Horner, Simon, 'Dossier: National Minorities', *The Courier* 140 (July-August, 1993), p. 49.

Houtondji, P., 'Introduction: Recentering Africa', in Houtondji, P., (ed), *Endogenous Knowledge: Research Trails*, Dakar: Codseria Book Series, 1997: 1-39.

Huntington, Samuel P., 'Political development and political decay', *World Politics* 17, 3 (April, 1965): 386-430.

Hybels, Saundra and Weaver, Richard L., II, *Communicating effectively* (New York: Random House, 1986); and 'The convergence model' by Rogers, *Communication Technology*, p. 199.

Ikhazuagbe, Duro, 'Riot Act for Clubs: Referees Threaten to Boycott the League: Pepsi League Fall-out', *Post Express* (May 18, 2000).

Inett, Pat and Shewchuk, John, 'Communication planning for organizations', *Factsheet* (April 2003): 1.

ITU, *World Telecommunications Development Report: Universal Access: Executive Summary*, Luzanne, ITU, March 1998.

ITU, *African telecommunications indicators.* (Luzanne: ITU, 1996). Http://www.itu.int/ti/publications/africa/afr96en.htm

Jacob, Philip and Teune, Henry, 'The Integrative Process: Guidelines For Analysis of the Bases of Political Community', in *The Integration of Political Communities*, ed. Jacob, Philip and Toscano, James (Philadelphia: J. B. Lippincourt Company, 1964).

Jahan, R., *Pakistan; Failure in national integration*, New York: Columbia University Press, 1972.

Jensen, Mike, 'African Internet Status', *The World Wide Web* (May 1999).

Kariithi, Nelson, 'Economics and business journalism in Africa', *Nieman Reports* (Summer 2002).

Kayigamba, Jean Baptiste, 'Rwanda to change flag in effort to bury past', *Reuters* (May 18, 1999).

Kelly, Kevin, *New rules for the economy: 101 radical strategies for a connected world*, New York: Penguin Books, 1999.

Keyton, Joann, *Communication Research: Asking questions, finding answers*, Mountain View, California: Mayfield Publishing Company, 2001: 9-10.

Kohls, L., *Survival Kit for Overseas Living*, Yarmouth, ME: Intercultural Press, 1984.

Kuo, Eddie, 'Language, Nationhood, and Communication Planning: The case of a multilingual society', in *Perspectives in Communication Policy and Planning*, ed. Rahim, S. A. and Middleton, J., Honolulu: East-West Communication Institute: 319-335.

Kupe, Tawana, 'Comment: New Forms of Cultural Identity in an African Society', in *Media and the Transition of Collective Identities*, ed. Tore Slatta, Oslo: University of Oslo Press, 1996: 118.

Lasorsa, Dominic L., 'Diversity in mass communication theory classes', *Journalism & Mass Communication Educator* 57, 3 (Autumn 2002): 246.

Lau, Richard R., 'Individual and contextual influences on group identification', *Social Psychology Quarterly* 53, 3 (1989): 220-231.

Le Roy, Etienne, 'Rethinking the State in Africa', *The Courier* 171 (September-October, 1998): 53-56.

Lears, J. T. Jackson, 'The Concept of Cultural Hegemony: Problems and Possibilities.' *The American Historical Review* (1995), pp. 568-593.

Lieberman, Devorah K., 'Ethnocogniotivism and Problem Solving', in *Intercultural Communication: A Reader*, eds. Larry A. Samovar and Richard E. Porter, Belmont, California: Wadsworth Publishing Company, 1991: 229.

Lijphart, Arendt, 'Preface', in *World Minorities in the Eighties*, ed. Georgina Ashworth, Sunbury, UK: Quartermaine House Ltd, 1980.

Lipset, Seymour Martin, 'The social requisites of democracy revisited', American Sociological Review 59 (1994): 1-22.

Lipsky, Richard, 'Towards a Political Theory of American Sports Symbolism.' *American Behavioral Scientist* 21 (January/February 1978): 348.

Liu, Alan, *Communication and national integration in Communist China*, Berkeley: University of California Press, 1972.

Locketz, L., 'Health education in rural Surinam: Use of videotape in a national campaign against schistosomiasis', *Bulletin of the Panamerican Health Organization* 10 (1976): 219-226.

Lukens, J., 'Ethnocentric Speech', *Ethnic Groups* 2 (1978): 35-53.

Mabogunje, Akin, *The Development Process: A Spatial Perspective*, New York: Holmes & Meier Publishers, inc., 1981: 250

Macdonald, Maryon, 'Celtic ethnic kinship and the problem of being English', *Current Anthropology* 27, 4 (August-October, 1986), pp. 333-347.

Macpherson, C., 'Changing Patterns of Commitment to Island Homelands: A Case Study of Western Samoa', *Pacific Studies* 17, 3 (1994), pp.83-116.

Majewski, J., 'Third World development: Foreign aid or free trade?', *The Freeman* (1996): 1-6.

Martin, Seymour Lipset. *The First New Nation, Expanded Edition*, Norton, 1979.

Mbaku, John Mukum, 'Bureaucratic corruption in Africa: The futility of cleanups', *The Cato Journal* 16, 1 (Spring/Summer 1996).

McHenry, Jr. Dean, E., 'The Use of Sports in Policy Implementation: The Case of Tanzania', *Journal of Modern African Studies* 18, 2 (1980): 237-256.

McCombs, Maxwell E., and Shaw, Donald L., 'The agenda-setting function of mass media', *Public Opinion Quarterly* 36 (1972): 176-187.

McCroskey, James C., 'Human Communication Theory and Research: Traditions and Models', in *An Integrated Approach to Communication Theory and Research*, ed. Salwen, Micheal B. and Stacks, Don W., Mahwah, New Jersey: Lawrence Erlbaum Associates, Publishers, 1996.

Makabakayele, Gupe, 'Radio training still under state monopoly', *InteRadio*, 9 (1998):2-5.

Makonnen, Raphael, 'Democracy or Autocracy?: Opinion' *Addis Ababa Tribune* (April 18, 2003):

Mangaliman, Jesse, 'Immigrants Send Kids Back to Homeland to Learn Culture: Indo-American looking to Defy U.S. Assimilation', *The Mercury News* (October 29, 2000).

Maslow, Abraham H., Toward a Psychology of Being, D. Van Nostrand Company, 1968.

Mauro, Paolo, 'Corruption and growth', *Quarterly Journal of Economics* 110, 3 (1995):681-712

Meisler, Stanley, ''Saints and Presidents:' A Commentary on Julius Nyerere', *One world News Service* (December 19, 1996).

Merkle, L. and Zimmermann, K.F., 'Savings, Remittances, and Return Migration', *Economics Letters* 38 (1991), pp.77-81.

Miguel, Edward A., *Ethnic diversity and school funding in Kenya*, Paper C01-119, Berkeley, California: University of California Institute of Business and Economic Research, Center for International and Development Economics Research, 2001: 1-50.

Miller, Jennifer, 'Language use, identity, and social interaction: Migrant students in Australia', *Research on Language and Social Interaction* 33, 1 (2001): 69-100.

Miller, John, 'History and Africa/ Africa and History', The American Historical Review 104, 1 (February 1999), p. 1-32.

Miller, Arthur H., Gurin, Patricia, and Gurin, Gerald, 'Electoral implications of group identification and consciousness: The reintroduction of a concept', Presented at the Annual Meeting of the American Political Science Association (New York, 1978): 18.

Ming, Chen, 'News Analysis: Africa ambitious to harmonize railways lines', *Xinhua News Agency* (August 12, 2002).

Minor, J. Douglas, 'The Moral Cost of Political Unity' (A New Visions Commentary Paper, National Center for Policy Research, September 1998).

Mngerem, Suleyol, 'Football as Metaphor for Nigeria's Unity', *The Gaurdian* (February 5, 2000).

Moemeka, Andrew A. ed., *Comunicating for Development: A New Pan-disciplinary Perspective*, New York: State University of New York Press, 1994.

Mogekwu, Matt, 'Overcoming violence in language in Africa', *Peace Review* 10, 4 (December 1, 1998): 593.

Momoh, Tony, Nigeria: The Press and Nation-building', *Africa Report* 32 (March/April 1987): 54-57.

Morrison, Minion, Ethnicity and Integration: Dynamics of Change and Resilience in contemporary Ghana, Comparative Political Studies 15 (1983) 4: 445-468.

Mosse, George L., *The Nationalizatioon of the Masses: Political Symbolism and the Mass Movements in Germany from the Napoleonic Wars Through the Third Reich* (New York: Howard Festig, 1975): 47.

Muller, Edward N., and Julian, Thomas D., 'On the meaning of political support', *The American Political Science Review* (1977): 1561-1595.

Murphy, Dan, 'US ads miss mark, Muslims say', *The Christian Science Monitor* (January 7, 2003): p. 6.

National Cancer Institute, *Making health communication campaigns work: A planner's guide* [Electronic Version], Washington, DC: Author, 1992.

Ndegwa, Stephen N., 'Citizenship and Ethnicity: An examination of two transition moments in Kenyan Politics', *The American Political Science Review* 91 (September 1997): 599-616.

Nelson, Thomas E., Clawson, Rosalee A., and Oxley, Zoe M., 'Media framing of a civil liberties conflict and its effect on tolerance', *American Political Science Review* 91, 3 (September 1993): 567-583.

Neslon, Harold D., Cameroon: Chapter 1. General characteristics of the society (01-01-1991.

Ngwa, George A., 'Communication and the empowerment of the people', in Eribo, Festus and Tanjong, Enoh, eds., *Journalism and mass communication in Africa: Cameroon*, Lanham: Lexington Books, 2002: 30.

Nkomo, Dumisani O., 'Consultation needed in formulating economic policies', *Africa News Service* (July 19, 2002).

Nwana, Henry, ' The railway I knew', *Vanguard* (June 26, 2002).

Nwanko, R. L. Nwafo and Mphahlele, Teresa K., 'Communication rule structure and the communication management of the South African crisis', *Journal of Black Studies* 20, 3 (1990): 288.

Nwosu, Ikechukwu E., 'Privatising Broadcasting for Rural Mobilization and National Development: A Qualitative and Quantitative Analysis of the Nigerian Situation', *The Third Channel: IBS Journal of International Communication* 5 (1987): 632-643.

Nyamnjoh, Francis B., 'Cameroon: A Country United by Ethnic Ambition and Difference', *African Affairs* 98 (1999), pp. 101-118.

Oatley, Keith and Johnson-Laird, P. N., 'Towards a Cognitive Theory of Emotions', *Cognition and Emotion* 1 (1987): 29-30.

Oatley, Keith, *Best laid Schemes: The Psychology of Emotions*, New York: Cambridge University Press, 1992.

Oboh, Stephen, 'Fans on Rampage in Jos', *Post Express* (May 1, 2000).

Oduko, Segun, 'New technologies upset the political communication balance in the Third World', Paper presented at the International Television Studies Conference, London, 1986, July.

Ogunade, Adelumola, Mass media and national integration in Nigeria. in *International perspective in news*, ed. Atwood, Leon and Bullion, S. J., Carbondale, Southern Illinois University Press, 1982: 22-32.

Okigbo, Pius, 'The Future Haunted by the Past', In Adebayo Adedeji eds., Africa Within the World: Beyond Dispossession and Dependence, London, Zed Books, 1993: 28-38.

Opoku-Mensah, Aida, 'The future of community radio in Africa: The case of Southern Africa', in Fardon, Richard and Furniss, Graham, eds., *African Broadcast Cultures: Radio in transition*, Westport, Connecticut: Praeger, 2000: 168.

Osaghae, Eghosa E., *Ethnicity, class and the struggle for state power in Liberia*, Dakar: CODESRIA, 1996: 19.

Osaghae, Moses, *Mass media and political integration in Nigeria*, Unpublished Ph.D. dissertation, Texas Tech University, Lubbock, Texas, 1989.

Oswald, Godfrey, 'The North vs the South' *Internet newsgroups: soc.culture.nigeria* (January 22, 1996).

Otenberg, Simon and Otenberg, Phoebe, *Cultures and societies in Africa* (New York: Random House, 1960).

Ouma-Onyango, Richard, *Information Resources and Technology Transfer management in Developing Countries* (London: Routledge, 1997), 9.

Owens, C., 'The developing leap', *The Wall Street Journal* (February 11, 1994), R15.

Packenham, Robert A., 'Political-development doctrines in the American Foreign aid programs', *World Politics* 18, 2 (January 1966): 194-235.

Paden, John, *Values, Identities and National Integration*, Evanston, Illinois: Northwestern University Press, 1980.Peng, S. 'Communicative Distance', *Language Sciences* 31 (1974): 33.

Pfaff, Francoise, 'Conversation with Ghanaian filmmaker Kwaw Ansah', *Research in African Literature* 82 (1995), pp. 186 (8).

Poindexter, Paula M. and McCombs, Maxwell E., *Research in mass communication: A practical guide* (Boston: Bedford, 2000), p. 5.

Porter, Richard, and Samovar, Larry, 'Basic principles of intercultural communication', in *Intercultural Communication: A Reader*, eds. Samovar, Larry A. and Porter, Richard E. (Belmont, California: Wadsworth Publishing Company, 1991).

Price, Vincent, 'Social identification and public opinion: Effects of communicating group conflict', *Public Opinion Quarterly* 53, 2 (Summer 1989): 197-224.

Ramsay, F. Jeffress, *Africa 9th Edition* (Guilford, Connecticut, 2001), pp, 1-234.

Ransdell, Eric, 'Africa's trek to freedom', *U.S. News & World Report* (August 10, 1992): 28-31.

Rao, Sandhya and Natesan, Chinna N., 'Internet: Threat or opportunity for India?' *Media Asia*, 232 (1996): 96-106.

Rashdi, Ibad, 'Communication and rural development', *Pakissan.com* (February 19, 2003).

Renda, Luca, 'Ending civil wars: The case of Liberia', *The Fletcher Forum of World Affairs* 23, 2 (Fall 1999): 64.

Renninger, John P., *Multinational cooperation for development in West Africa* (New York: Pergamon Press, 1979), p. 2.

Renninger, John P., The future of economic cooperation schemes in Africa, with special reference to ECOWAS', in Shaw, Timothy M., ed., *Alternative futures for Africa*, Boulder, Colorado: Westview Press, 1982: 153-177.

Rodgers, Harrell R., 'Towards explanations of the political efficacy and political cynicism of black adolescents: An exploratory study', *American Journal of Political Science* (1974): 257.

Roe, Knut and Aadland, Oyvind, *Assessment Study on media educational involvement in Ethiopia: Media involvement in building democracy and civic institutions in Ethiopia*, Gimlekollen School of Journalism and Communication: Extension and Consultancy Department, Holland: November, 1999.

Rogers, Everett M., *Communication Technology: The new media in society*, New York: The Free Press, 1986: 199.

Rosenberg, Scott, 'Monuments, Holidays, and Remembering Moshoeshoe: The Emergence of National identity in Lesotho, 1902-1966', *African Affairs* (Winter 1999): 49-74.

Ross, Edward Allsworth, 'Socialization', *American Journal of Sociology* 24 (1919), pp. 652-671.

Sawyer, Amos, 'Social Stratification and National Orientations: Students and Non-students in Liberia', in *Values, Identities and National Integration*, ed. John Paden, Evanston, Illinois: Northwestern University Press, 1980: 285-303.

Schultz, Daniel and Felter, Maryanne, 'Reading Historically in a Historically Illiterate Culture', College Teaching (2002), pp. 142.

Sears, David O., and Freedman, Jonathan L., 'Selective exposure to information: A critical review', *Public Opinion Quarterly* 31, 2 (Summer 1967): 194-213.

Seton-Watson, Hugh, *Nations and States*, London: Longman, 1968: 5.

Shepherd, Jr. George W., 'National Integration and Southern Sudan', *The Journal of Modern African Studies* 4, 2 (1996): 194.

Shivute, Mocks, 'The Media in posit-Independecne Namibia', in *Communication & The Transformation of Society: A Developing Regions Perspective*, ed. Nwosu, Peter, Onwumechili, Chuka, and M'Bayo, Ritchard, Lanham, University Press of America, 1995.

Sidanius, Jim, Fesbach, Seymour, Levin, Shana, and Pratto, Felicia, 'The interface between ethnic and national attachment: Ethnic pluralism or ethnic dominance?' *Public Opinion Quarterly* 61, 1, Special issue on race (Spring 1997): 102-133.

Simmons, Anne and Montagne, Renee, Nigeria's Political Transition, *NPR Morning Edition* (July 21, 1998).

Singhal, Arvind and Brown, William, 'Entertainment-education: Looking backwards and forward', *CommDev News* 6, 2 (1995):1-5.

Singletary, Michael, *Mass Communication Research: Contemporary methods and applications*, New York: Longman, 1994: 48.

Skinner, Elliot P., 'African political cultures and the problem of government', *African Studies Quarterly: The Online Journal for African Studies* 7, 1 (Spring 2003).

Smith, Brian, Federal-state relations in Nigeria. *African Affairs* 80 (July, 1981): 377.

Smock, David, and Bentsi-Enchill, Kwamena, eds. *The search for national integration in Africa* (New York: Free Press, 1975).

Sonaike, Adefemi, 'Communication and Third World development: A dead end?' *Gazette* 41, 2 (1987): 83-103.

Souley, Adboulaye Niandou, 'Sub-Saharan African Under pressure from the West', *The Courier* 171 (September-October, 1998): 48.

Spates, James L., 'The sociology of values', *Annual Review of Sociology* 9 (1983): 27-49.

Spicer, Edward H., 'Developmental Change and Cultural Integration', in *Perspectives in Developmental Change*, ed. Art Gallaher, Lexington: University of Kentucky Press, 1968: 1-16.

Spitzberg, Brian H., 'Intercultural Communication Competence', in Somovar, Larry A. and Porter, Richard E., eds., *Intercultural Communication, Sixth Edition*, Belmont, California: Wadsworth Publishing Company, 1991: 353-365.

Starosta, William J., 'Communication and family planning campaign: An Indian experience.' in *Communicating for development: A new pan-disciplinary perspective*, ed. Andrew Moemeka, Albany, New York: State University of New York Press, 1994: 244-260.

Stock, Robert, 'Environmental sanitation in Nigeria: Colonial and contemporary', *Review of African Political Economy* 42, 15 (Summer 1988): 19-31.

Strouse, Jeremiah, Buerkel-Rothfuss, Nancy, and Long, Edgar C. J., 'Gender and family as moderators of the relationship between music video exposure and adolescent sexual permissiveness', *Adolescence* 30 (September 1, 1995): 505-522.

Subramony, Deepak Prem, 'Communicative Distance and Media Stereotyping in an International Context', Paper presented at the AEJMC conference, Phoenix, Arizona, August 2000.

Suberu, Rotimi T., 'Federalism and Nigerian's political future: a comment', *African affairs* 88 (1988, July): 431-438.

Suchman, E., *Evaluative Research*, New York: Russell Sage Foundation, 1967.

Tafawa-Balewa, Abubakar, 'Nigeria looks ahead', *Foreign Affairs* (1962, October):131-140.

Tanjong, Enoh, 'Using survey methods in communication research', in Eribo, Festus and Tanjong, Enoh, eds., *Journalism and mass communication in Africa: Cameroon*, Lanham, New Jersey: Lexington Books, 2002: 105-119.

Tehranian, Majid, 'Communication and development', in *CommunicationTheoryToday*, ed. David Crowley & David Mitchell, Stanford, California: Stanford University Press, 1994: 274-309.

Tempels, Placide, *Bantu Philosophy*. Trans. A. Rubbens (Paris: Presence Africaine, 1959). Cited in Bourgault, *Mass Media in Sub-Saharan Africa*, 5.

Tersigni, Joe, 'Taking pride in our National Flag', *The Toronto Star* (February 15, 1999).

The Inter-Africa Group, 'Social Development in the Horn of Africa: Challenges and Prospects, March 1995' (paper prepared for the World Summit on Social Development, Copenhagen, Denmark, 1995), p. 6.

Thunberg, A., Nowak, K., Rosengren, K., and Sigurd, .B., *Communication and Equality: A Swedish perspective*, Stockholm: Almquist & Wicksell, 1982.

Tichenor, P. J., Donohue, G. A., and Olien, C. N., 'Mass media and the differential growth in knowledge', *Public Opinion Quarterly* 34 (1970): 159-170.

Tololyan, K., 'The nation and its others: In lieu of a preface.' *Diaspora* 1, 1 (1991): 3-7.

Traiger, Lisa, 'Dancing Their Stories', *The Washington Post* (February 22, 2002), pp. T28.

Ume-Uwagbo, Ebele, 'Broadcasting in Nigeria: Its Post-independence Status. *Journalism Quarterly* (1986, Spring): 585.

UNCTAD, *Economic development in Africa: Performance, prospects and policy issues*, New York and Geneva: United Nations, 2001: 5.

Ungar, Stanley and Gergen, David, 'Africa and the American Media', *Occasional Paper No. 9*, The Freedom Forum Media Studies Center: New York: Columbia University (November 1991).

Uyo, Adidi, 'Communication research: An African discourse', in Festus Eribo and Enoh Tanjong, eds., *Journalism and mass communication in Africa: Cameroon*, Lanham, New Jersey: Lexington Books, 2002: 82.

Uzoigwe, G. N., *Uganda: The Dilemma of Nationhood*, New York: NOK Publishers International, 1982: 227-228.

Valente, T., 'Evaluating communication campaigns', In Rice R. E. and Atkin, C. K. eds. *Public communication campaigns*, Thousand Oaks, CA: Sage, 2001: 105-124.

Verma, M. M., *Ghandi's Technique of Mass Mobilization*, New Delhi: R. K. Gupta & Co, 1990: 117.

Vinokur, Martin Barry, *More than a game: Sports and Politics*, New York: Greenwood Press, 1988: 1.

Wanyeki, L. Muthoni, 'Promoting socially responsible finance, trade and investment', *Africa Economic Analysis* (2000).

Waters, Malcolm, 'Citizenship and the Constitution of Structures and Social Inequality', *International Journal of Comparative Sociology* 30 (December 1989): 159-180.

Weber, Max, *The theory of social and economic organization.* Translated by Henderson, A. M. and Parsons, Talcott (New York: Free Press, 1947).

Wedell, George, 'Radio Broadcstsing in Developing Countries', *The Courier* 105 (September-October, 1987).

Weisfelder, Richard P., 'The Basotho nation State: What Legacy for the Future?' *Journal of Modern African Studies* 19, 2 (1981): 221-256.

Weiner, Myron, 'Political integration and political development', *Annals of the American Academy of Political and Social Science* 358 (March, 1965): 52-64.

Wimmer, Roger D. and Dominick, Joseph R., *Mass media research: An introduction*, Belmont, California: Wadsworth Publishing Company, 1991: 11.

Windahl, Sven and Signitzer, Benno with Olson, Jean T., *Using Communication Theory: An introduction to planned communication*, London: Sage Publications, 1992: 19.

Winland, Daphne N., "Our home and native lands?': Canadian Ethnic and the Challenge of Transnationalism' *The Canadian Review of Sociology and Anthropology* 35, 4 (November 1998): 555-577.

Wright, Bonnnie, 'The Power of Articulation', In Creativity of Power: Cosmology and Action in African Socities, ed. W. Arens and Ivan Karp, Washington, D.C.: Smithsonian Institution Press, 1989: 39-59.

Yearwood, Gladstone, 'Mass media in Nigeria.' The Nigerian Media Journal (1985):8.

Yemsi, Alufa, 'War against indiscipline and corruption', *U.S. African Eye* 9, 12 (June 15, 2001): 39.

Young, John, 'Regionalism and democracy in Ethiopia', *Third World Quarterly* 19, 2 (06-01-1998).

Zeleza, Paul Tiyambe, 'The politics of historical and social science research in Africa', *Journal of Southern African Studies* 28, 1 (2002): 9-23.

Zenawi, Meles, 'Democracy and Development Have to Come from the Grassroots', *The Courier* 145 (May-June, 1994), p. 23.

Index